MORE PRAISE F

D0863473

910.41 Mordu.M
Mordue, Mark.
Dastgah

Dastgah: Diary of a H

Mark Mordue has written a poetic and memorable love le_____ ____ ____
breathless, seductive and full of exuberantly remembe
reflections on the planet at its best and worst. This is a
that opens up possibilities, the sort of work in which you find pieces of
yourself.

author of Wild Plan_ 1, o_____ ordinary Ev_nts for the __sp___ __ _____

A lovely, fascinating book. —DAVID ALMOND
author of The Fire-Eaters and Whitbread award winner 2003

Sydney Morning Herald Bestseller List – Non-Fiction:
    #8 January 5–6, 2002
    #6 February 2–3, 2002
    #10 February 9–10, 2002

A lovely impressionistic book … idiosyncratic, entertaining, vulnerable
and unpretentious … Mordue skitters between worlds, not sparing his
readers the contrast. —NEWSWEEK

Meticulously assembled … Mordue has elevated *Dastgah* beyond the realms
of the traditional travelogue by sharing not only what he learned about cultures he visited, but also his brutally honest self-discoveries. —ELLE

In the chapters on the Middle East – to me the most fascinating part of
the journey – he intertwines local histories and politics with the daily
record of endemic incomprehensions. In a suite of sympathies-in-transit,
he gives us that rare point of view, the literate sensitive backpacker.
—SYDNEY MORNING HERALD

Stirringly vulnerable … *Dastgah* is as raw as punk but definitely not as
loud. —AUSTRALIAN STYLE

FEB 1 0 2005

As travel displaces us physically, so it displaces us emotionally and it is this experience that Sydney writer Mark Mordue captures so powerfully in his first book. —VOGUE

Mark Mordue has embraced the random logic and existential ethos of the wanderer … sharp intuitions, combined with the quality of the descriptions, make *Dastgah* a great read. —SOUTH CHINA MORNING POST

Anyone who calls chapters of his book 'Day of the Dickhead' and 'Is Terry Venables Evil?' knows how to get a reader's attention. The trick, of course, is to keep you hooked. Mark Mordue does so with ease … In this debut book his short stories and poetry fizz. He is sometimes intense, sometimes distant, but always compelling. —NEW ZEALAND HERALD

Dastgah is much more about what it means to be a traveler than a travel book. This is brave writing, unafraid to open itself to awkward emotions with honesty and passion. —MARIE CLAIRE

Travel round the world for a year, keep a journal, write it up into a book, find a publisher, hey presto, you're a travel writer. Only thing is, you have to be able to write. And Mark Mordue can. — GLEEBOOKS SUMMER READING GUIDE

Mordue, an innocent abroad, dives into the black hole of Calcutta, and with a backpack full of good wishes, crosses borders that wiser men fear to tread. —HQ

Dastgah might have worked better as a novel, and Mordue may well go on to write first-rate fiction. His literary gifts take time to emerge, but then do so emphatically. Mordue's mosaic of daily life in Calcutta is quietly but compassionately drawn. He is similarly gentle, but also keenly observant, in chronicling bystanders' reactions to a boy's death on a Nepal highway. He captures the edgy revelry of an Indian cricket crowd at Eden Park and the 'gloomy glitter' of Edinburgh. —CANBERRA TIMES

This book, like the elaborate form of traditional Iranian music it is named after, moves through tempos and moods – poignancy, humour, fear and excitement ... This is a compelling read – part rock lyric, part love poem, part road novel – and it should be required reading for those who seek to vilify the entire Muslim world in the wake of recent horrific events in America. —AUSTRALIAN BOOKSELLER & PUBLISHER

Mordue is a people watcher of the first degree and that, combined with a journalist's eye, is what makes his tales so enticing and interesting to read. —CENTRAL WESTERN DAILY

DASTG

AH *Diary of a Headtrip*

MARK MORDUE

EVANSTON PUBLIC LIBRARY
1703 ORRINGTON AVENUE
EVANSTON, ILLINOIS 60201

 HAWTHORNE BOOKS & LITERARY ARTS | *Portland, Oregon* | MMIV

Copyright ©2004
Mark Mordue

All rights reserved. No part of this book may be reproduced in any form or by any electronic or mechanical means, including information storage-and-retrieval systems, without prior permission in writing from the Publisher, except for brief quotations embodied in critical articles and reviews.

Hawthorne Books
& Literary Arts

1410 NW Kearney St.
Suite 909
Portland, OR 97209
hawthornebooks.com

Form:
Pinch, Portland, Oregon

Printed in China
through Print Vision, Inc.

Set in DTL Albertina.

First American Edition

9
8
7
6
5
4
3
2
1

Library of Congress Cataloging-in-Publication Data

Dastgah: diary of a headtrip / Mark Mordue. – 1st American ed.
p. cm.
Includes bibliographical references.
ISBN 0-9716915-6-8 (alk. paper)

1. Mordue, Mark – Travel.
2. Voyages around the world. I. Title.
G439.M67 2004
910.4′1 – dc22
2004014833

To Lisa Nicol, who showed me the way.

Publisher's Note

MARK MORDUE'S *DASTGAH: DIARY OF A HEADTRIP* HAS been reprinted exactly as it was in its original Australian edition, complete with Australian spellings and punctuation. Any attempt at an Americanization would have comprised the reading experience. We invite you to enjoy this global journey courtesy of Mark Mordue and all of us here at Hawthorne Books.

Contents

Preface

IN FEBRUARY 1998 MY PARTNER LISA AND I SET OFF ON A journey around the world.

Inevitably I started writing down notes, impressions, entire stories. What follows is a collection of those pieces, some quite personal or interior, others more involved with reflecting the environment around me – a mapping out of a year of our lives.

It was hard to find a title that grasped this fragmented sensibility. But when I thought back to experiences in Iran and my encounters with the extraordinary music there, the word *dastgah* came to mind.

I liked the sound of the word, its exotic suggestions of another universe. I also liked the way it echoed the word 'dust,' swallowed it whole into another language (Farsi/Persian) and another meaning.

On a more technical level the word *dastgah* had a strong connection to ideas I was playing with structurally. Iranian classical music is identified by twelve major *dastgah-ha* (plural for *dastgah*). Each *dastgah* is made up of numerous segments that can be connected melodically or modally. They are in effect shifting labyrinths, where an almost endless array of musical combinations weave, echo and reconnect in a fluid yet always identifiable realm. Out of the same base material musicians can form an entirely new composition. It is all a matter of interpretation.

The complexity of each *dastgah* has been likened to that of an underground bazaar. Once you learn a particular 'map' it is possible for you to move through that bazaar at will, choosing this street or that lane to walk down, signaling for others to join you, improvising your journey each time you make it. The next time you pass through you may go an entirely different way. Paths are crossed and re-crossed, familiar places are glimpsed, new directions are found or agreed upon. The notes played build up what I'd call 'a geography of the mind,' something a musician must be prepared to traverse creatively every time he approaches this 'place.' To understand where you are going and what you are doing is a grand feat of memory as well as skill. You must know each *dastgah* like the back of your own hand.

I liked this as a metaphor for the collection I was bringing together, for it was what I was trying to do with words: to represent not just our physical trip, but also the transitory, seeking spirit that underlined it. I was mapping out a movement with words, to be experienced and hopefully reinterpreted again and again. Divining a way through these places and stories and moments to find something more complete at their end.

MARK MORDUE
Glebe, March 2001

DASTGAH

One moment in Annihilation's Waste,
One moment, of the Well of Life to taste,
The Stars are setting, and the Caravan
Starts for the dawn of Nothing
— oh make haste!

THE RUBAIYAT OF OMAR KHAYYAM
Translated by Edward J. Fitzgerald

People who come here see either death or life.

WOMAN IN A CALCUTTA TAXI

India Death or Life

Lightning Storm Over Calcutta

IT'S ALMOST MIDNIGHT AND LIKE MOST VISITORS WE ARE already in bed, asleep and trying to sleep. In my drift I hear the storm building, catch spinal flashes and sheets of brightness in the window. Rain begins to fall as the lightning and thunder increase, but I close my eyes again and keep drowsing. Only as it hits the window, harder and harder in thin waves, do I begin to wake and see the fingery rain on the glass, the delicate slow patterns at odds with the torrential source.

It's raging steadily now, and the lightning is permanent and rickety in the sky.

A dripping – a running – sound.

And I realize the storm is coming inside our hotel room.

I move to my desk in the darkness, fumble for a lamp, try to be silent for my sleeping girlfriend. Flick the switch and get nothing. Look out into the backstreet and see nothing – nothing but blackness broken by lightning glimpses of dead streetlamps and a madness of wires and cables tangled along the outside of the buildings. India's way with electricity reminds me of pasta thrown against a wall. Like I should be surprised by what's happening now? It's a power failure.

In the dark I feel for our torch and shine it towards the running sound. I see the leaking roof by the window join, streaming down to a large, neatly placed vase of flowers on the table. The leaves are bouncing water all over the place, so I quickly move everything off the table onto a chair, with the exception of a red makeup bag, a silver ring, a black camera cover and a sealed deck of playing cards, each object under the torchlight wet and waterproof, somehow holy looking.

I think about the reverence we sometimes have for objects. How even the most mundane things can become magical. And I decide to make this accidental night time arrangement my little offering to the gods of India.

By now the storm is enticing me outside as it thunders and flashes and trickles through into the room. I search for other leaks, move our books and clothes into piles that can be more easily protected by an old coat and the day's newspaper, with its headlines promoting an upcoming atomic test. They're calling the bomb 'Agni' after the Hindu goddess of fire, planning to hand out sweets to thousands of children on the streets of Delhi, Varanasi, all the big cities. Beating Pakistan in the cricket and nuking them on the borders of Kashmir are the current leap this country is hoping to make into the divine. I scan the ravings with my torch for common sense, but there is none.

A rumble of light bursts over me. At the back of my mind are thoughts of Calcutta's vulnerability. Is it the monsoon season? How wild does it get here? It is easy to imagine the city swamped, pounded by nature.

I shift the bolt away and open one of the two swinging doors, then the other some five minutes later. I'm surprised by the coolness of the air outside. Calcutta's humidity, its continuous heat, is finally gone. This could be a fresh night at home in Sydney.

The rain is sweet sounding on the guttering, running and breaking onto the concrete directly below our first-floor room. The smell of it on the warm stone is clean, almost scented in a city I more usually associate with spices and shit and sweat.

The lightning has moved off now and I can see Calcutta being outlined like a jumpy photographic negative. Despite the flashing in the sky there is no thunder anymore, even as the rooftops are continuously lit up for miles around. As the rain also eases, the sky turns a rosy, smoky colour with each pale splash of light.

I want to go out into the streets and see Calcutta in a storm. Put on a raincoat and shrug down the streets, yet another watcher of the city.

Just how many watchers has this city seen? I wonder.

But Calcutta is bigger than any definition or journey, beyond containing by any writer or photographer, any tourist, any saint for that matter. Let alone me.

I'm frightened of what might be out there too. The deformed beggar who stands perpetually at the hotel gate, with a crooked arm and a nub for a hand and a mouth like a half-broken dinner plate. The leprous fingers grabbing from doorways, the forms beneath sodden blankets, even a common beseeching for rupees given new night energy. A deserted street with me. A dog without eyes…

My dark visions run on without me. I don't want to leave my girlfriend either. What if she worries? Wonders where I have slipped to?

I begin to use her as an anchor, a blaming point for my own fears, and yearn for the chaos of the lonely world, the free world, to just do as I please.

I click pointlessly at the dead fan. Completely open both doors to let the rainwashed air in and the heat of the room escape. Lisa sleeps on, her back still visible and pure in the shadows.

A pang of sadness shoots through me, a longing to kiss the base of her spine and whisper, 'I'm sorry.'

It's then I hear some sickly meowing. Walk barefoot out onto the balcony with only a towel pulled to my waist. Look down the stairwell.

In the darkness a white cat is calling. One kitten comes out complaining, then another, then another. Still she calls, stalking her babies, licking each of them, counting them in with her tongue. It feels like a secret shared between us: a cat, her kittens and me.

I start listening for other sounds. A rowdy car horn – probably a black-and-yellow taxi, the automotive thugs of Calcutta's roads – blares long and repeatedly down Sudder Street with typical 'out-of-the-way!' indifference. Out-of-the-way sleepers, fearers, cat mothers, beggars, half-awoken dreamers... out of the way, there's work to be done, fares to be collected.

Dogs are barking. Voices cheer or moan. I feel guilty for hearing the city's sounds as animal and in unison. As if my ears are degrading the individual souls of the street, canine and human alike, into a great bestial shaking off of water from the skin.

More car horns. More shouts. More dogs. Rain is still falling, but Calcutta is starting to move again.

Then, for just a minute, I hear the crows. The perennial black crows of Calcutta, a bird for every soul it is said. As if they have woken up at the wrong time or come to lie to us about a dawn that is still some way off. There's a wave of their cries, cawing at space, then they fall away.

Servants are moving below. Cranking up the generator. A sewery smell begins to rise as if something foul has been stirred. And as the noise of the generator roars I move back inside and close the doors, trying to slide the great bolt back in as quietly as I had slid it out.

Within seconds there's a flutter of light on the balcony and the overhead fan begins to turn. Power is restored to the hotel. Outside our window the alley is still dead black, hard to see into.

I check for more leaks when I feel some water at my feet, but it all seems okay. Throw the day's newspaper over the flooded section of floor; let its A-bomb dreams die in a puddle.

My bedside lamp is now burning low beneath its green shade. So I open my diary to try to remember what I did. In Calcutta. In a lightning storm. Before I fell asleep. When my eyes were heavy. And the world recalled the sky.

After the Rain

THE STREETS AT EVERY INTERSECTION AROUND CHOWRINGHEE are rivered up to the knees and long with water. This is not a time for shoes.

A girl in a freshly-ironed school tunic raises hers neatly above her head as she wades through sensibly. A cyclist, bare feet lifted to his handlebars, sluices across a shallow lake nearby, clean and fast and free as a bird. I see their pleasure as they look down into the heavens, how they loom across a liquid mirror. Rain turning girl into woman and man into child at play.

The lake that has formed along Sudder Street is breathing, sucking in drops of air. Circles appear and disappear, light parting shots of drizzle after last night's storm. The torrential downpour has slowed Calcutta down this morning, shutting it off into smaller pieces, distinguishing the pockets of neighbourhood life that make this place a wild jigsaw of villages bucketed together into a makeshift metropolis.

In the aftermath of the deluge I amble around my own little tourist block with less and less determination, always to another watery dead-end.

A black-and-yellow taxi scuttles up and down and around the same streets with me, testing the depths, gears cranking forwards and reverse, like a drunken beetle trying to escape the inevitable. There is nowhere to go this morning, nothing to do but wait.

Families are reestablishing themselves on the sidewalk. Hoarding their lives under green sheets of plastic, using raggy strips of material for rope, attaching the plastic to the eaves of closed shopfronts, even a weary-looking rickshaw, then securing their newly improved roofing to the ground using bricks and stones, whatever is around. So this is home: shelter for a day.

A young woman with five children gestures towards me with her hands, but I shake my head. No small change today. She nods at me and gestures again carelessly, starts to laugh. No harm in trying. Underneath the plastic she is cooking something in a small pot that steams out of the shadows while her children sleep off the morning and she pulls an ever-falling veil back onto her face, hiding her smile again and again from me.

'Smoke?'

A young man in a cheap brown suit starts to make a sales pitch in my ear. 'Very good quality, sir. Excellent smoke.'

He flashes a small green parcel bullet-bound in Glad Wrap. Gathers it back up into his sleeve again as if a hydraulic system is working his fingers invisibly from the cuff of his jacket. Quite the magician.

I shake my head at him but he won't give up and starts hassling me all the way down the street. 'The very best, sir. Smoke. Excellent quality, I assure you, sir!'

Finally I say 'nahee!' so sharply a few people look out from under their plastic homes to see what the fuss is all about. The young man stops and stares at me coldly, a who-the-fuck-do-you-think-you-are? look that makes me tremble. Everyone shrinks back under their coverings and evaporates. Suddenly there is just the two of us in the open, the bitty rain blotching his suit and adding to the aloneness between us.

I escape from the salesman down a side street that turns into an alley and yet another dead end full of water. Some sodden rubbish stinks it out. This is the dark street I was staring into from my hotel window during last night's power failure. There's nothing here except silence. But in the human mania of India, silence moves on you with a distinct presence. It feels bad.

I backtrack my way out into the street again. The salesman has gone. A couple of boys are talking on the corner in Bengali. I point to the sky and smile. They nod, so I ask if it rains like this all the time in Calcutta? They freeze up and just smile back at me. Clearly they don't understand what the hell I am saying, though one of them knows enough English to say, 'Hey Shane Warne!'

I nod wearily to this perpetual Indian greeting. It marks me out as an Australian tourist, forever associated with one of my country's most famous cricketers, a man who openly detests India and is nonetheless revered across the subcontinent as a hero for his playing skill. His current piggish behaviour – demanding cans of baked beans be flown in for him rather than eat the local muck – is shamefully ignorant. A perverse streak makes me feel like putting on an American accent just to escape the low burden of his fame.

A few rickshaw wallahs rap their bells on the wooden handles of their carts to get my attention. The unusually high chassis makes them an effective means of transport in a flood. They know I have no way out of Sudder Street with my boots on. I'm an easy mark, a likely ride.

Again I say *nahee*, more happily this time. I'm surprised by the communication inside such exchanges, the humour. It's a game.

A woman with a child in her arms is shouting at a man who is filling a jug from a street pump. She looks well dressed and walks on, speaking quickly to a parked taxi driver who leans out of his window and starts yelling abuse as well. The man at the pump is indifferent to their anger. He finishes his task and walks off with a huge cask of water pressing down over his shoulders.

What a strange crime in a flood: I can't interpret it.

I find myself gravitating back to a coffee shop on the corner opposite the Fairlawn Hotel where Lisa and I are staying. She's still asleep in our room, as if the cool smell of the rain has drugged her. I've been up and down all night, disturbed by the storm, writing, then waking at the crack of dawn to go wandering, well, not far at all.

As I take a bench and sit under the café awning, a few raindrops stroke me. Despite my run-in with the marijuana salesman, the morning is very tender.

I notice a sloppy European girl dressed in a sari is with a tight-looking young man, scalp shaved athletically. They exude a queer energy, one that makes you reluctant to breathe the air near them and catch whatever mood it is they relish. An erotic misanthropy, I suspect. Certain travellers can be so intense their physical being stains everything around them. How to escape them?

At the back of the café, an Indian businessman, or maybe just a well-dressed student, reads his newspaper quietly below an advertisement for *Titanic*. The film poster – an obviously new decoration – features Leonardo DiCaprio and Kate Winslet in a swoon that is Indianized like the swarthy, melodramatic images promoting Bombay musicals.

As Lisa and I travel the country and become aware of *Titanic* fever everywhere we go, these two actors emerge as fresh gods in the Indian landscape. Sitting in a packed cinema watching the film a few days later, we enjoy a crowd whose biggest laughs are reserved for jokes that involve class barriers and English table manners, such as the choice of knives and forks Leonardo struggles with over dinner. Despite the last gasps of the twentieth century, India's memories of English colonialism are still fresh and influentially absurd, a thick paste over their own caste system. They laugh as if from inside another time when these things mattered and marked you. Perhaps here they still do.

The tight couple beside me pays up and departs and I am relieved to have the café and the street more or less to myself. A typically Western thought when the street is so busy. I'm hardly alone here, just culturally distant. What makes me think of it as 'mine'?

More people, barefoot or on bicycles, are now making their way through the floodwaters. Another taxi driver plunges his vehicle in and out of a narrow section of water, creating a tidal wave that laps over doorways and causes an explosion of words and raised, knotty fists. The driver quickly escapes around the next corner, honking his horn sluttishly.

One of the rickshaw wallahs from across the street hovers nearby, studying me. As I sip my steaming glass he finally approaches.

'Good morning, sir.'

'Good morning.'

'It rains very much tonight in Calcutta, sir.'

'Last night? Yes. The lightning was amazing.'

'Oh yes,' he says. 'Very good for business.'

He stands there before me, improbably optimistic in a grubby *lunghi* and a dirty, slightly torn singlet so sheer he must have been wearing it for years.

'Tell me, sir, how much is a glass of Nescafe in Australia?'

Here at the café I appear to be paying roughly US $0.40 for an espresso coffee. So I do the calculations, increasing them a little to emphasize how expensive it is for me to live back in Australia. In other words, to let him know I am not a rich man at home.

I finally say that the price is about five times what I am paying here, and go on to explain how this affects me in Sydney. But he is not interested in the excuses for my life. Merely astounded by the price of a cup of coffee. I suspect he already thinks the café is exploiting a ridiculous European indulgence as it is. The madness of the West when one can just drink chai!

He keeps staring at my glass like it might be a pot of gold, so I offer to buy him one. 'No thank you, I cannot drink,' he says, holding his stomach to indicate a vulnerability or illness. 'Thank you for your kindness, sir. But I was just curious to know this price.'

He jiggles his head side to side in that bobbing Indian way somewhere between a yes and a no. I look at how skinny he is. Too skinny to be pulling a rickshaw around Calcutta. I picture him straining every muscle to get people, sometimes very fat people and their luggage, from point 'A' to point 'B'.

Yesterday I bargained a rickshaw wallah down from 80 to 60 rupees for a trip, the equivalent of quarrelling over a dollar. Once that was done, Lisa and I climbed aboard and watched the rickshaw groan with our weight as the wallah lifted the handles to his waist. Bowing his head, he started to step forward, gaining momentum, sandals thudding down the road 'till we arrived at our destination some fifteen minutes later. By which time he was heaving with the need to breathe and so drenched in sweat I thought he might pass out. We gave him 100 rupees and ran away, ashamed of ourselves for having beat down his asking price. Even our belated generosity made us feel like gluttons gorging ourselves on a false kindness.

Some Europeans won't take the rickshaws at all in Calcutta – it's too much like indentured slavery. But the awful truth is they are just denying the poor a few rupees they desperately need. And these are men who are willing to work, who have struggled hard at the bottom of the heap to get this most menial of jobs. Forget the beggars if your conscience is strained by the poverty round here, these guys will give you their backs to ride on. I can't help but acknowledge some pride, or at least determination, in their efforts. Maybe it's not so bad to let them rip you off a little.

My new friend stands quietly beside me looking out at the street and the sky. Three more rickshaw wallahs cross the giant puddle to join us, leaving their carts lined and covered by the white walls of the Fairlawn. Most of their customers are shut away inside, still snoring their arses off. Business will be slow for the time being.

The wallahs are equally friendly so I offer to buy them all coffee. But I soon realize there is not the same warmth in their communication – and that they are understandably milking me for whatever I might be willing to give. The Indian café proprietor gives them the evil eye, tolerating, just, their presence outside his door.

As they crowd in around me asking questions about Shane Warne (oh no, not him again) and who my favourite Indian cricketer is (I always say 'Srinath' because I love the sound of his name) they push my friend to the back of their huddle. Eventually he saunters away to his rickshaw and sits quietly inside it as the rain continues to sprinkle down. I see that they are much harder, physically and mentally, and it pains my heart to think of him as someone lower on the pecking order.

I start drinking my coffee quickly despite its scalding heat. I don't like being king of the rickshaw wallahs this morning in a flooded Chowringhee street. I am able to step outside this scene and look at it from across the way as if through the eyes of a floating stranger – and I do not like the man I see big-timing himself with a few cheap coffees. So I burn my tongue and refuse entreaties for 'a tourist ride' through their watery world. And I walk back to my hotel and a security that threatens to defeat me once more, grieving for a friend I barely know. Praying Lisa will be awake to hold me and help me feel human on a foreign morning. Hand bells jangling

in the rain, calling to me in vague hope despite all my refusals. *Nahee,*
nahee…

First Ride/Blue Wallet/Day of the Dickhead

THEY SAY YOU NEVER FORGET YOUR FIRST TAXI RIDE IN ANOTHER
country. Mine was into Calcutta. To get there, Lisa and I had flown out of
Sydney and on through a typically shapeless 24 hours, all stratospheric
space and airport shuffle, with a torturous six-hour morning wait at Mumbai before finally catching our connecting flight across India.

Tiredness weighed on me like a slab of lead, but the weight lifted from
me that morning as easy as opening my eyes and breathing.

Despite what should have been excitement, I'd been grieving after
moving the last of my things out of a huge terrace house on Bourke Street,
inner-city Sydney, home to me for over twelve years. I felt like a big old
tree being pulled up by the roots, leaving my much larger and more permanent brethren behind on that green parade, the wind singing in their
branches for me one last time as I shut the door. My life fell away from
me in great big sorrowful clods with every gust. I wouldn't be back.

Now I was attached to nowhere but a storage warehouse, the state of
my bank account and a brand new email address. I was pure electronic
aura, a not entirely transcendent condition. It was like I had left my past
and hadn't joined my future yet. Call it 'travel zone aftershock': moving,
yet not part of the feeling of movement at all.

Lisa had helped me to finish packing in a last mad rush while I fetched
clothes from the laundromat and went on to meet her at the airport, throwing shirts and jeans from a rubbish bag into my already overweight backpack then boarding the plane. There must be calmer ways to leave a country,
but when I collapsed into my seat I knew this day hadn't seen one of them.

We had tickets that would take us on to Kathmandu after a one-week
stopover in Calcutta. Australia was playing cricket against India and we
thought it might be fun to see the big match at Eden Gardens, one of the
most famous sporting stadiums in the world.

I'd never been overseas before. But I thought of India as the place where people tried to 'find themselves,' only to end up going loopy, if not insane. From what I understood, India's mass of humanity exerted a gravitational pull which crushed individuals who couldn't resist it. Even Hindi spirituality bordered on the feverish and tentacled, all those half-human half-animal gods with glowing eyes in their foreheads and endless arms waving hypnotically. How not to get pulled in?

Calcutta was meant to be the darkest, heaviest place of all. The 'black hole.' A reputation founded in the Bangladesh crisis of the 1970s that flooded the city with war and famine refugees. It gave the world a new and evil iconography for poverty: garbage trucks moving through the streets at dawn, loading up the dead while the starving and the sick looked on, knowing the trucks would be round again for them tomorrow. An image strong enough to deter tourists right up to this very day, despite Calcutta's post-apocalyptic efforts to improve itself, and a native Bengali enthusiasm for life, art and poetry that had made it a cultural capital of India and, once upon a time, colonial Britain's administrative centre of choice.

Now we were here for real – arriving in a bright morning torrent of images while our driver sang Hindi pop songs beneath his breath and his crackling radio begged – oh, how it begged! – for a steady hand on the tuning dial.

I looked out the window into the morning peak hour. Hump-backed cows wandering carelessly, traffic like spaghetti on the boil, horns honking in semaphores of impatience and familiarity, buses teeming with passengers, literally bursting with humanity, men standing on the bumper bars and clutching at the windows as they rode to work, giant hoardings clouded by sooty plumes of monoxide – 'Phillips: Let's Make Things Better'; 'Blues Kings: Attitude is Everything'; 'Good Luck India: 50 Years of Independence' – tatty and frequent posters everywhere for a magician who had long since been and gone in a blaze of spiralling street publicity, farmers planting in wet padi fields right next to half built or half falling down apartment blocks, beggars wild with deformities, businessmen in beautiful blue suits, street carts oozing smells of cardoman and masala, cow dung on the sidewalks, women in saris floating through the slow dust, gold in their ears, gold on their wrists, gold studs and gold rings in their noses, a dull white statue of Queen Victoria looking fruitlessly down upon them…

Calcutta went on and on, growing out of its own chaos and decay, constantly and ecstatically in a state of self-salvage and renewal.

But my notes on all this are shit to read now. I look at the incoherent scrawl, the excited words 'INDIA IS GREAT' written in my pocket book as the taxi jumped over potholes and swerved past other vehicles – and see the descriptions as futile. What excites me is the physical condition of the writing, an incoherent calligraphy scratched and scattered across the page. It's truer than the words themselves, which keep getting lost in jags of ink and scribble and the tidal rush of impressions. I'd need to be Jackson Pollock with a pen to get it all down.

In the end I surrender and simply look.

Lisa is beside me in the taxi, calm as the sunlight. Reminding me to move my shoulder bag into the middle of the seat between us – to avoid having it ripped off through the open window as it slips to my side and I lose concentration. She then pats my arm without saying anything. It makes me feel young.

I'm amazed by the vitality of the street. Far from the pessimistic visions I had expected of an unvarying misery attended to by the saintly ghost of Mother Teresa and her Missionaries of Charity. Lisa's just happy I'm happy. I always feel humble when I see that empathy in her, the way she celebrates me with a smile. It's a light I struggle to raise my face to some times, almost too bright for me; a way she has that can just lift me in a second to a whole other place.

'People who come here tend to see either death or life,' she says. 'Depending on how you see India pretty much decides whether or not you will be able to cope with it. It's not to say all the poverty and begging and suffering aren't there. God, you can see that. But I always get excited by the energy, not depressed or frightened. Not often anyway. We're gonna have a good time here, I think. Life, not death,' she says again, putting her hand on my leg.

I take her hand and hold it. Enjoy the softness of her skin. Watching multitudes.

WE HEAD ON THROUGH THE PULSATIONS OF THE CITY TO Sudder Street in Chowringhee, the heart of Calcutta's backpacker district. To the Fairlawn Hotel, a mildly infamous establishment caught in a colonial time warp. We've heard that staying here is like being lost inside an episode of *Fawlty Towers*. Perhaps only India could make a British sitcom about an eccentric hotel come to life, then push the circumstances even further into farce. How could we not love it?

The place is run by an old couple – he English, she Armenian – who are so *pukka* it is hard to believe: walking canes, little dogs yapping, imperious gestures, like two people prepared to walk out and perform a vaudeville stage show. Getting a room here is neither certain nor impossible, but whimsical, as they look us over approvingly and decide we are best suited to 'Room 16'.

Outside the hotel the temperature is rising. Once we've settled in we go looking through the street markets at a 100 different varieties of sandals, most of them designed for a Persian genie or a German hippie, not entirely my style, and all of them too small for my heavily-booted, overheating big feet.

Suddenly a man throws a bright blue wallet to a small clearing on the table in front of me. Squirts fuel from a tin container as if he is pissing on it. 'Look! Fireproof!' he shouts, and flicks a burning match through the air, landing it on the wallet with acrobatic precision. It erupts in a quick whoosh, the fire as blue and bright as 'the genuine coloured leather!'

I buy the wallet without hesitation. Who needs sandals? This is what I really want!

I am then offered old padlocks, cheap sunglasses, a smoking pipe, horrible synthetic shirts, more sandals that would fit a child's feet but not mine – 'for you, sir, yes I think it is possible' – pictures of Bombay film stars, mixed nuts, ice cream, today's newspaper in Hindi, scented candles and some old postage stamps in quick succession. No, no, I'm fine, thank you. The wallet is good, plenty, enough, *nahee*. The Indian word for 'no' is a joy to use with confidence once I get the courage to mouth it. I seem to be integrating.

I will love flashing my blue wallet about on our further travels, its deep luminosity a none-too-subtle signal of my individuality. This wallet tells the world exactly who I am, a sophisticated yet somehow psychedelic kinda guy. Till I test its fireproofing strengths one day, scorching it badly and immolating a few hundred rupees into the bargain before stamping the whole thing out on the ground. Indian salesmen are pure technique, and I clearly lacked the sleight of hand involved in that first little circus of flames in Calcutta. It's all over now, baby blue.

WITH MY WALLET STILL FRESH IN HAND, THOUGH, WE'D GO TO Eden Gardens a few days later for the Australia versus India test match. Initially it had been hard to get tickets, despite the 120,000 capacity of the ground. But by the last day Australia was being slaughtered so embarrassingly two New Zealanders at the hotel happily parted with their VIP passes to the grandstands. They couldn't bear to watch this one-sided game any longer.

They warned us about sitting with the Australian contingent, a group of about twenty guys who had so angered the cricket mad locals they now had a police cordon stationed around them. Mostly the friction had been good-natured ribbing between the fans, and handmade banners on the Indian side such as 'India is the best, but Australia is no less' were so polite as to be ridiculous.

Things, though, had taken a decided turn for the worse thanks to one Australian supporter: his shirt permanently off, bad tatts displayed, non-stop shouting and insults yelled apace at both the Indian cricketers and the crowd.

'The Supporter,' as I began to call him, had escalated the fractious intensity between the home crowd and the visitors. At roughly 118,980 to 20, these were bad odds. Apparently a young boy had kept running up to the Australian contingent the day before, taunting them with an Indian flag and running away again. The Supporter made the mistake of tearing the flag out of the kid's hands. The locals had wanted Australian blood for this insult! And though the flag was quickly returned, police protection had to be put in force – and yet that loud mouth kept flapping unchecked in the face of murderous feelings.

Thank God India was winning. Otherwise it could have got really ugly.

Okay, I said to Lisa when we arrived, let's sit up the back and look as Bengali as possible.

We picked a spot with some well-dressed types and their families, mostly men and their sons. On the field things were still going poorly for Australia as batsman after batsman cringed in the face of the Indian bowling attack.

The fear factor was hugely enhanced by the Eden Gardens crowd, who began a grunting chant with each step the bowler took towards the wicket, getting louder and louder till the moment the ball was unleashed and they erupted into a hideous explosion of roaring and whistles and fiercely-beaten plastic containers. You could see the Australian batsman flinch under the barrage of noise, the ball a terrible messenger of the mass slaughter being sought. It had been decades since Australia had won a Test series on the subcontinent, even when playing the weakest of teams. Now I understood why.

Down in the stalls, we could see thousands of Indian fans streaming to different parts of the ground every change of over. We were told the great Indian batsman Sachin Tendulkar was in the outfield and that his presence attracted adoring crowds excited to be within even a few hundred metres of him. Each time he moved it was as if the crowd were made up of magnetic filings drawn to his energy.

Inevitably The Supporter got up and bellowed something. He was the kind of guy who could make 'Happy Birthday' sound gross and unpleasant. I tried not to hear him and we slunk lower in our seats.

'Excuse me, sir,' an Indian man said, turning to me. 'But why is this fellow here so rude? He is really most unpleasant gentleman. Nobody here likes him one bit. We think he should go home now please.'

I shrugged my shoulders as a line of men and boys turned around to get my insights on this 'fellow' Australian. 'Ahhh, he's just a dickhead,' I said, groaning. 'People wouldn't like him at home either.'

'Dick head?'

My Indian inquisitor made the words sound as crisp and sharp as the ironing creases in his stonewashed jeans. He raised his eyebrows towards me. 'What is this "dick head"?' he asked, mimicking the way I had held my fist to my forehead and moved it in a repetitive back-and-forth jerking motion.

This was going to require careful explanation. 'Well, in Australia we sometimes call a man's penis his "dick",' I said, pointing between my legs discreetly. About a dozen guys all looked at my groin and nodded.

'But when someone is very stupid, we call him a "dickhead" – you see?' I repeated the jerking action from my forehead again and pointed to The Supporter, who stood up as if on cue.

The man nearest to me nodded. I began to see he and his friends elbowing each other and making actions with their fists to their foreheads. I could hear the word 'dickhead' getting passed along the line, till people began tapping each other on the shoulders throughout the grandstand, men and boys by the score muttering 'dickhead' and sniggering and pointing, fists bobbing back and forth from their foreheads with a mighty enthusiasm.

I felt immensely proud of this. It was becoming 'the day of the dickhead' and not a complete loss to the bored sports fans I had met here watching a dreary match with no surprises. I felt as if I had made some great contribution to the game, perhaps to the history of Indian obscenity and linguistics. This was what creating a cultural bond was all about!

My amusement was stopped short by the fall of the last Australian wicket. It was all over, a crushing victory to India.

The men around us began picking up the newspapers they'd used to cover the concrete seats they were sitting on. In seconds they had rolled them into cones, and were setting fire to them like torches. This action was being repeated across the stadium. All of Eden Gardens was asmoke and aflame, thousands upon thousands of fans cheering wildly amid the flying embers. People were clearly in a good mood, but Attila the Hun and his hordes couldn't have been scarier to see. It was time to go home to the hotel.

We left the grounds in a great throng of chanting. Only to have a group of teenage boys harass us on our way through a park nearby, throwing stones, then bricks at our legs while they laughed into their cell phones. I finally reached for a brick and hoisted it back half-heartedly, puffing with frustrated anger. Lisa dragged me on to safety and the main street as I shouted abuse back at them and wondered if they understood a word.

The Big Match

UNDER SIGNS FOR 'NEEM TOOTHPASTE INSURES YOUR SMILE' and all the tat and fade of billboards smoked and dusted by Calcutta's air, boys play cricket on the road.

There are two gangs. The older boys, teenagers, almost young men, have a 'pitch' at the prestige end of Lindsay Street in Chowringhee, near trucks coiled with masses of straw or stuffed with cages full of chickens for the New Markets. The younger boys, maybe as old as ten at most, are closer to the open end of the street, where it is more likely they will be forced to stop their game because of increasing traffic.

It is early Sunday morning, their regular game. 'Always Sunday only,' says one of the boys.

Despite the day of rest, Calcutta's endless mercantile seethe is still tooting and rolling around them as they play, the black-and-yellow cabbies beseeching for trade, men unloading chickens in great fistfuls (twenty at a time, all bound by the legs, alive, dumb-eyed and clucking wearily), people bathing in the street, beggars sprinkling water lightly in circles to settle nearby dust.

Every waking moment is on display. From cleaning teeth to layers of soapiness lathered up under running pipes or sloshing buckets, a dozen or more people washing themselves along the sidewalk, heads crowny and bodies white as the foamiest surf. On steps, in gutters, the sweet, fiery bubble of Nescafe and chai, the breakfast sizzle from shops that look like the sheds of blacksmiths.

Calcutta's streets may rot with piles of rubbish and the wafting smells of open sewers jabbing like a telegram to the nose, but the people still sweep and scrub and feast with a dedicated sense of everyday pride.

While the neighbourhood cleans and feeds itself, the boys shout and argue, fired by India's battle with Australia in the previous day's Test Match here at Eden Gardens. Names like 'Srinath' and 'Sachin' and 'Kumble' are in the air as they clap each other sarcastically. Boys paying backhanded compliments to each other's batting strokes and bowling deliveries by calling on the names of their heroes and slowly becoming them.

The older boys play a meaner game, moving tight and fast onto the ball and the batsman. The younger ones scatter and weave like mosquitoes, less hard than the older boys, looser in their pleasure.

Even younger boys, barely five years old, beg for money – one with a *bidi* (handrolled cigarette) hanging from his fingers, smoke pluming lightly from his nose. A man binds sugar cane on a cart, his back to the two street games. The bells of a rickshaw man ploughing through the fieldsmen are struck bluntly against his cart handle for attention. Black-and-yellow taxis continue to roll by and blast their horns – the monoxide rulers of Calcutta's streets are coming through!

On high and broken-windowed concrete apartment blocks that surely must be uninhabited and are most probably full of people, black birds land in scavenging spirals. Amid Calcutta's decaying architectural bones, one of the younger boys scoots a ball skyward and down a steaming alley. The batsmen break for two runs. A crow is forced from a mound of rubbish by the ball and flaps vacantly onto an open windowsill. The boys cluster. Argue over the shot. A slightly taller boy with an exercise book and a pen is encircled in a chattering rage.

'C'mon, c'mon, c'mon,' shouts one of the older boys with hard repeated claps – a rare moment of English amid the rushing Bengali of both games. Two of these older boys approximate a look of professionalism, dressed in near whites heavily blackened with the street. A stocky looking fast bowler whips a tennis ball down the bitumen at a wicket driven into a pothole they've smashed into the road. The slight, tiny batsman gets an edge to the ball, and the boy who was shouting for action dives and hits the road hard with his shoulder, reaching out – fast – to his right, while a taxi trundles by his head with casual indifference, distracting him. He fumbles the ball, cursing, hoisting it back at the wicket for a futile, pride-restoring stab at a run-out.

Meanwhile a man sits quietly against a wall, red-bearded, running his fingers through grape-green beads. He rests on an empty potato sack and has a plastic bag and an old plastic mineral water bottle hanging from his neck on a worn piece of string.

He seems at home.

Someone drops a coin in his purple bucket and he reaches in, picks up the coin, rubs the face with his thumb and forefinger, then leans his ear back to the boys and their games. A blind man.

The boys who were begging, including the one smoking a bidi, come back and hassle me for rupees, gesturing with their small hands and making scooping motions to their mouths. I say, 'No.'

A stall holder finishes scrubbing down his metal food cart and washing his glasses. He sweeps away the refuse and the water with a broom made up of loose, hard straw bundled into a fanning circle from the fist to the ground. He hisses something and the boys leave me as indolently as they had approached.

There's a splash.

One of the older boys is suddenly a foot from me, jagging back and forth between the rubbish, the cart, the blindman and the puddles of water. All cat-confused and quick, he looks furiously for the ball, then realizes it's half-submerged in one of the puddles, sights it, grabs it, blinds himself with a stringy splash as he swoops on it and throws it back.

Both games go on. Balls pound the street signs, get stung down side streets, lope up into buildings and don't return (for today at least). There are still a few tennis balls of varying quality, from phosphorescent green to bald and black, held in reserve. But there seem to be penalties for breaking the perimeters of the game in ways that bring about any loss of balls. Bonuses for hitting particular signs make the risk worthwhile, just as belting the ball into a moving taxi is considered a consummate act of point-scoring by the batsman.

More and more bells ring, more and more horns thump and blare. The taxi cabs bully. Motor scooters quack. Calcutta is waking up to a busy Sunday. Both games begin to accelerate as time runs out. Crows and parked cab drivers playing Hindi pop music from their car radios watch. The world jangles and crackles and pumps and sings.

A packed shout signals someone is out in the big game and a busy looking boy marks the grubby, but highly official, cricket scoring sheet. It's decisive. One of the younger boys meanwhile rushes by, pursuing a wild shot past a cinema billboard for *Titanic*. Their junior game also freezes before they too break into a final applause.

It's 8 a.m. A blind man turns his ear. From end to end of Lindsay Street the boys of Chowringhee are calling out. Well played.

Now you make fire.

TIBETAN TRADER with a burning stone in his hand

Nepal Fire

Superstition Kills Woman

Rajbiraj, Nepal, 1 April 1998, *The Kathmandu Post*

Sheer superstition that a blend of extracts obtained from the bark and the seed of the bakaino fruit will absolve her from severe stomach ache ultimately proved costly to Narayama Devi Karki, a resident of Rajbiraj Municipality, Ward No. 4, who passed away at the Sagarmatha Zonal Hospital.

According to her son, the 40 year old Mrs Karki fell unconscious two hours after taking the deadly concoction and was rushed to hospital but the physician on duty there said that he was helpless since the concentration of poison was so high in the body to be neutralized.

He quoted his mother as suggesting he also take the mixture 'to kill the germs in the stomach.'

The late Karki had stood as a candidate for the Town Council membership from CPN (UML) in the local elections.

Roadkill

SOMEWHERE ON THE ROAD BETWEEN KATHMANDU AND Pokhara in Nepal, at the bottom of a series of sharply declining, ravinous valleys, down past hairpin bends and switchbacks and precipices adrenal with careless traffic, past plummeting views of river rapids and rock gorges, on a pulse-thin strip of bitumen that has finally gone flat and straight after so much fearful turning, lies the body of a boy.

I can see the white soles of his feet darkening at the heels, a palm pale and still, the lifeline cross-hatched on his hand.

The rest is just a shape beneath what I initially think to be a blanket.

It's not long before I realize the body is covered by an old towel, with some dull gold braiding forming a track of squares around the perimeter. Despite its regal airs, this harvest-green towel seems a pathetic offering to cover up a mountain boy's death. Not even a blanket here in this small roadside village – not a blanket they can afford to use, at any rate – for such a loss.

Back up the road for a few miles on either side of the village, deep into Nepal's Middle Hills, arriving or leaving this cluster of mud-walled shacks and the small drama at the centre of it all, a long and paralyzed parade of trucks, buses, motorbikes and just a few cars, mostly tourist hire-cars at that. They sit surrounded by people waiting obliviously for things to change or walking along the road to find out what has happened.

It's been storming all morning, a wild grey turbulence sweeping the hills with rain, adding to the gnarly game of nerves this trip along the Prithvi Highway requires. Now that the storm has passed and the road is ready to straighten out for the home stretch into Pokhara, this blockage.

A washout somewhere? A burst river bank? A truck overturned? A bridge gone? Conversations telegraph themselves along the road, speculations that vary from the workaday to the more dramatic. But amid the idle chatter no one seems especially surprised by such a problem in the foothills to the Annapurna Himalaya. It's a place where people have got used to all sorts of interventions from man, nature and the gods, be they Hindu, Buddhist or some animist hybrid of the local tribes-people.

And the tourists, well, even they know that time is a relative thing in 'these kinds of places.' The funny thing about travel is how much of it gets consumed by waiting, by stasis. It's all part of the adventure. We know that much.

Way above us the peaks of the ice-capped Himalaya (Sanskrit for 'the abode of the snows') glare coldly out from under a fresh and blinding burst of afternoon sun. The white light beckons us on, to trekking, mountain climbing and mythical Shangri-las. Down below – in the afternoon shadows of a roadstop farming community slapped up to capitalize on passing traffic – Kali, the Hindu goddess of blood sacrifice, has the body of a boychild in her teeth.

NOT TOO FAR FROM THIS SMALL AND NAMELESS PLACE IS Gorkha, the former home of the ninth Shah king, Prithvi Narayan Shah. Most guidebooks repeat the mythology that after he was crowned there in 1743, he set about uniting the divided principalities of Nepal into a single state, using his considerable military and political skills to force or forge alliances across the country.

A few centuries on from Nepal's harsh path to statehood, Prithvi's name is symbolically tied to Nepal's busiest highway and another kind of cruel, ambiguous dominion: the centrality of Kathmandu and its financial and administrative control of development across all of Nepal.

Based around what is now a constitutional monarchy, Nepal is a fledgling democracy barely ten years old. During that brief time it has experienced eight prime ministers and what economist Devendra Raj Panday calls 'multiparty chaos.' The recent history is depressing, marked by unstable governments and bureaucracy rife with corruption at every level, an unholy mess.

Nepal has also been plagued by Maoist extremists waging a 'people's war' for the last four years. This has involved bundhs (strikes), beatings, intimidation, the odd murder and bomb explosion, with the equally unpleasant and indiscriminant police responses capturing the attention of Amnesty International. But to quote *The Kathmandu Post*, 'the Maoist problem cropped up in the first place because of long neglect of the mid-west and far-west regions of the kingdom. It has been nurtured by poverty, want, illiteracy, social injustice and perceived or real discrimination. The Maoists seek to establish a more just, not necessarily a more liberal, set up.'

Despite the Himalayan brochure images and Freak Street nostalgia for the 1960s, a more troubling reality thrives in Nepal today. To me it feels like a country living on a fuse.

It's certainly ironic that the highway between Kathmandu and Pokhara should be named after Prithvi Narayan Shah, part storybook hero, part brutal despot. This desperately poor, mountainous nation needs the infrastructure of decent roads to assist in development and tourism, that's inarguable. But despite the eco-friendly platitudes of Kathmandu officials, a corrupt, unplanned and devastating cycle of rabid urbanization and development continues to damage both the landscape and the people. Roads have become a part of that vandalistic tide.

Completed in 1973, the Prithvi Highway is an established and major arterial pathway, hardly a thoughtless new development. But the refugee settlements that sit like tatters along its magnetic path advertise the suffering that has brought rural people to its edges in the hope of tourist scraps and fleeting business opportunities.

For many travellers this might be mere background noise to the real pleasures of Nepal. But these changes increasingly impinge upon tourism, as any recent visitor to the diesel-choked atmosphere of Kathmandu will tell you. For now it may be easy enough to escape that blighted city (which still holds patches of genuine Nepali magic in its monkey palace of attractions) and light out west for Pokhara, the starting point for a trek into the Annapurnas.

How to stem the tide of abuse and ruin is not so easy to answer. Like all tourists we want to push outward from the known into the unknown. In doing so we might have to ask that the unknown be protected from our need for comfort and speed. From the rush to get there. The irony is that to appreciate that, all we have to do is take a ride and look out the window.

OUR BUS IS A 20–SEATER COURTESY OF THE PEACE & HEAVEN Travel and Tour Company. It's 300 rupees (US$5.00) a ticket for the eight hour, 200 kilometre ride along the Prithvi Highway from Kathmandu to Pokhara. You can take your pick from a variety of local companies, many painting over the discomforts of the trip with words like 'DELUXE' or 'LUXURY' brazenly on display at their shopfronts, on their ticketing, and even the sides of their most dubious vehicles.

There are bigger air-conditioned monsters to ride. And much cheaper ways to travel too, like the local buses which dispense with the idea of seating and crowd in as many people, chickens, goats and children as possible, piling those that don't fit on top of the roof with the baggage.

Lisa and I opt for the middle path. And take Peace & Heaven with blessed thanks as the bus company for us. Our vehicle is manned by a happy crew of three or so. I say 'or so,' because this tourist bus with no scheduled stops except breakfast (Nescafe) and lunch (Coke and cheese balls is the safest buy) also services other demands along the way: delivery of a dozen loaves of bread from one place to another; a free ride or two from village to village for local friends; periodic road taxes to be paid to men who sit idly beside rickety card tables set in the dirt at dusty buildings. Each stop giving a new individual the chance to involve himself with the bus and its progress in some way.

Before we first leave from Kathmandu at 7a.m. it becomes apparent two people have slept in or had too much of a party the previous Friday night. For a ticket-price equivalent to the cost of a burger and chips, you can imagine the thinking after a big night on the town – oh fuck it, let's sleep in, we'll go tomorrow, it's nothing. Kathmandu has a way of eating tourists up this way. Some people never go further than getting smashed watching bootleg DVDs at the local Thamel restaurants.

There's a bit of conferencing among the crew about the missing passengers, then the bus gets rolling at a few minutes past 7 a.m., a surprisingly prompt start. While the driver does a spin of Kathmandu, two young men hang from the open door, beating the outside of the vehicle, making a piercing, birdlike double-whistle to call for attention, turning up their hands and casting out the word 'Pokhara' like fishermen looking for a catch. There are two seats here to spare and they're in no mood to waste them. But their appeals are useless today.

It won't be till a village somewhere in the rising hills just outside of town that we pick up a thin young boy with a blue parka pulled over his head to protect him from a brief drizzle of rain. It has a lightning bolt on the back etching out the words 'KISS ALIVE.' He bounds on and walks up the aisle with a pile of eggs in his arms, looking frightened and out of place among us. Sits, hangs his head down, and drops off instantly into a semi-sleep.

Our young passenger's jacket is prophetic as we see storm clouds brewing ahead of us. The Tibetan word for thunderbolt is *dorje*. It's regarded as a symbol of male power. At Buddhist temples you will find ornate objects called *dorjes* that are shaped something like hand weights (often with bells attached, a balancing symbol for female wisdom). This boy is declaring his modern manhood, rock 'n' roll style.

The road starts narrowing as we clear the Kathmandu Valley and arrive at its head, broaching a final crest and descending into what will become an ever-spiralling world that plummets and rears up again in front of us. These are, after all, the foothills to the Himalaya. But the terrain, the road and the density of traffic are still a shock to the safety system and the imagination.

Most people's homes – or the villages constituted of maybe a dozen shacks strung like pieces of rope on the edges of innumerable cliff faces – are made of old, raw wood and mud-brick with tin roofs weighed down by stones and bricks. There's barely a spot that isn't farmed, housed, played on, somehow used or traversed.

It would be wrong to characterize the landscape as crowded, however. There is an undeniably wild sense of space to it all, especially as the valleys we pass through open out from the deep river-hugging hills into misty expanses. Yes, there is a strange aloneness here, a sense of man *and* nature. But a sense, nonetheless, of a world populated and used to its fullest.

Periodically we catch glimpses below of the Trisuli, the Marsyangdi and the Seti rivers and their tributaries. Women wash clothes or themselves on their cold banks, while children stumble over flood plains of water-smoothed stone. Clothes and blankets are spread out neatly to dry on the rocks, in one case like a rapture has taken the owners out of their garments and directly to heaven, leaving the pants and shirts to fall where they once stood.

In the villages the men are particularly idle: sitting around benches at tea houses and smoking endlessly; or gathering excitedly about a large round table at about waist height where they play a game called *carom* with what look like poker chips, knocking them outside a circle in the local equivalent to snooker.

Passing by a few sheds, we see a group of men gathered around a large pig, its pink-stained, hairy flesh blotchy with mud. Their mood is casual, even bored, about-their-business as they watch it fighting and squealing for its life when a few of them grab it by the legs. It hits the dust on its back with a crude thud, a *khukuri* (curved knife) is gripped firmly and its whole belly shivers with fear before we pass on from sight.

Just ahead, a child is hounding a small goat up and down a hill for fun. A woman's breast slips out from her loosened sari as she washes her back and hair in the shadows away from the road. A man takes a piss up against a busy highway rockface as indifferently as he takes a mid-morning stroll. The images come and go.

Once you hit the small towns the feverish confusion of shacks, shops, vegetables, clothes, bargaining and people temporarily changes the tempo of your vision. But these places rise and disappear again like dusty dreams: local eyes watching you as you watch them.

Children and women with baskets of fruit, ice blocks you can't eat (water! always polluted, always sneaking its mutable and varied way past your lips) and folded paper bags full of nuts all wave their wares at the bus windows. Some people buy, some *try* to buy, some mock the gaunt, frenzied sales pitches. The bus pulls away again quickly as food is raised up in one last futile gesture at the windows. Clouds of dirt and litter float back over their cries.

Now the hints of rain set in heavily, and our hill roads take on an even more nervous, deadly edge. Most turns are blind and, as is the Nepali way, all vehicles deal with this by blowing their horn and careening around corners with abandon. Here we come!

Our driver has metal-rimmed modern glasses and dresses with a smoothness that differentiates him from the rest of the crew. He wears pressed black trousers with ultra-sharp creases, imitation patent leather shoes and a silky white shirt with brown and red dragons. He also talks and laughs a lot, honking his horn with a brash certainty that inspires your confidence despite the dangers. He knows the road, he knows the other drivers, he knows the villagers on the way who wave at him and acknowledge his passing. You feel you are travelling with a hero.

On permanent guard at the door is a slightly tubby young guy with a moustache and a close-cropped haircut full of knicks that expose his scalp. A home-done haircut to be sure. He'd get a better one in prison, poor bastard. Suddenly he hears a rattling noise, worries about something on the roof and climbs out through an open window with his sandals on, thumping around up above us in the rain and coming back down again through the window in a slithery instant. On the steep, mountainous road he makes his gesture seem breathtakingly mundane.

He also has access to what looks like a light switch. It turns out to be the bus horn. As he hangs freely from the door, he alerts buses and trucks that we are overtaking by pressing the switch and honking with gusto (in tandem with the driver), sometimes hitting the sides of other vehicles with his hand as we swell past in a competitive roar of metal and air. Real cowboy stuff. Yeee-hah.

The bus itself is occupied by all kinds of travellers: Israeli backpackers loud and overbearing, the brash aftermath of compulsory military service in their country; an American working for a non-government organisation (NGO) in Nepal doing reforestation and plantation work to stop erosion and assist in the endless need for firewood; a superior English guy listening to The Verve's *Urban Hymns* playing loudly on his Walkman; an Australian girl from Tasmania who looks a little lost, all apple-cheeked and scratchy-skinned as if life itself is worrying the pleasure of living out of her.

It's one of the curious fruits of travel that travellers often don't like each other very much. They certainly seem to be a rude, stupid and arrogant lot to me on this bus today – to be honest, the very sight of them arouses my instant hatred. I don't think this intolerance is exclusive to me either. There's a secret superiority to this kind of backpacking and adventure. A hermitic drive at odds with any group dynamic and the *Lonely Planet* congestions we all suffer under, an anti-social and misanthropic urge for oneness with nature and escape from our own cultures. And so we travel together as a team forced on each other, with an ambivalent *bonhomie* as we feed off each other for information, in that competitive atmosphere of bragging at and refusing each other which always comes when a grump of travellers merge as one. Friends are thin on the ground indeed.

This grudging mood lifts as the rain begins to clear and we start descending out of the wild hill turns. A banked-up line of traffic doesn't deter our driver who simply swings around it and continues down the wrong side of the road. But what seems like a handful of trucks and buses turns into ten, twenty, thirty and more, with ever-increasing numbers of people milling about on the road and parting as our driver pushes our bus further along, though some people try to stop him while others simply look on stunned as he pumps his horn and laughs his way through their indignation.

Eventually we pull up beside another bus in the same company – 'Peace & Heaven' emblazoned across its side – and somehow squeeze into a formerly invisible gap between it and a Nepali water truck painted up with a typically lush, Eden-like vision of Himalayan blue purity. The painting makes for a contrast to today's newspaper scandal, which has a shot of one of these trucks siphoning up 'kani-pani,' pure water for hotels and private homes, directly from the Kodku Khola, a polluted creek outside Kathmandu.

What's going on?

The road is horribly blocked. And we aren't going anywhere for quite a while. That much is obvious. So we get off the bus and start walking with the NGO American, who seems to know what he is doing, and the girl from Tasmania, who doesn't. At first it's a pleasant stroll, but as we keep walking and walking and walking, we forget about asking what has happened and become hypnotized by the sights along the roadside itself.

Much like our bus journey, there's a detached feeling to it all as we slowly move along. Past 'Adventure Tours' where two young guys swagger around against their travel van clutching their guidebooks like bibles. Past timber trucks loaded violently with wood. Past other tourist buses spilling bored and impatient Westerners everywhere. Past local buses that carry everything from village people to ducks to a lonely looking goat bleating on a roof. Past a bus full to the brim with stacked cardboard boxes, from which can be heard hundreds of baby chickens all crying and chirping in a chorus of vulnerability. Past those beautifully painted water trucks and their false idylls of Nepal. Past Tibetan monks and dishevelled motorcyclists and men hunched in circles around cards.

There is a constant sense that just around the next corner we will find out what is happening, but the blocked line of traffic goes on and on. Just when our trudge seems truly god-forsaken, we meet a woman from Holland who tells us in halting English that a boy has been killed by a truck and that the villagers haven't been letting any traffic through all morning since it happened. She didn't actually reach the end of this snarl of loss, just glimpsed a gathered crowd off in the distance.

The NGO American, Lisa and I decide to keep walking on into the village. But the Tasmanian girl is expressing her reluctance in a way that starts to drag on me and divide my will. I get that creepy feeling fate is laying a hand on me, making me choose which way to go.

Suddenly a pulse moves through the long stream of drivers and passengers, and people are rushing back up the hill to where they came from – things look like they are about to start moving. The problem for us is we're too committed now. We've passed the point of no return and may as well get to the end of our walk. Our bus can pick us up, we hope, as it goes by.

We finally see the village at the very bottom of the valley, after having walked for an hour in all. It is round the proverbial last bend, across a small bridge, directly beside a creek. People are gathered in a stony silence that fills the valley sky, while an opposing stream of traffic sits head to head, segments of a long, sleeping snake shining in the sun.

As we get closer to the bridge and the road completely straightens, we see that a platoon of riot police is waiting. They are wearing blue-grey protective combat gear – and look like toy versions of what they are supposed to be: their tiny Nepali stature heavily padded with insect menace around the shoulders, chest, groin, knees and elbows. Despite the ominous baggage, black batons, automatic guns and bamboo shields (a curious echo of ancient times), the long clear PVC visors on their helmets are flipped open and they stand around sloppily, only half-ready for action.

A few more scattered riot police are posted along other parts of the road. We move past them, push through the crowd and parked vehicles to get into the village itself, which is barely more than a patch of small houses on an incline. A flood plain sits immediately across the road. On this flat grassy field a large semi-circle of peasant women sit quietly. Behind them, a clear 50 metres back again, are the men and the teenage boys of the village. Only the children seem to be moving freely between the male and female groups, in a subdued but irrepressible state of play.

We look back across the road to the houses and a delegation of about a dozen men standing bunched in front of them. My eyes reach down to the road itself and the body of the boy covered in the green towel, his feet poking out from underneath, his hand reaching towards Kathmandu.

A motorbike throttles by and the coughing exhaust ripples up underneath the towel, leaving an entire ankle bare. A man crouches beside the body, tidying the placement of the towel, covering the body again so that only a few toes and fingertips are visible at the edges. The body lies half on its side – there is no blood or gore – it could be someone sleeping. Some bricks and stones are placed around the edges of the towel to try to keep it in place. Next to the body is an old blue sari with a few crumpled rupees.

The traffic on our side of the road has begun to move very slowly as a man in the village lets them pass one by one. He wears a faded *topi* (hat) and has one eye damaged and milky from the effects of trachoma. With tentative authority he stops each vehicle, points to the boy, then the pile of money – the village wants a donation, reparation for this loss, for this road fatality.

Not far away is a bus with what looks like a flat tire. The driver is fat and stunned, standing aimlessly within a circle of riot police. From the markings it is clear that the bus is from India – a bad sign in a small country that sometimes resents such a big and dominating neighbour. The women on board have drawn the curtains and hold their hands over their faces.

Apparently it is not unusual for villagers to attack a vehicle and set fire to it after an accident like this. You can only imagine what they might do to a bus run by a foreign interest. Luckily for them there is a police training camp based just five miles down the road. They've got to the scene with phenomenal speed. You can hear their walkie-talkies radiating soldierly static. But their mood is fragmented – from tense to negotiable to laughing with locals and drivers. The crowd's unease has small pools of tension and indifference. It's clear everybody has been through this before.

The Tasmanian girl begins tugging at our sleeves to leave as if there is something improper about our part in the spectacle. She has been voicing her increasing doubts all the way down this final stretch of road, and won't look at what is happening, preferring to stand back deep in the crowd. Eventually she tells us she is heading back to the bus – her tone is accusing, a little angry, as if to force us to do the same. We refuse her bluntly and she walks off like someone who wishes she could run, tossing shame back at us like an invisible aura of pornography.

It seems to me, though, that these people want us to witness everything that has happened. That this is the whole point of their road blockade. I can't help but reflect on how we treat accidents in a Western country, quickly moving the debris, the dead and the injured, away so that traffic might flow quickly again. This is not the way it is here.

Later I will hear about 'chakka jams,' roadblocks staged by villagers to try to gain restitution after a death has occurred. 'Chakka jams' are also enforced by Maoist groups in the hills as well as small independent transport companies with grievances. But they mostly occur spontaneously, and are the only effective way poor local people can make a protest, to strike against the vehicular tide that they live by. It's the closest thing they have to direct political action.

Today, it all seems under control. A serene weight grips and unifies us. With a few other men I cross the road and donate what I think is 101 rupees. I've been told that giving an even number of rupees to a monk in Nepal is considered inauspicious – that it is always good to include an odd, single note. So I adapt that knowledge to the present situation.

Lisa tells me I've actually donated 1,001 rupees. She thinks I am feeling emotionally overwhelmed. Instead my mistake is part of the muting, reverent blur that compels me blindly forward to give like everyone else. Oh well, it's a good mistake.

A young teenage boy in a red tracksuit crosses the road to thank me. He's almost cheery. I say 'Your family?' and he nods and smiles at me. I look down at the ground and get stuck in my silence as I don't know what else to offer, but a vague feeling of guilt. By the roadside a few people are talking and laughing now. The boy keeps smiling at me. It all feels inappropriate, too casual for me to deal with.

Back down the road, a bent old woman with a fully loaded *doko* (woven basket) on her back, bound to her forehead by a long strip of jute cloth, is walking towards the body. A riot policeman tries to stop her, but she ploughs her way indifferently around him without lifting her head. She senses the body at first, stops, then sees it. Pulls the basket down to her side and pauses in a half-hunched posture, clucking her tongue. For quite a while she stands bowed before the boy, saying something, looking down at him, never up or around at anybody. The police try to move her along with a gentle nudge, but she refuses to take a step, and continues her utterances over the body. It seems a lonely, painful prayer is being wrought from her lips, a blaming thing that cannot blame anyone but fate itself. Then she picks up her *doko*, bends to support the weight and simply starts trudging down the road again. Slow as a turtle. Looking at no one. Taking her load home.

The man tending to the body moves forward to pull the towel over the boy once more. Exhaust fumes keep displacing it despite the stones. He crouches over it in a more permanent way now, like a man eating rice. The other man with the *topi* on his head and the accusing wall-eyed stare continues dealing with the vehicles, one by one. A group of solemn men stand behind the scrappy, gathering pile of money, all dirty and crushed, watching it grow in the late afternoon sun.

The bus loaded with boxes full of chickens comes by and their small, myriad crying can be heard floating through the crowd like a confused song. Our own bus is not far behind and when we see it we run back and jump on board. We try to say what has happened, but there is no time for people to grab for their wallets or peel open their money belts and contribute a donation. Most of them don't even understand what we are talking about till we are passing by. The Tasmanian girl looks away from us in angry disgust. Another girl looks out the window at the precise moment we are beside the boy's body. She turns her head back into her boyfriend's shoulder, cries 'Oh no.' Others crane out the window for a quick glance at the drama.

The man in charge of the money collection stares at us through the bus windows. He opens his tooth-bare mouth, not shaping any words, stuck in the middle of a silenced speech. He can't cross the language barrier. So he tries to point to the boy and the money, but our bus driver says something quickly to him and waves him crudely away. Before anybody knows what has happened, we've already been kicked into second gear, then third, and the scene is frozen and lost behind us. We're barely a hundred metres down the road before our driver is honking his horn and laughing and waving to traffic on the opposite side. Pokhara is just an hour away. And the cold whites of the Himalaya are in our eyes.

Fireman

THERE IS A MAN BEHIND ME. I FEEL HIS PRESENCE FIRST. Everybody looks and I turn to see. He is Tibetan, dressed easy in a workman's blue shirt and cut-off blue trousers, with an army-green shoulder sack and a small backpack as well. He holds a rag in his hands, sweats, mops his face like a long day has passed. He smiles. Without words his gestures say, 'I've just arrived.'

We're blowing a joint in the sun and giving in to our third bottle of beer for the afternoon, waiting for vegetable and egg chow-mein, the hotel specialty at Pokhara's extremely blissed-out Shanti Guest House.

You could call our mood receptive – to anyone, anything.

The Tibetan is possibly a fellow traveller. So we freeze up, used to bartering first with his kind and befriending them second. How do we find a social etiquette beyond buying and selling? We're confused.

He sits down shyly. Begins to talk. I can't join my English to his idea of English, let alone his Tibetan or Nepali. But words aren't completely necessary. By now people around me see better what is happening. He is selling something after all, and he is asking if we would be interested to inspect his wares?

A young, fair-haired man who has had all his gear stolen on the bus into town can't resist the Tibetan's seductive reticence. 'Well, I'm curious about what's in the bag?' he says, pointing to it and nodding.

The Tibetan smiles, lifts his bag. You can see the weight inside. He places it back down with a thick *chink* on the stone platform where we are all sitting in a circle.

Before he will open the bag fully, he pulls out a piece of white fabric. He lays it out neatly on the ground. To his back and mine is a sapling casting delicate shade. I notice the way he folds the white fabric loosely to create a velvety thickness, an illusion of lushness from a cheap piece of linen.

He then puts his hand into his bag, fully pushes open the mouth. He reaches in and plucks out some beads as slippery and smooth as an eel, dangles them above the cloth. Holds them between his thumb and forefinger, drops them down with his three middle fingers so that they fall gently into a lazy spiral.

'Ah, you've done this before,' I say.

He laughs. Eyes shut. Skin brown and tough from sun and wind. Eyes open again. Close, sizing me up. Laughing eyes. Charming eyes.

Then comes 'fossil.' He opens a black rock cleaved in two and touches something Jurassic, makes a movement with his hand like a fish. Nods. Bone bracelets clatter forth. There is one with a laughing head on a large tooth, its smaller bones painted with burnt skulls. Then plain sandstone medallions. And a set of lone black beads, strung on thin orange-stained string that he pats for value.

A silver bird appears in his palm: for opening beer bottles, he shows us, closing his fist around it, flipping his wrist. Holy bells for prayer. He taps them and they hum for a long time. An ornate flint pouch for making fire is laid down. A metal rooster atop a silver tray is placed beside me. He unscrews it and shows me how its eight silver feathers open up to hold a spectrum of paints.

The display on the white cloth begins to dazzle and turn like a story. Capturing eyes.

I spy an orange bone bracelet that matches the patterns on the silver Navajo bracelet I have on my wrist. I slip off my bracelet to show him. He admires it, weighs it in his hand, feeling the silver, overwhelmed. 'American Indian,' I try to explain. 'Navajo people,' I say to him. He quietly repeats, 'Navajo. Navajo. Navajo.'

I point to the maker's name inside the bracelet. 'Emerson Bill.' He says nothing this time and looks at me and for some reason I feel I am hurting him. I take the bracelet back and slip it on my wrist and he smiles again and the moment dissolves.

As the sun climbs, the tree shadows lengthen and protect us. I am stoned and drunk now. Happy to be bold with our new trading partner. He reaches into his bag and I ask what else has he got in there, as I gesture ridiculously to indicate how bottomless it is. Maybe the next thing you pull out will be a BUFFALO, I say, making a huge shape with my hands and mooing. He laughs, shakes his head, then makes a quizzical motion with his shoulders as if to say maybe, let's see?

He passes his hand over the cloth, dropping something quickly. My girlfriend reaches down to two fish carved from a single piece of bone, arched and diving into a heart burnt with shapes I can't decipher.

'You want?' he asks Lisa.

'No,' she says, 'I'm just trying to think who would like it.'

The man who lost everything is drawn to a blue jewellery box with a single green stone on it. Inside the box is a rough ruby-red stone that gives off a citrus scent when you rub it with your fingertips, an odd mixture of earth and fruit.

Two silver eggs. A string of pure silver beads. Smooth stones, 'smooth as water' he says, letting me hold one in each of my hands before lifting them lightly from me and placing them back in the old wooden box to which they belong. He sets the box down, leaves it shut. Maybe we might look again at them later.

'When did you come from Tibet?' I ask.

He does not quite grasp the question. 'Yes. From Tibet,' he replies.

I repeat my question. He nods, understanding this time, answers, '1959.'

He thinks hard. 'I was eight… eight,' he says, holding his fingers out in front of me to confirm this is the right word. Then ten fingers again. '1958. I was eight…' He looks at me, trying to be understood. The three of us say, 'eight-teen' and show our fingers, counting them out. He nods in agreement. 'China,' he adds, one word explanation enough for an eighteen year old to cross the Himalayas and never go back.

His father was 'same' as him. He also sold jewellery. 'Dainsun,' he says, touching his chest.

Dainsun lifts out another small blue bag with traces of silver showing through the laced opening. 'What's in there?' I ask.

He jangles it and smiles humorously and pulls the lace in a single gesture that unloosens the bag entirely, spilling the contents out in a long pile – more bracelets, a tied piece of cloth with rings hooked along it, many in plain silver, some planted with blue stones, others with the imprinted pattern of two cats joined head to head, tail to tail. He leaves them on the ground, to be touched, explored.

The silver bird that carries eight different oil colours in the bell-shaped hollows of its feathers – just unscrew the bird and flip it open, he shows us again – is moved towards me like a pawn in a game of chess. He has noticed my curiosity in it.

At the same time he pulls another leather flint pouch from his shoulder bag. This pouch is very rough looking, very used. It has a half-moon shape and a large curved blade attached to the base. Half purse, half tomahawk. He unbuttons the pouch and plucks out a tiny stone the size of a baby's fingernail. He holds the stone and strikes it with the blade fast and firm in a hard downward stroke. Sparks fly out everywhere, some small, some meteorite intense.

He hands it to me. I can barely cope with this fire-starter, lest I lose half my hand trying to create the friction necessary to get the same result. We all laugh at my efforts. Everyone has a go, everyone fails. Dainsun enjoys watching and laughs very much. He waves his hand. We've got it all wrong.

He says he will bring me a larger rock to work with 'tomorrow.' Hands me back the flint pouch like it is mine already. Pushes the silver bird closer again. I take both. My girlfriend says she will 'think about' the fish. The man who has lost everything buys the jewellery box, adores the smell of fruit inside a stone.

Dainsun starts folding everything away. It is a ballet in reverse, but much slicker and faster. His movements are very quick, very soft. Silver and cloth and bone. Everything back in its place. Till the white cloth itself is folded up and gone.

He nods and smiles. Puts the small backpack over his shoulder. Stands and nods again, not quite a bow, but goodbye for now. Picks up the larger sack and walks over to greet the hotel manager before waving to all of us and leaving through the main gate. We stare at our gifts and I try to create sparks with my new toy – very unsuccessfully.

A day later he returns quietly through the gate and walks up the stairs to our room. He knocks at the door and I am surprised to see him. I had forgotten his promise. Dainsun opens his hand to pass me a large stone and smiles. '*Chakma*,' he says. 'Now you make fire.'

The Angry Hand

I DON'T SEE HER WHOLE FACE AT FIRST. HARDLY ANYTHING of the face at all. She has a shawl, exceedingly black and heavy in the mountain heat, that she uses to shield herself from my gaze. In the barest flash of her profile I detect the possibility of a great beauty, a line of perfection any man would covet.

The only thing I am able to examine in detail is her hands. Reaching out from the darkness of the shawl, these lean brown hands are firm and strong, her wrists delicate, even erotic.

Along the mountain trail I've seen Nepali men stand slack-jawed at the sight of a girl washing her feet under a tap. Found myself with them, staring too.

Now here I am again, hypnotized.

On a stone doorstep to a hut behind her, three young girls are conducting a dance competition, swivelling absurdly and squealing, then covering their eyes in mock embarrassment. I can hear Aqua's 'Barbie Girl' straining out of an old boom-box, flattened batteries speeding and slowing both the song and their laughing moves. It's the anthem to the Annapurnas this trekking season, the tune that greets you when you finally reach the roof of the world.

She rocks to the music, continues spinning goat's fur into wool. A basket of loose white hair gathers itself into soft tufts, is grabbed by the handful and pulled towards a rotating wooden peg. She runs her thumb and forefinger down a long strand as it turns and twists and binds itself. Her gestures are quick and graceful, with the three unused fingers poised upwards as if she too were a woman dancing on a stage.

Finally she glances in my direction and the shawl falls away.

Her face is heavily scarred. The whole right side looks as if it has been pulled off and turned, as if an angry hand had pushed its fingers into wet clay.

It is hard to take in all the damage. I feel as if a sudden deep breath has been taken from me. There is not enough sky to fill my mouth.

She pulls the shawl back into place, patting it self-consciously. Then she takes more goats' hair from the basket. With her head down now – no part of her face visible at all. Just those fast moving, sensual hands. The flickers of wool being spun.

I have seen my mountain woman and she wears the mountains in her skin and bone. A small chicken has wandered onto the warm stone pavement at her back. Girls are singing. It is time for me to look away and breathe.

The Pole

HE SITS HALF IN THE SUN, HALF IN THE SHADE. WEARS A
grey woollen jumper tied by the arms around his neck. Grey shirt, green
army pants. Grey hair, grey blue eyes. Face like a pale, fat balloon. A self-
satisfied man, around 50 years of age.

'Books!' he exclaims. 'May I see?'

He leans over and takes them from us without quite waiting to hear
our answer. 'Do you mind?' he asks again, having taken possession of
our reading. 'Books are too heavy to carry when you are trekking in the
mountains.'

He smiles presumptuously, even sarcastically. Examines them both.
He knows Milan Kundera (my copy). 'Oh,' he says glancing down
upon the cover and twisting his face like a squeezed lemon. Decides to
begin reading Michael Ondaatje (her copy). I feel a little judged and dis-
pensed with, shunted off into a socially undesirable oblivion. But he only
browses the pages of Coming Through Slaughter as if looking for a pertinent
quote long forgotten. He really wishes to talk. And then talk some more.

We're in the town of Marpha, coming down off trekking the highest
and hardest part of the Annapurna Circuit. This section is called the Jomson Trail, the land of apples, the place where life gets easy again. Apple
jam, apple wine, apple pie. It's all so wonderful. Or it was until now.

He begins with a résumé of who he is. At first he tells us he is a lecturer
in computers in America. But then it evolves that he has not been in the
USA for four years now, 'so that is not really true, but I say it anyway.'

For the last four years he has spent all his time travelling. 'Around
India twice. Nepal now three times! China once. Northern Laos, I like – by
train I went through.'

He holds a burning cigarette towards the ceiling, a mark of his urbanity or an old pose. 'I don't like Americans, they are too neurotic,' he declares, pulling a tense face and boggling his eyes like they might explode
out of his head. He laughs, scoffs, the slight trace of a European accent
rubbing on his words.

The thought of neurotic Americans sends him into a treatise on modern Nepali history and the intrigues that distinguish it. He says the CIA built all the bridges on the Jomson Trail in the 1960s after China invaded neighbouring Tibet. 'For guerillas to use so they could go and blow up things. Originally the hippies and the CIA had to share accommodation here. They were the first tourists,' he laughs again. 'All sleeping together,' he adds lewdly.

This is his preferred version of human history: terminally ironic. You can hear the taste for it in his mouth.

'Accommodation was in dormitories,' he explains. 'Ten beds to a room. You did not pay for a bed. Just for food. This is the primitive beginning of the way lodges are run now – you must eat where you stay. That's how they make money. Not through rent. They don't believe in rent here. That's why they get so upset when you eat outside of the hotel. Accommodation is cheap, but not cheap for nothing!'

He knows a lot about Nepal, Tibet, trade, overpopulation, international espionage – everything else as well if you'd care to name a subject. Says he is 'a self-confessed political cynic. Who gives a shit?'

He chews on some nuts. Jokes about knowledge being lost between generations, spitting shells into his hand. 'The grandparents die, the parents die,' and then he opens up his face with a gay spark of insanity and squeaks highly, 'and then *you* die!'

With the last comment he looks right at me and cackles. It's a little death wish for me. There's that air of shrill absurdity peculiar to the kind of Eastern Europeans you usually find in bizarre arthouse movies. I start wondering how I can get away from him, but Lisa seems fascinated, keeps prompting him with the odd question or two. He's only too happy to respond.

He does not return home to Europe much he says. 'Four years ago the last. Poland is below Thailand in development,' he explains sniffily, clueing us in to his origins. 'Poland was not a country for 150 years. It became a country again after the World War One. They are very scattered. Polish people think let's go somewhere else,' he shrugs, dismissing the place permanently.

He reads philosophy and psychology mostly. 'I stay away from radio, television, newspapers too. The world has been in a partial hell for 300 years. Not much matters in that, except a nuclear explosion,' he laughs, 'and poof!'

Never married. 'But I have a nine-year relationship. She is my financial manager now. She could bankrupt me if she does not like me,' he mock-whines, needling out a phrase: 'Please, one more slice of apple pie.'

He is obviously turned on by this self-perpetuated powerlessness, by the management relationship he has established with an ex-girlfriend. As if not handling his own money makes him less materialistic. I get the feeling he has made this poor woman his surrogate mother.

We begin to discuss with him the way Tibetan children are chosen to become monks and use the word 'compulsory.'

'Compulsory? No! Bullshit word. Nothing is compulsory.'

But ideas of freedom and compulsion fall to the wayside. He has other thoughts to play with. He likens the monasteries in Thailand he has visited to mental hospitals. 'In the West we have mid-life breakdowns and you go to a mental institution. People with mental problems can go to a monastery there.'

An altogether healthier solution he believes. He has lived in monasteries there he tells us. And in an ashram too. Practised yoga postures. Drank 'lots' of lemon tea. Stayed at the ashram for three months. 'If I tried to piss them off, they would laugh. That's Eastern philosophy,' he says, approving strongly. I imagine lots of frustrated Thai monks shredding their saffron robes at night, hoping he might be gone by morning.

He especially hates Catholicism. 'It's like bloody Special Forces,' he barks at me after asking if I am one (I say yes with Papal zeal). But then he admits he stayed at a Catholic monastery too once. Learnt the finer elements of Zen Buddhism from a priest there, 'although he did not use those words. An Italian who liked spaghetti.'

Above the Pole is a scenic horizon picture of the Himalaya. Quiet and white and blue.

He is talking much more to Lisa now. Reassures me that he will not try to steal her from me. Says he is trying to transcend all desire. To live purely on a metaphysical plane, something I probably find difficult to appreciate.

Which is why he can tell my girlfriend – as he stares intently into her eyes – that she is someone 'gifted.' A fellow psychic traveller. Unlike yours truly, a lumpen Catholic throwback and an obstacle to his romance of the higher mind.

For most of the time I am barely there in the conversation at all. In fact I'm taking notes, which shows you how interested he is in me. But the Pole gravitates towards me again on the issue of my Catholicism – he's like a young boy wanting to smash a toy that bores him.

He has persistently expressed his hatred of Christianity in a variety of ways throughout the conversation. 'I used to teach Comparative Religion. So I compared Christianity with totalitarianism, and Hinduism to a liberal democracy – they have all these gods, if you don't like one you can just go to another.'

Similarly, there is his definition of Jesus as 'a motherfucker. This Virgin Mary, if God entered her, and God and Jesus are one, then this makes him a motherfucker. So *you* believe in a motherfucker,' he says, jabbing a finger at me and smiling.

Finally there is his analogy of icons. 'Buddhism is this big fat happy man sitting cross-legged. Christianity has this guy nailed to a cross who looks like he came out of a concentration camp. Who would you follow?'

The sunlight is moving on his face as he talks. Maybe an hour has passed, his thoughts spraying out from one subject to another. I look at his mouth and wonder if it is a time machine.

This is a monologue. We are not required to speak at all. The air is friendly but intense throughout his speechifying. Like being caught in a heavy drone. And though he talks a lot, he also pries with his eyes. Can-opener eyes that see what he wants them to see.

He goes on and on, tells us he is continuing his studies into all religions. Likes Tao the best. Recommends *The Celestine Prophecy* to us as 'Indiana Jones and spirituality. I know it's for fucked-up people, but it's all right.'

An only child, he is also 'teaching' his parents by not giving them any means of contacting him. This distancing process has been going on for years.

One time back in the USA he said he would only see them if they went to a psychologist. 'They did. And they told me it was the best thing they ever did. Maybe they put some slime on me or kiss my arse,' he says, patting his backside, 'to make me happy?'

I don't say a word.

Another time he admits he had a tantrum and made them travel from New York to LA by train rather than plane to visit him. 'They were frightened of the train. And of changing at Chicago. But I said I would not come and meet them in LA if they arrived by plane! So they did it. And when I met them at the station I had to drive them somewhere with friends they made on the trip.'

I see an opening and go for the jugular. His rejection of Christianity sits oddly with his treatment of his parents, I suggest. 'You seem to believe that redemption lies in pain. That's very Catholic of you,' I say sarcastically.

'There's nothing wrong with the philosophy of redemption through pain. It's true,' he replies, completely ignoring the allusion. 'The Buddhists will tell you that life is pain, life is suffering.'

Then he smiles. Like a fat child. Clearly he seeks to become a jolly Buddha himself, transcending us all. He has had out-of-body experiences. Flown all over the place. He does not know how it happens. But he laughs about it. Call himself 'a fuck-up.' Calls us 'fuck-ups.'

'And if you don't know you are a fuck-up, you're even more fucked up.'

I notice both his shirt sleeves are frayed at the cuffs and torn above the elbows. Like a well-dressed businessman down on his luck. 'I don't care,' he says, pulling self-consciously at his clothes after seeing my eyes drift along them.

One must get away from the material world. As he is trying to do. And yet there is something ostentatious about his abandonment of materialism. 'I have turned my back on America, on the West. Sometimes I even beg to make myself humble,' he confesses, asking me if he can eat the leftovers on my plate, which he devours with superior relish.

It all started four years ago, funnily enough. 'During an earthquake in LA. Someone yelled get under a desk. I have never felt so alive. I grabbed a pregnant woman and pulled her under the desk with me. When it stopped I realized I was laying on top of her to protect her. Right across her womb,' he says, a little stunned by the memory, the insight he has been chasing ever since.

'I did this without thinking. There was no thought at all.'

A Matter of Interpretation

I'm in two minds about it. –AUSTRALIAN
I am double thinking this. –NEPALESE
I have my arse between two chairs. –SWISS FRENCH

Patron Saint

I'VE GOT A DEAD FRIEND IN MY HEAD.
I don't know why she won't leave me be.

Or why I don't let her leave me – not just yet anyway. I must need something from her. But I don't know what it is.

It is six months, maybe a year, since Ellen died. Already it is getting hard for me to put an exact time on her death. Maybe that's the first sign of something slipping away despite these haunted feelings.

I'm sitting here on a bed in the Red Planet Hotel in Kathmandu, listening to the noise of the street, how busy and alive it is – yet she still comes to me from another world and drags me back there.

For some reason I wrote her name out again last night as I was entering my contacts into a new address book. Keeping names I felt I'd need again, dispensing with those that were irrelevant or long gone or who I'd just as easily and casually catch up with again if I ever returned home to Sydney.

It felt important to write Ellen's name out again. Like I was keeping faith with her somehow. I seemed to need it, to see her name on the page even though I knew she was dead. I put her mother's address and phone number down beside her name – there was nowhere else to record a contact for her. Even though I knew I'd never call her mother and felt ashamed of not being able to make such a call. Ellen would have wanted me to check in on her mum, but after a while it just gets too late and all you can do is nurse whatever it is you knew of someone.

I remember Ellen one mad night when she invited me down the road to her house for dinner, disappearing for minutes, then whole half hours, re-appearing spasmodically, her whole household running up and down stairwells and round corners, nothing but footsteps, whispers, buried laughter. She was cooking pasta for me. It took four hours and tried my patience to the limits. Her world had gone into drug-fucked slow motion. A night and a house as tangled as the spaghetti in the pot. And just as badly cooked.

I think of the beautiful painting she did of me wearing a hat, with bits of dream bric-a-brac sailing about my head in a blue-coloured wind: poems on paper, a bird's wing, leaves, light globes and fish. Then I recall a large dark photo she scratched, heat distorted and painted over, a room full of our friends being slowly overcome by their own amphetamine voodoo. She was big on ghost things.

Ellen took one of my favourite photos ever of myself. I was sitting barefoot in a chair, and she was looking at me through a fish-eye lens that grasped the junkyard of books and records and shelves and piles that I called my attic bedroom. Later we got stoned and she looked out the window to a great tree fresh with spring leaves shaking in the breeze. She shivered a little and said, 'Gee there must be a lot of people in that tree.' I had always thought so, but it surprised me to hear someone else say so.

Back in Sydney I kept seeing her after she died, walking the streets of our mutual past. Still out there, living secretly. Mostly on her way out of a train station, about to take her camera somewhere and do something, always on a mission. As if she hadn't stopped working at all.

I remember the first time I'd seen that she was really in trouble. Her little broken voice talking to me in the back yard as we sat in the sun, how embarrassed she was about going to rehab to get help. Her smallness in the world shocked me.

What had happened to the big mischievous laugh? The terrible red-headed temper? The creativity that was best when it was on the move? The presence behind those kinetic wedding photos where all our friends gathered at one big celebration and she blurred the vigour of dancing and conversation into the matrimonial heart of the day?

There was a feeling Ellen could be great, but she didn't feel it enough herself. Now she comes running at me from nowhere, an avalanche of old air and whispers: there, there, there she is, no.

I think we find pieces of ourselves when we travel, pieces we don't even know are still with us. Being in a foreign place sees them float up out of us – old arguments, spent lusts, lost faces and lost words. I'm surprised this is happening to me now. And that I seem to be falling back into myself with these memories, moving away from Lisa into a zone that can't be lived again, just remembered. Somehow stuck inside myself like I've missed my own life.

Outside on the street all kinds of journeys are ready to begin and end. Kathmandu calls me with its throttling midday life. Lisa is amongst it all, eating, reading, waiting for me to come and join her.

I know Ellen would have loved the worn hands of men here, their fingers like rope, the smell of the local cigarettes, the hint of snow in the wind and how it flies into your skin like fine glass. She would have got it all in a photo. And laughed with me about unseeable things.

But she's back in Sydney now riding the ghost trains. I can only imagine what we would do together, the story we might tell. The things I wish we could speak about because we were such good friends. Something's bothering me. Come back baby, come back and take a picture for me.

Don't go to another country and be single.
Take me with you. Don't be alone in another country.

A song for lovers and travellers as sung by
A VARANASI BOATMAN

India Take Me With You

Not Far From…

I CAN ONLY SEE A MILE OR SO. TO WHERE THE HEAT HAZE, the dust, the pollution, the smoke, the sky get condensed into a single air. Joni Mitchell's 'Coyote' is on the stereo, crackling out of a small set of speakers attached to my Walkman. From our hotel room I can see that in the nearer distance two people are walking along a sandbank on the opposite side of the Ganges.

It was over there that someone else in the hotel had seen 'something in the water. I thought it was two dogs fighting,' he told us, 'till I saw the baby's arms and head drooping in the dog's mouth and I realized what it was.'

Vultures mark the sky, annihilating charcoal strokes over this nearby horizon. It's an island graveyard for those who aren't burned: bodies buried, or washed up on the shores. The birds come, so too do the dogs. The divine and the feral finish off the matter at hand.

Cricket is being played out on the stone esplanade directly below us. A crowd of boys claps. It's a big game with a big audience, between two of the river *ghats*' (stairs) best teams. The winners get a colour television set, but the prize is less important than the honour – and less divisible.

I don't know how they can do it. It's been 48 degrees Celsius every day here. So hot your eyeballs dry up if you go out in the middle of the day. Yet they play and play, fantasizing about Test matches, acting out their heroes' roles. It can feel as if your skin is being cooked in an oven even when you are in the shade. How can they even move, let alone run?

The heat of the day may finally be going with the afternoon, but the wind is still dry and warm. Out there the winners are being celebrated over a bitter, crackling microphone. Everything lingers, dangles, struggles. We've been splashing buckets of water on the concrete floor to cool off the room. Water everywhere. In an hour it's gone. Evaporated.

It's an oddly silent room. An old personality in and of itself. The marks of candle flames run up the wall from blackened holes.

The fan above us turns in a yellow *thut thut thut*, the cord and wires attached to it in a confused, dirty knot. A poster shows an idealized picture of a tree by a river. This kind of message art is popular all over India and Nepal. It says, 'Like a tree we each must find a place to grow and branch out.'

Dusty children are washing cups and plates in the hall by a stone basin too tall for them to reach. It is full of fresh, cool water. They use a tap lower down at the base. The adults simply grab a bucketful, refresh themselves first with the sound, then the wet weight of the bucket as it comes back to them, then the water itself.

On a balcony outside a man cleans his teeth and spits, squirting out a white stream like a piece of string. I can see him through a narrow window to the side of our room. I wonder if he's been watching us.

A newspaper flutters on the bed. It has a front page about 'two miscreants' who killed a man and kidnapped a boy. The use of the word 'miscreants' amuses me, as if the journalist purposely insults the criminals' dignity with some old English abuse.

The bed itself has absorbed the heat, absorbed it into the sheets, the mattress, the frame, as surely as hot, heavy stone.

She is to one side, recovering from diarrhœa. An empty bottle of 7-Up is on the table.

The tape has played on now: 'trouble man' 'don't you cry' 'spread your wings' 'I can't abide'… pop phrases leap up and dissolve into the stilling heat. No longer part of distinct songs anymore, the lyrics break off and turn adrift into a numb and fragmentary poem that pushes itself periodically into the brain.

A drop of sweat stains the page I write on. Outside a bell repeats itself. It is hard to say if the colour of the river is blue or grey.

Varanasi Morning

SIXTEEN PAIRS OF SUIT TROUSERS AND TWO TOWELS DRYING on a handrail in the sun. A grandfather teaching a boy how to bless himself with water from the Ganges, both of them waist deep in its slow flow. A charred skull and body being struck with a bamboo pole by a 'man of fire' at a funeral pyre by a riverbank *ghat*.

Varanasi is rising.

Men beat clothes, ankle deep in the river, swinging the knotted material down on smooth stone. Ten, twenty, thirty of them in a line. Pounding, grunting.

The horizon is dusty and smoking. The sun egg yolk-ish, muted in the low quiet morning sky.

A woman, fully dressed, is pulled from underneath the water dripping from head to toe. She mutters and stumbles, helped by two younger women, holding her hands together and nodding to the sun, once, twice, then a third time again as she stumbles. Praise the sun, praise the sun.

Varanasi is rising.

Up on a hill of stone slabs, white sheets are uncoiled from the shoulders of a boy. At the directions of his young mother, dressed in parrot green with shining black sandals, the edges of the sheets are seized and neatly squared, fast and floating, to the ground. Their precision is a delight. They cover the hill like a Christo work of art, sixty white squares, unrippled and damp.

Boatmen sleep on their craft, heads and torsos wrapped away from the sun in T-shirts and rags. Their sleeping, dishevelled bodies informal, sloppy brothers to the golden-bound forms of the dead brought down to the burning ghats and left to await a ceremonial dipping into the Ganges before they are finally cremated.

The man of fire cracks open a skull, a lick of flame pokes its tongue through.

Embers splash upward into the smoke as he continues to strike it. The legs have already perished from the knees down, and he tries to beat off the stumps as well. The whole body jumps to the blows and more flames leap around it, refreshed by the movement.

The pyre itself is in three tiers. Logs criss-crossed on two levels so that hot ash and bits of flesh and bone can fall into the white cinders. The body itself sits atop the pile, falling away at the legs and the arms, slowly going at the centre. The neck leading to the blackened skull, akin to a charred knob of wood, is thin like a cord or a branch.

How long can the body last? How much of it is left?

They say when a woman burns she leaves behind a hip bone. That a man's thorax will resist the flames. It all takes about six hours.

Nearby smoking piles of ash, fine and hot, betray subsiding fires. Other men of fire, cloths tied to their heads and across their faces – against the smoke, against the smell – sit down in a circle, talking in a crouch like men at a barbecue.

Relatives sit on stone steps above them, about a half a dozen men in all. They could be waiting for a bus.

The men of fire are actually standing on a black slope that leads down into the river. Old ash accumulated and trod on. More ash floats in the river, in coal grey surface pools. Smouldering logs from the finished fires are rescued and dipped in the Ganges, splashed and saved. They dry in the sun to be used again. Their gnarled shapes not unlike that of the human bodies they consume.

Some people are not burned. Their bodies are wrapped in material and simply thrown into the Ganges. A ritual reserved for baby boys, holy men, and people who have died of leprosy or a cobra bite.

Here at the holy city of Varanasi (Hindu), Banares (Muslim) or Kasi (an even older Hindu word), the pilgrims come to wash themselves in the Ganges, to purify themselves for the next life. And if they are lucky, to be burnt and thrown in the waters and go on to *moksha* or nirvana, liberation from the cycle of death and rebirth.

My boatman leans over to one side. Spits a greenish, beetrooty gob of chewed *pahn* into the face of the river.

Another man in a smaller boat pulls up alongside to try to sell me a candle flickering among marigold blossoms on a banyan leaf, an offering to the gods that you are meant to set afloat, calling out to your mother or your grandmother or your sister, whichever one of them is dead. 'The river will answer back to you.'

Not far away, children swim. At another set of stairs, a bathing *ghat*, women and men wash side-by-side in two distinct clusters.

I can feel the heat of the rising daystar on the skin of my face. Its awful strength.

I see a fellow traveller from the Hotel Sunview in another boat, smiling and waving. I see trousers washed and drying in a line on the handrail. The slender legs of a man, back arched, pounding clothes on a stone, his body thin and sleek from behind like a woman's.

Boys call out 'hello', their only English word. A sadhu with two white finger marks on his forehead sits cross-legged on the shore, holding a trident, staring straight into the sun, God-mad.

My boatman turns us around with a lazy stroke of one oar. We have seen the dead burning and Varanasi by the Ganges as it wakes. One hour for 50 rupees, a bargain in the off-season.

He sings me an Indian song as we splash slowly home. 'A good song,' he says, smiling the bloody grin of a *pahn* chewer. To a man from a woman. He sings it then recites the words in English.

'Don't go to another country and be single. Take me with you. Don't be alone in another country.'

Notes on a Train from Varanasi to Delhi

I.

Peacocks in ditches
    people in rags
    and smoke
Man in white
    on a bike
    cycling the dawn
Boy with oxen
    near a yellow field
    walking ever
    so slowly
Brahmin in the bunk
    opposite me
    spitting in his hand
Wipes it behind his seat
    goes back to sleep
    superior man.

2.

Last night a doctor
joined us from Lucknow
with his daughter's folded hands

For company
he offered us sandwiches.
She averted her gaze,
spoke only when spoken to,
prepared for her exam.

His 'friend' the gynæcologist
burst upon us at another stop.
Wore a green sari.
What a woman,
big as a mountain,
talked the legs off a chair.

She spoke in 'Hinglish,'
joked the by now
half-sleeping daughter
from behind her modest
prescription eye-care.

Hinglish: the habit
of speaking in
both Hindi and English

Unconsciously.

'Half of India
does it you know.
Haven't you watched TV?!'

We listened to
the woman's speeches
masked as conversation
tracing the spine

of everything!
Oh on and on
she went like the wheels,
would she never end?

Through the window,
we watched a blind man
walk an unknown station,
rub the train with a stick,
carry a sack on his shoulder,
find his way to a door
without a helping hand.

Now the daughter begins to talk
of the chemical table,

alcohol, physics and grades.
The gynaecologist
of logic and ethics
so proud of this girl's
bright rationality.

Father beaming
for his child
and a new wife
in the making.

India you kiss us
with your family.

The Searchers

AT THE MOONDANCE CAFÉ IN OLD MANALI A GROUP OF
Indian boys masquerading as men sit around in bad denim and crap
techno gear, acting cool, mixing with tourists, looking sleazy and wise
to the world they know.

A beggar with shrunken legs knuckles his body along in the dust beside them. A beautiful tree thick with small, tight green leaves provides plenty of shade. 'Hello, hello, one rupee, one rupee.'

The cripple's face is fresh and young and tanned. He does a good trade.

Pink Floyd's *The Wall* is pumping out over the open-air stereo: a guitar like a jet plane soars into a recognizably cold melody and the first dull mantra of 'Comfortably Numb'.

A girl with a scarred face – a splashed-through-a-car-windscreen look – sits at a table sucking back hard on her cigarette, legs crossed to show off her Tibetan cowgirl boots. Sex appeal has replaced beauty. She declares it as a permanent fit of anger at the world.

Nearby a Japanese couple by the café entrance look as if they just walked off the pages of *Dazed & Confused*. Nose piercings, sinister tribal tattoos, expensive designer backpacks, clothes out of a Grand Royale catalogue, a cute print of Astro Boy on the girl's T-shirt, a real fuck-for-Ecstasy indifference to her sensuality, something X-treme sports about the boy's whole demeanor, your modern degenerate samurai going all the way out there. I can't help but feel envious and intimidated by their completeness.

A younger boy approaches the teenage Indian gang at the table nearby. He tries to approximate their gaudy take on rave culture, but he can't quite cut the look. Instead of being fashionably baggy and futuristic his clothes are ill-fitting and tawdry, the cheap copies that they are, further dated for being obvious hand-me-downs from one of the older boys. He mimics their toughness, a certain scammy cynicism they all mistake for being cool as they ostentatiously palm a buddha stick of dope from one hand to another. One of the older boys punches him playfully in the stomach, hard enough to hurt, light enough to excuse the violence. He bends with the blow, laughs it off, holds his stomach and breathes tensely. Got to be tough.

Two English guys nearby us sit around with their shirts off, all muscle and milk fat, white as sheets. Why they think anyone would want to see their bodies is a mystery. They soak up the sun and the undisguised envy of the Indian boys. The admiration makes them feel even more like the backwater kings they are.

Two Dutch girls pass by, their voices cooing with rounded European vowels. One is fat and badly dressed, stuffed into tight cut-off jeans and a t-shirt that says 'NO HASH, NO TIGER BALM, NO MONEY, NO GUIDES, NO THANKS.' The other is a slim, attractive blonde, wearing shorts and an orange bikini top.

One of the English guys nudges his friend, who flips his sunglasses up and eyes off the bikini babe. He chews gum, says something back to his mate while the gum sticks to his teeth like drool. With their cleanly shaved heads they literally look like cocks, white and hard in the light of day. A fact they are extraordinarily proud of.

Who owns this fucking place? This alternative universe?

Outside this dropout zone, cars pass by squirting sleepy clouds of dust up from the side of the road. Hawkers try to sell off cheap clothes, hideous hippie knockoffs and rave t-shirts, a mix of tie-dye and smiley prints and 'shiny happy people' patterns and plain bad tourist slogans for beer, pot and trekking.

Small A4 posters decorate a few trees and walls with far less forced cheer. Desktop publishing efforts that we will see again and again all over town. 'Have You Seen ... ?' they ask desperately.

The names and accompanying images change but the message is always the same. Young Israeli, English, Australian and German backpackers who have disappeared in the region while trekking. We see the same posters often enough to start feeling as if we know the people who have disappeared, like they might be friends of ours, might even be us in some other, parallel twilight zone.

All the details are there – how old they were, the places and parties at which they were last seen, where they had planned to go or what had been heard about them, along with a message from their families or their lovers, whoever the searchers might be. The appeals for help, somebody help them, please.

Photos on the posters show fresh faces in their late teens and early twenties studying for university exams by a computer or sitting next to a tent smiling independently. One of a delicate looking Scottish boy waving goodbye before he hops onto a bus feels particularly grim. Some have been missing for years; others are much more recent. You wonder when hope runs out for these people's family and friends. When the search ends in futility?

I look up to the densely forested hills of the Kullu Valley, feel some sense of their green menace as Manali's frenetic sprawl intrudes into them like ugly fingers. Everywhere here the scent of shit, piss, rotten fruit and diesel fumes, the scenes of furious building to make yet another guest house, the scattered smell of rotting apple blossoms from trees that were once part of thriving local orchards, the sounds of booming techno floating up into the valley and the sky like a relentless insult.

You know with awful certainty that they are out there somewhere – dead and maybe buried, robbed and murdered for their boots, their camping gear, their clothes. Killed for small change in Kullu Valley. Lost from us all.

On Temple Road:
The Way, the Truth, the Light

'DANGEROUS DRIVERS KILL AND DIE, LEAVING ALL BEHIND to cry.'

The warning signs are many on the steep and winding road from lower Dharamsala to McLeod Ganj, home to the Dalai Lama since 1960.

It's easy to be impressed – or simply terrified – by the efforts of your car or bus to get there and the reckless attitude of those behind the wheel. Some drivers exceed all hope of common sense, ignoring the advice emblazoned along the road and crashing into the safety signs themselves. A truly Zen way to go, blowing their horns to the last.

As yet another billboard puts it, this is 'The little Lhasa in India': a cool holiday retreat from the intensity of the Indian summer and a pilgrimage destination – partly spiritual, but also political – for Buddhists and travellers of every ilk.

Up here in the clouds, in the foothills to the Indian Himalaya, there is a feeling something still survives of old Tibet – a remnant Buddhist culture over the mountains and beyond the reach of the Chinese. That this 'something,' not only a Tibetan government in exile and a great religious leader, but an actual feeling, an aura, even, might some day return from whence it came and flower again.

As you get closer to McLeod Ganj a circular male drone can be heard washing down the hills along with the repetitive *doof doof* of techno: the sounds of Tibetan monks chanting and at play. We will discover saffron-robed novitiates with pictures of football players pinned on their walls next to the Dalai Lama, incense burning beside their Bob Marley CDs as they pray. Up here Buddha's children still follow the satellite broadcasts of the World Cup soccer and enjoy the latest Massive Attack remix. It hardly seems like a contradiction at all.

On the narrow streets the Tibetan facility for trade is in full swing with market stalls and shops full of handicrafts, beads and the odd religious 'antique' battered into shape. There's also the inevitable frenzy of cheap building, a spate of new hotels and businesses trying to cash in on a Western tourist boom that shows no sign of abating.

This makes McLeod Ganj an easy town to misread and a strangely pregnant destination filled with the feelings of its visitors as much as the inhabitants who live here. One has to look past the noisy commerce to something else inside the mood of the town. Despite the modernizing trends and the rush to accommodate tourism, you still feel – physically, if nothing else – a little closer to heaven with each turn higher up the road as the air cools sharply among the pine needles and fluttering prayer flags.

After a while you see that even the backpackers here are of a better quality than anywhere else in India (not a hard thing to achieve, admittedly): they're more purposeful, educated and respectful in both their character and conversation. They have not come here for the dance parties or the drugs or the wild sights, but for something you might call an ideal, even an apprenticeship. The Tibetan cause and its spiritual current exert a powerful pull over the imagination.

So it is that we climb the heights of northern India, defying grimly philosophical signage and the traffic madness that matches it. Hoping to catch a glimpse of His Holiness, the Nobel Peace Prize–winning fourteenth incarnation of the Buddhist deity of Universal Compassion, who by all accounts is quite a card, a veritable laughing saint. Or to at least taste a slice of a Tibetan life long ago suppressed in its homeland.

Tibetans address the Dalai Lama as *kundun* when they meet him, a word which translates roughly as 'presence.'

You sense this presence throughout McLeod Ganj. Rumours abound wherever we walk that the Dalai Lama is not in town, that he has just arrived from overseas, that he has left, that he will make an appearance soon. The whole community pulses to when and where he might emerge, to the very thought of him. In such a tiny place, this feeling is infectious, exciting, sometimes even soothing.

IT IS JUNE 10TH, THE DAY OF BUDDHA'S ENLIGHTENMENT AT AGE 35 and his later 'paranirvana' or 'final disappearance' – a death explained in terms less than final, and in his divine case as 'a candle goes out'.

Local Tibetans refer to the event colloquially as 'full moon day', the necessary astrological movement in their calendar to signal the onset of this most holy of moments. A light, cool rain also signals the start of the monsoon season, an auspicious change in the weather.

It's said the effects of positive and negative actions on this day are multiplied ten million times. Which is why a program of 'virtuous actions' is expected from all people, most especially the monks of the town. Goodness is essential.

We arrive in McLeod Ganj by Ambassador hire car but there is absolutely no room on the tight and muddy streets to park our vehicle. So we literally drive into the hotel, and I mean all the way in, parking our car in the unfinished lobby. No one seems to mind. We could almost reach out of the car window and sign the register.

We are still unaware of the great day proceeding quietly around us. Once settled, we follow the ritual habit of most travellers and set off looking for an email centre. A place we will never find.

Instead we walk out of the main section of McLeod Ganj, down the hill and into a long roadway strewn with hundreds and hundreds and still more hundreds of beggars. Families in all their wretchedness. *Sadhus* muttering and waving tridents and tin cans. Lepers reaching out, if they can reach at all. Old men and women with rotten teeth and empty mouths. The young and the sick. The grossly deformed. They're all here, hands outstretched, a thickness of hushed voices blending with the smoke of their fires and the spattery rain, rising up into the pine needles, filling this dank forest with need. In his wanderings the Buddha once declared himself 'one of the beggars,' absolving himself of a material life and declaring his sympathy for the suffering of others. Where might he be were he among them today?

I see a boy who has an arm missing from the elbow, the bony stump pushing through the flesh to create a wet, red star inside the dry bubbly skin. Another man who has two completely white irises like horrible eggs seated in his face. A girl in a dirty brown skirt walking past them, carrying two glasses of what looks like strawberry milk on her way back to her waiting mother. Despite the images of horror, it's like some awful picnic out there.

Hands are cupped, grabbing. Everybody looks skinny and desperate – and yet there is a settled quality to the crowd as they wait compliantly for the generosity of passers-by. We estimate 2000, mostly Indian, people have come here, dressed in rags and draped in garbage bags and plastic to protect them from the rain.

A group of monks in red robes extracts change from a grateful beggar, returning a small portion to him for his troubles. They then proceed to walk down a line giving one rupee or 50 paisa pieces to each person. Such kindness seems futile. There are more monks coming, but so many more people waiting.

Just off this road two Tibetan women are making their way through the forest. It smells richly of pine needles and fresh rain, as you'd expect, with the pungent addition of human shit. They prostrate themselves again and again along a stone path, making their way by knees and bellies and breasts and palms to the Dalai Lama's temple. The women wear aprons covered in moisture and mud, moving head to toe as they bow, marking their way precisely with a stone. A ten-minute walk to the temple will probably be an afternoon's crawl for them. More devout people than they circle a holy mountain the same way every year.

An old man in a makeshift hut is located about halfway along the path, surrounded by parchments and stones. Young men are paying him to write down messages upon them, either their most secret wishes or their prayers for the dead.

A monk called No Ang stops beside us on the road. He tells us all this is happening 'because of *Sakadawa*, Buddha's birth and death day. This is why the people have come.'

But these are Hindi people?

'Always Indian people,' he says in an uncertain English.

How does it make you feel?

'Heart depressing – yes,' he says, and then he laughs.

His laughter has a fatalistic, monk-like way about it. The tone is oh-well and what-to-do-but-do-what-we-do. He hands out his small coins. Goes on down the road adhering to the good will of *Sakadawa*. Ironically it is the Indian people who act as refugees here, not the Tibetan priests and people moving serenely among them, casting good will into desperation.

At the local shops a few of the monks buy biscuits and food, or seek more change for their rupees in order to disseminate them among the crowd. We do likewise and find ourselves overtaken by a feeding frenzy as a small mob sees an opportunity – mostly children who can't and won't control themselves. There is a distinct sense of consciousness to their hunger which surprises me, a licence to madness. They grab and crowd in around us with greater and greater intensity, mucous-y, hair lousy, calling words I do not understand. My hands are wet with their grabbing, with whatever it is the beggars have on them: spit, snot, rain.

Eventually the packet of biscuits is wrenched from my fingers and someone darts off viciously, pursued by a few others. The crowd fragments, discontented but quick to go. A man with a child on his hip keeps following me, gesturing to his child, pushing his hand to her mouth, making me feel as if I have shortchanged him. I yell at him and he backs away.

Wisps of smoke continue to rise off the tiny fires and fight against the rain. Mothers and children seek cover from the increasing downpour by crouching under sheets of black plastic that have been supplied by someone. A *sadhu* climbs a tree to watch it all like a dark bird, as if it is his kingdom to survey.

Others stay standing in the rain, nowhere to go, touching their foreheads in a holy assignation, then reaching out with the same familiar hands towards me. It is starting to really pour down now. We decide to turn back and head up the road again to the safety of McLeod Ganj.

Another tourist with biscuits is mobbed in front of us. He is luckier than we were – protected by an old man who keeps whipping back the children with a pine branch. Even as they are beaten off the biscuit pack gets torn open and the contents fall on the road. The monks and the beggars all look and laugh together at this chaotic scene.

It is as if this were Christmas and these were the gifts.

We walk further on with a ten rupee note clutched tightly in my fist. People have spotted me pulling it from my wallet and pursue me and beg and appeal and beg again as we walk up the road. I clutch it tighter and feel the wetness of the children – the wounds, the sweat, the sickness, I imagine – still on my hands from before. We are going to give this money to one person, give them something that might matter rather than all these crumbs.

Finally we see a woman with her back to us, a group of four children waiting as she boils some mixture in a pot, a husband looming beside her nastily in a ditch. I don't want him to see the exchange, but there is nothing I can do. I lean over the edge of the road, make one of the daughters grab the mother. She turns, I pass the note to her and she lifts her hands to her forehead in a quick blessing before tucking the money away.

We keep walking back up the hill till McLeod Ganj takes over and the beggars' road is well behind us, still thrilling to other visitors. All I can think of is washing my hands, washing my hands and getting clean.

No one is completely useless.
They can always serve as a bad example.

GRAFFITI in toilet,
Glastonbury Music Festival, 1998

United Kingdom No One is Useless

Electric Avenue, Brixton

A BLACK MAN AND A BLACK WOMAN ARE HAVING AN ARGUMENT on Electric Avenue. He is calling her a *'bumbo claat,'* Jamaican patois for 'blood clot,' an insult to women derived from some unflattering West Indian slang for menstrual blood.

She is bending over, pointing to her vagina from behind, encouraging him to 'Give me *lickspect*. Lick it. Lick it gooooooood!'

He is furious. He threatens to 'kick it.' Calls her a *'labba mout, yah.'* Moves towards her and begins to raise his foot.

She has walked over his posters laid neatly on the ground for sale: Bob Marley, Hailie Selassie, Jimi Hendrix, James Brown, Tricky, all the big heroes, accompanied by images of swirling smoke and psychedelia and wet cosmic fantasies of drugs and sex.

With a trail of footprints.

Her footprints, little heel marks indenting their way blithely across his hall of fame.

He is young and shiningly handsome with his hair Rastafaried and curled up inside a loose-knitted, striped cap the size of a small house. Like Dr Seuss' *Cat in the Hat* gone ganja wild on his head. Like one of his Bob Marley posters.

She is young and beautiful, all in white. Tight white t-shirt, drum firm stomach, tight white jeans. When she bends over everything is plain. 'Lick it, liiiiiiick iiiit!' she taunts him and points again at her hot cunt, wiggling her arse at him while she is at it.

He burns with rage and embarrassment. Flusters around without going forwards or backwards. Hot stepping about – his anger shaking his bulging cap full of hair back and forth in slow motion seconds after his head has moved.

The whole street is watching – vendors of fish, mandarins, vegetables, torch batteries, socks, second-hand books, cheap jewellery, assorted meats, bootleg cassettes, boxes of superglue 'at bargain price' – everyone and everything is there to witness the scene.

He blusters some more about her 'fuckery' while his friends laugh at him, bunched together in a funky mix of Curtis Mayfield zooming and reggae insouciance: tan leather jackets, flared green jeans, bright red running suits with yellow stripes, full radioactive colours and natty dreads. They look album-cover-great, awesome.

Her girlfriends, real Foxy Brown types, pull her away. One of them wheels a pram like she's swinging a handbag. Blues and silvers flicker around their eyes, creating the impression of futuristic sexual birds. 'Lick it, lick it,' she calls out to him from all the way down the avenue, tugged along laughing by her 'sistren' until she is gone. She yells one more time from out of sight, a great booming shout that fills the street and bounces off the buildings: 'LICK IT!'

He is leaning over now, picking up and dusting off his laminated posters with disgust. Cursing her under his breath. 'Bumbo claat. Woman! Look at this. Chuh!' He has lost the argument. But he keeps looking down that street. If not for another fight, then certainly for sweet, sweet love.

Himbasha

SHE IS BAREFOOT. HE HAS GOLD-RIMMED GLASSES AND A sensible blue business shirt. Black. Respectable. I ask them to mind my bags while I go to buy a coffee. There couldn't be two more trustworthy people on the whole damned train.

Lisa has split for Istanbul via Paris today, where a connecting flight awaits her tomorrow morning. I've seen her through to London. Watched her go through the Channel gates to the underground, parting from me. Only to go running back to misty Edinburgh again, somewhere I can feel safe. Or so I hope, shivering with feelings, struggling with them in my rib cage.

It's a funny thing: to have the space I've been craving. Is it ever what someone wants for long? The space to define exactly what it is that makes you feel weak or uncertain about a relationship or even yourself?

Even though the train is overheated, I can feel the cold lands outside entering into my mind, my body. The further north we go the wetter and greyer it gets out there. And freer somehow. Brutally, wildly free.

Somewhere near Newcastle a giant sculpture appears to take wing on the landscape. It's hard to make it out at first: Jesus Christ, an airplane, what is it?

The train rocks closer. I lose my balance in the aisle. Say something obscene. As I do I see the statue again through the window, much closer this time. An angel of steel some twenty metres high, towering over the green hills and up into steelier skies. A nowhere angel built for I don't know whom.

I buy coffee 'to go' in the service carriage, percolated shit with a bag of sugar. I know I won't enjoy it but it's something to do, a response to train trip entrapment.

When I get back to my seat I say thank you to the black couple who've looked after my bags. The man says, 'No problem,' and waves his hand at me in a delicate upward motion from the wrist to the middle finger. Next to the stockiness of his body his limbs are surprisingly slender and graceful, almost womanly.

He pulls a plastic bag up from the floor beneath his seat. Opens it up and starts tearing apart some bread for himself and his wife. 'Would you like to share in our bread?' he asks me formally.

I say yes. It does not seem right that I would dare say anything else.

They are just married, he explains. Travelling by train from London to Scotland for their honeymoon, hoping to catch the last week of the Edinburgh Festival. She smiles each time he finishes speaking. I say congratulations. She leans forward and says her only words to me, 'Thank you.'

The man beside me explains everything to me – then to her in amused asides – as we talk. They laugh with each other privately. Not just a matter of their language, but a closeness I am only able to watch rather than know.

He is from Eritrea. Near the Red Sea. He draws the shape of Africa in the air, points to the corner his country hangs on, squeezes his fingers together gently – just so, here it is, so small you might not notice. He left ten years ago because of war and drought.

'It's fine now,' he reasons wistfully, 'although it is a very poor place.' An American girl he met last year told him she feels safer on the streets of Eritrea than at home. 'Maybe,' he laughs, 'this is not so surprising.'

In London he works on computers. He hints that it was not easy at first. That he has spent a long time on his own. Ten years he has been in England. Ten years alone. I privately wonder if he returned to Eritrea for an arranged marriage, to find the love London did not give?

Lisa will be stepping off at Gare de Nord by now. Maybe eating a croissant in Paris while I talk to this couple and stare out of a train window, watching the rain and the steel pointless angels of these cold northern fields.

The man breaks a piece of bread off for me. Explains it is Eritrean bread. That it is called *himbasha*. Shows me how it is baked into sections so that it can be cleanly separated into triangular portions. 'Then everybody can have a piece,' he says, gesturing around the carriage as if we were at an imaginary banquet table. 'Actually in Eritrea, this is more like cake, really. It is for special occasions. The bread we usually eat is not so tasty.'

I nod and take a bite. It tastes a little dry, oddly sweet and salty at once. He is right: not really bread, not quite cake either. I don't know if I like it but I continue eating to show how happy I am to be sharing this moment with them. I see that I am in need of their company, the slow politeness they mete out to me.

'Actually this is our wedding cake,' he reveals. 'My wife made it for us yesterday. For the journey.' He lifts the bread up with both hands and nods to her proudly. She leans forward and smiles towards me again. He smiles with her.

Then he asks me the inevitable. 'Where are you from?'

'Sydney, Australia,' I say. It surprises me how I stumble over the name of my own country like I don't quite know how to pronounce it. An experience I've had before.

I look out the window again. We are passing close by the coast now. Bits of land are violently cut away by inlets that drop into raging waters below. Oh my ocean, I think to myself, I forget how much I love you, that I've lived on coastlines all my life in Australia. That even the deserts I have loved in all my travelling are just a shadow of you.

I say these words over and over in my mind: 'Ocean, ocean I belong to you.' The mantra, or the prayer, makes me feel better, even though another part of me feels ready to rise up inside and start sobbing. I push the feelings down again. Wrestling with emotions bigger than me.

'Do you know Fred Hollows?' my fellow passenger asks me keenly. He is referring to the human rights activist and crusading opthamologist who died a virtual saint in my country. Despite Hollows' fame in Australia, I am surprised an Eritrean man has ever heard of him. It seems an obscure connection.

'Oh yes, he is very famous in my country,' the man tells me. 'He paid for an eye hospital in our capital. We love him. After he died, our government invited his wife and all of his family out to see the hospital opened. His whole family!'

He is clearly proud of this gesture. 'Oh yes, yes, Eritrea and Australia are very close,' he says, meshing his hands together like a house, rocking them gently in front of me.

'You must go to Eritrea,' he urges me, still holding the home of his hands in front of me. 'People will see where you are from. People will like you very much.'

Then he opens this home and takes his wife's slender right hand gently, till her fingers are turning among his.

No Stars in the Sky

'THERE ARE NO STARS IN THE SKY SO BEAUTIFUL AS EDINburgh street lamps.'

Robert Louis Stevenson's words are carved into sandstone stairs not far from the Royal Mile in the heart of his old hometown. Edinburgh Castle shades over them – bagpipes, fifes and drums rising above the battlements, cartooning the air with Scottish history as an unseen parade practises for the world famous Military Tattoo.

A Friday night is just beginning; I'm walking slowly behind two old women taking their own tour of the so-called 'Athens of the North.' Writers' words rest on steps and in paved alcoves here and there along Edinburgh's Literary Walk. A map wrinkles between their hands like chocolate wrapping.

We can hear each other's progress on the stone pathway, boots and stilettos, heavy and sharp. It's surprisingly quiet in this nook of the world, given it's the middle of August, the peak of the Edinburgh Festival. Hardly anybody seems to know this peaceable place is here. A blessing, really, such unexpected solitude.

I do my best to hang back from the women, to avoid hating them for loving the same words as me and appreciating these same things in a naive way that makes me contemptuous of their conversation.

I end up laughing to myself: what an asshole I can be! Hungry to be special, to inherit these writers' words in private. And so angry, too, at the queer, vocal innocence of these elderly women, their banal enthusiasms. What do I hate, after all, but a common feeling for uncommon beauty?

Maybe the old just need to talk more in order to remind themselves they have some final breaths still left in them? I laugh out loud this time. If that's my idea of a kind thought, I am in a particularly mordant mood. Oh fuck off you old bitches – fuck off and leave me in peace anyway! I let myself enjoy this unexpected streak of malevolence. But as I pass by the women I nod and smile towards them and wonder if they suspect me of such evil thoughts? A little guiltily I call out, 'Beautiful, isn't it?' They look at me as if I'm a pervert and say nothing, a response I find curiously pleasurable.

The air feels damp with the evening's oncoming weight, an in-the-bones coldness that gets into the stone and brickwork of Edinburgh itself, those slab-sided big-blocked walls of the large tenement houses which take in the cold like darkening ink blotters. You feel a sub-arctic brutality in the architecture at such icy moments, a defensive need to hive off warmth and keep the cold world out, the world I will go walking aimlessly in tonight in all my misfortune.

August is mostly a pleasant month in Edinburgh – but a cutting wind and a bad turn can hint at a winter day and a cold that makes you feel you've been banished from humankind. Defying all common sense, the local girls wear mini-skirts, sandals and skimpy tops, sexy as hell on the barren 2 a.m. streets, arms crossed tight against the nipping wind, freezing their cute arses off while their drunken boyfriends pursue a lone fleeing taxi winking away into the night. It's not very hip, you see, to wear a coat or show you feel the cold when you're a girl here. The hottest babes dress like they are going to a disco in Cuba. That takes some real Scottish attitude.

It's a strangely pretty town, Edinburgh. All lit up at night. The sombre made dazzling. They make the place even prettier to greet the tourists who come from all over the world. Illuminating the architecture, beaming the sky, draping fairy lights over awnings, across trees and streets. Finishing off the month with the inevitable fireworks display over the castle walls. Aye, the place fairly glitters and glows.

The castle itself is set on a hill at the centre of Edinburgh. Highlighting a medieval and modern townscape that cleaves into a far-off cliff face. That's how I saw the place when we first arrived, climbing out of the railway station one crystal morning, standing on Queen Street getting cold ears – I turned around to see that big stone jewel of a building, letting my gaze slide out to the cliffs and a wild sky braying.

Anywhere else they would have built something, anything, between your eyes and all that raw space out there. A car park or a multi-storey monstrosity probably. Not in Edinburgh town, no. They've kept a piece of the sky. And I love them for that.

I look down now from the steps of the Literary Walk, back to where I first stood on Queen Street, to the town switching itself on in the dusk, lighting up as in Robert Louis Stevenson's words. Think how queer it is that Edinburgh can be so intimate and tight in its cobbled back lanes and yet so open to the elements above. A moody place: picture perfect or brutal as a bashing. And they reckon Glasgow's tougher, 'a real city, not a postcard,' as one girl told me proudly at the P.J. Harvey show, handing me a leaflet from her nightclub a hundred miles away. That's regional optimism for you.

I already knew Glasgow had the better music scene – bands like The Jesus and Mary Chain, Primal Scream and Belle and Sebastian all came from there – and that Glaswegians considered Edinburgh 'stuck up' and pretentious or, worse still, a wannabe English town riddled with class affectations. But I wasn't going to get around to visiting Glasgow on this trip. In my mind it was a bunch of working class razor blades to Edinburgh's cobbled tourist stones. Call me lazy, call me a coward, but I'll be taking the easy road and the nostalgic Scottish lies.

In Edinburgh I liked walking across The Meadows each morning, watching lads play soccer on the wide greens, losing each other in the mist, a game of invisibles based less on skill than on shouting to find either another player or the ball as it thudded out of the clinging oblivion; or a girl just ahead of me with an umbrella fending off the moisture on her way to university, parting cloudy swirls as if the whole town had started raining lazily from the ground upwards.

Each day would get busier and sunnier (maybe) as the weather cleared (maybe) and the students all started marching back and forth from the university to Marchmont, Tollcross, Morningside... all those suburbs where they partied and studied and gathered over pot and beer and pills. A life I could imagine living. Not many places really offer that sense of home up to you when you are travelling.

I knew this place made me nostalgic, not for its own history, but for mine as a student, a teenager. Crossing The Meadows made me feel strangely, sadly young again. It was sweet there in the day.

Then comes a little twist of night. Till The Meadows is peaceful or lurking. And humanity frays out to nothing on the pathways like ants retreating down a piece of string. Under the trees, off on the edge of the fields or your eye, a man, a dog. How late do you wanna cross tonight? Does it feel good out there?

Edinburgh is a place where people *see* things – they're either watching you or you're watching them from an array of vantage points around the town. One senses a life of secrets, inchoate and unconsciously collaborative, amid all this watching. From across The Meadows or above on the castle hill overlooking it all, or just gazing down streets like Lothian Road, all over Edinburgh, one lives with and joins in a city of voyeurs.

I had bought a book of Scottish detective stories called A *Good Hanging* before I came north from London. In it the writer Ian Rankin summarized residential life in Edinburgh through the eyes of his favourite character, Inspector Rebus: 'Nowadays, a tenement might contain the whole of society in microcosm – the genteel spinster on the ground floor, the bachelor accountant one floor above, and above the barkeeper, always it seemed right at the top of the house, the students.' In these kinds of places, the worldly-wise Rebus observed, 'the stairwell walls had ears.' I was living in just such a place. And had heard it for myself. A lovers' hissing argument, plastic shopping bags crinkling with angry static, their words rising up to me from the landing below until they went and shut themselves inside with a deadening slam. Me listening from behind my own heavy door, a guest in the archetypal student's home, top floor (dead right, Inspector Rebus, as always!).

At festival time people who had large houses often turned them into bed-and-breakfasts, taking in visitors, tucking them into single beds with frilly pillows and a greasy breakfast to come. Others let their entire homes or apartments out to what less enthusiastic locals referred to as 'Festival poofs!'

The place was so inundated with tourists throughout August it doubled the entire population of the city for the month. Just try walking the pavement in the opposite direction to a crowd headed towards a major event. To make matters worse there was always a bundle of Apocalyptic Christians doing the rounds, clogging up the pedestrian flow, holding up a giant placard that announced, 'There's a way back to God from the dark paths of sin, there's a door that is open and all may go in. At Calvary's cross is where you begin, when you come as a sinner to Jesus.' Most people were just trying to get to the theatre on time. Salvation was not in the festival program. Nor in my line of thoughts either.

I thought about the crowds and how I had best be on my way.

It was going to be a wet night. Not raining, just cold and misty. So I left Robert Louis Stevenson and the old women for the gloomy glitter of the town itself, cutting quickly across the The Royal Mile through a throng of tourists who had surrounded a black busker adeptly squeezing himself through the head of a tennis racquet.

At a corner pub I decided to stop in for a quick drink. It was a tiny place, stuffy with nicotine smells and about a dozen or so men idly watching a stripper do her act on the only stage available: a green six-foot by six-foot pool table. She was down to her black g-string, straddling a corner pocket, giving Thin Lizzy's 'Rosalie' her best effort, an arse-grinding, fuck-me rock 'n' roll show if ever there was one.

I only had enough small change in my pocket for a glass of Snakebite, not the cover charge, so I was hunted back out again by a barmaid, somewhat shamefaced at my naivety among Edinburgh's hard men. A horny-looking girl still giving it out good to the last pump of Thin Lizzy while they looked on as if they were bored. Not clapping. Paying for more. The door shutting, closing me out altogether. Damn!

I headed back across The Meadows to my temporary student home in Marchmont to change into something warmer for the night ahead. To get more money too. To pop a tab of acid in my pocket that I wouldn't bother with for the rest of the evening, but you never knew. I was ever the optimist right then when it came to the possibilities for self-destruction. A part of me would have loved to fry my mind; a part of me felt ashamed even of that escape. It was like I shouldn't be having any fun here at all.

It might have been festival time in Edinburgh, but the loneliness of the city, its solitary touch, had me in its grip. I thought of an old friend who once lived here for five years, who wrote to me all through that time, urging me to visit him. And now that I was finally here, that friend had packed up and long gone. I wondered about myself now and if I was doing similar things? Stalking old footsteps and the same self-appointed loneliness that tormented my friend – 'a bad atmos' I always made fun of, as in the hand-drawn birthday card I sent him one year, a picture of a man caught eternally below a thundercloud while the rest of humanity enjoyed the sun. I'd always thought of this as 'the Scottish temperament.' Now here I was, walking the same walk, talking the same black talk. Crying, or feeling like crying at least, in the same town, maybe even in the same places. Moving into my friend's solitary way of life.

Sometimes it's hard to know when loneliness is truly heartbreaking for you – and when it is just a beautiful over-indulgence. Grieving can be a wonderful ocean to float abandoned in. I had told my girlfriend Lisa I needed a break for a while, using that dreadful phrase 'some space.' That I was feeling 'divided' about things when she really pressed me on what

I wanted from the relationship. She'd held on to that word and when I'd tried to tell her later that I didn't necessarily want to end things, that I still loved her, she'd said I was 'divided not devoted' and that she needed something better than that. She wasn't gonna wait for me in Edinburgh to make up my mind. She was blowing on ahead. I could catch up with her later if I wanted. Frightening as her actions were, some part of me was relieved.

We had skated through the city after that fatal conversation like low clouds, fading into ourselves over the next few days. At the Café Graffiti we'd watched a young group called the De K-Band do something jazzy and sweet, flower-power rock 'n' roll that didn't dominate you at all – just drew you in. A song urging everyone, 'let's go back to the prayer of touching.' We'd gone back to see these American and Dutch teenagers strut their stuff once, twice, three times, amid all the hurly burly of what the Edinburgh Fringe Festival had to offer, soothed by each delicate performance and the boyish belief in something tender which underlined their sound.

Later, after Lisa had left, friends from Australia arrived in a band called Leonardo's Bride. They set up residency at Beck's Famous Spiegeltent on Queen Street, that street I kept coming back to. It became an Aussie hideaway, as well as a late pulse in the festival's dying days. The crowds swelled from nothing to a full house over four days, that word of mouth thing that makes everyone feel they're involved in a community discovery. I was proud of my friends.

On their last night I sat right in front of them, getting pissed on red wine. Looking up from my glass and the absurdly heavy thoughts that seemed to lie within it, I found myself staring at their shoes. As they tapped their feet I noticed they were all wearing Blundstones, Australian working men's boots that rocked something about home all the way through me. They were singing a song I knew well, though I hadn't really noticed the words before: 'He who lives more lives than one, more deaths than one must die. Oh yeah, I get this feeling, oh yeah, I get this feeling, will it ever leave me alone.'

As their feet touched the stage their boots seemed to press in on my heart and I struggled not to burst out crying in front of the world. I was way too over-emotional to be out and pouring in this way, barely holding myself inside my own skin. I wanted her back now – back at the table, sitting beside me, saving me from this song. I wanted it all back and yet I didn't know what I wanted at all.

Afterwards, Dean, the band's songwriter, and I stood on a small observation lawn immediately behind the tent. We blew a joint and leant against a rail and started talking about love and the fathomless stuff that goes with it, feelings that roll out when you are not looking to talk at all and find that you need to. Some girl in New York that Dean couldn't stop thinking of, how they had sung a song together one night in a club, things that were going wrong in his life and if he was a decent human being. It was like the two of us were swapping talismans, bits of stone and glass and bone with no particular meaning, little moments of ourselves. Sometimes we spoke only in this fractured code because we could not speak the real words, and it was enough to understand the signals rather than say what was going on deep inside.

Edinburgh was starting to disappear before us in an increasingly heavy mist, heavier than I had seen before.

'They call it the Haar,' Dean said to me, leaning on the word. 'It comes in off the North Sea. Can't you smell it?'

'Aha!' I said, sniffing to the air, making an obvious joke.

We started 'aha-ing' together like drunken pirates. Laughing madly. Till the rest of the band came out and exclaimed variously, 'How come you guys are standing there? That's where Leo Sayer and his band always piss. It's their piss trough. They use it every night!'

Dean and I looked at our feet in horror and the damp gravel on our boots. It suddenly didn't seem so contemplative or melancholy out there anymore. I kicked up my heels frantically like a loon, jumping from the trough back onto the lawn, and started singing an old Leo Sayer song while I jived. 'You Make Me Feel Like Dancing' never sounded so intense.

We all started laughing, our breath swirling the mist. The town was mostly gone now. A few bright lights still pushed through the Haar like blurry satellites till they finally died too. We could barely see each other as we kept talking. I could feel myself getting slowly soaked to the skin. Smell the salt in the air as if we were drowning.

The others went inside again while Dean and I continued to watch the mist roll in. We could see it turning inside itself. I felt myself turning with it. Until Dean laughed and slapped me on the back for no apparent reason, waking me out of my thoughts, which had no form really, were hardly even thoughts at all.

'Come on,' Dean said wickedly, 'let's go back inside and talk to some girls!'

I followed him in and watched Dean disappear into the crowd, everybody talking and drinking and flirting. It was the last night of the festival, a joyous, crazy night, and I looked on from the edge of the room and wondered how I might join them.

Never Enough

I've walked across the Himalaya
and seen the dead in flames,
hit the road to the Dalai Lama
watched your face through Scottish rain,

bought jewels from Tibetan traders
felt a stone-throwing Jomson wind!
known the reds of Mustang plateau,
then urged London just to end,

stood by while you were all night sleeping
in a Calcutta lightning storm,
drunk my coffee with the rickshaw men,
made lover's question marks to keep you warm,

sat with mad-eyed sadhus raving,
heard P.J. Harvey sing aquatic sexy blues,
met gypsies on jet aeroplanes,
saw a boy dead where we passed through.

But I've never seen enough of you;
I've never seen enough of you.

Κατα Τον Δαιμονα Εαψτοκ
(To the divine spirit within himself)

GREEK INSCRIPTION on Jim Morrison's grave
Cimitière du Père Lachaise, Paris

Paris Divine Spirit

The Dead

IT HAD RAINED THE NIGHT BEFORE. THE GROUND WAS DAMP.
Some blue was in the sky. Some sunlight for a while.

I set off for Cimetière du Père Lachaise, the most famous cemetery in
the world. But what did I know of the world it held? Very little, other than
this was the place where Oscar Wilde and Jim Morrison were buried. It
seemed enough.

My love of graveyards dates back to childhood. To the long, ritualistic
visits my family made to my grandfather's grave on the outskirts of Newcastle, my home town in Australia. My grandmother would be with us,
directing proceedings as we washed down the tiled black marble and laid
down fresh flowers for my grandfather with a sense of stiff duty, a dry
wind blowing across the aptly named Sandgate Cemetery.

Sometimes my sisters and I would wander off and play between the
row of graves while my grandmother and my mother (her daughter) held
onto their breath in gulps and dabbed at tears in the corners of their eyes.

I remember it was part of my job to steal a vase or a glass jar from
some other grave. They were often filled with old flowers, either dried
out or decaying and wet with stink. I'd throw them away, then use the
jars as containers to get the necessary water from a nearby tap to clean
our grandfather's grave.

It seemed a little criminal, and once the job was done I took great care
to return the vases and jars, placing them in the same dry, sand-marked
circles where they had previously, preciously stood. It sticks in my mind
how often these containers were already broken and beaten and bleached
by time. As if the dead were slowly touching them with something of
their own world. I was aware of their emanation, unhappy and reluctant
to touch them, yet forced to by duty.

Eventually my grandmother entered Sandgate as well. Her colour portrait was installed on the tombstone opposite my grandfather's black and
white shot, both of them dressed in their Sunday best. When I think of
my grandmother's portrait, I think of the way happiness can dry up in a
person's life, in a person's face, when love goes away forever. My grand-

father's face seems more alive and robust – or maybe just younger – and certainly not marked by a decade alone and grieving. Or by the flickering memory I still have of him in a hospital room, dying of cancer, his grey-trembling request that I kiss him, the way I fled the hospital room frightened and crying, a mere eight years old, feeling this was not what men asked of each other, knowing that something much bigger and more terrible than I could grasp was happening. I ran. I ran.

It frightens me to think of the days when I must follow them to Sandgate. First to tend the graves of my not-yet-dead parents, with that same catching of the breath as my mother and grandmother. And then, of course, to enter my own grave.

And yet the strange thing about graveyards, at least during the day, is how reassuring they are to me. To sit in a cemetery in the sunlight is akin to sitting on a beach and looking out to the ocean: there, right at that moment, death doesn't seem so frightening at all. There's the feeling that you are a part of something much bigger, and with it a calming gentleness to be found in one's own smallness, the tides that take us to these stone-crested seas of the dead, this world we all (finally) belong to.

There are other graveyards I have known and loved since Sandgate. The quiet sunlit respite of a cemetery off King Street in bustling Newtown, Sydney, my first big city home, where one night I tried to drunkenly fuck my old girlfriend by a stone wall. The miles of crosses overlooking the Aboriginal Survival Day Concerts in La Perouse, Sydney, like strange witnesses to the old crimes of settlement and colonialism, the replacement of one people with another. A loamy graveyard near a small-town airport in western New South Wales that I slowly realized told the generational history of the whole community, from great-grandfathers and municipal visionaries to Depression-era wives and Vietnam sons. The windswept sprawl of the dead at Waverley's beach cemetery on a summer's day, salt and seagulls and the sounds of surf resounding in the huge blueness of the sky. The elegant stillness of Japanese pearlers' graves in Broome, the shin-high, neatly lined tombstones, like large stone hands poking out of the ground, kabuki-graceful in their petrified symmetry. A hundred unknown country cemeteries that have held the souls of everyone from Les

Darcy, the famous 1930s boxer, to hours-old babies. Coastal stories of ships and the drowned.

No doubt you have your own graveyards written somewhere in your heart as well. Places of sun and silence, of holy scripts and poems, stone and prayers, marble and wilted roses, trees and weeds, the wrought iron, the fresh mounds, the people walking quietly, the children playing too loudly... To claim, then, that a graveyard is the most famous and visited cemetery in the world, well then, it must invite a genuinely deep stirring of the soul in order make it so memorable. Père Lachaise does not disappoint. Nor does it depend for its attraction on its fame as a resting place for the famous. No, Père Lachaise is something else again.

Commissioned by Napoleon and established in 1804, it was meant to relieve the pressure on the Cimetière des Innocents, whose full-to-capacity condition would service the bends in a David Lynch grotesque. Les Innocents became so crowded corpses would stick out of the ground after heavy rains. A wall on one side of it gave way, pouring bodies and earth into a public house. The dead had to be moved. And Père Lachaise was part of the answer.

It now stands at a hundred acres, with a million souls, some famous, many once wealthy, even more anonymous and forgotten. A kind of glamorous sister to the lesser known Cimitières Montparnasse and Montmartre, which are enticingly described as 'gloomy and bizarre' on a website of Parisian walking tours. I didn't make it to these sites (how obsessed do you think me?). But on reflection I wondered why I should choose the word 'sister' when comparing the undulating Père Lachaise to these two unseen places. And I can only say there is something curiously feminine about Père Lachaise. When I reflect back on it I think of words like lush, shadowy, cool, decadent, refined, ripe, tangled and wet, all words I associate with a feminine otherness.

The cemetery was named after Père (Father) Lachaise, a Jesuit priest who was the confessor to Louis XIV. Lachaise owned the land, which two hundred years ago was simply another wooded hill in the Twentieth Arrondisement on the eastern side of Paris. You still feel that you are entering these woodlands – and the atmosphere of political and religious intrigue of nineteenth-century Paris – when you cross over from the city into the graveyard's perimeter.

I enter mistakenly from the rear, by the Porte Gambetta, where I ask a guard *'Parlez-vous Anglais?'*

'Only a little,' she happily indicates with an offhand squeeze of the thumb and forefinger.

So I say, 'Oscar Wilde?' It sounds more like a talisman than a name, a way to identify myself as much as where I am headed. It makes me feel more refined, more literary and elite than if I had asked for 'Jim Morrison,' though I will certainly visit him as well.

She gives me a map and points me on my way. Père Lachaise is a mix of wide, easy avenues and small pathways to nests of the dead. It's a matter of how deep you want to go along its cobbled thoroughfares and side-streets. My map is numbered, annotated, and alphabetically arranged. It's clear there are more famous people here than I could have ever imagined: Colette, Chopin, Proust, Balzac, Piaf, Bernhardt, the list goes on.

When I walk along Père Lachaise's Avenue Circulaire, I immediately feel a strange electrical grieving. There's a strong breeze running through the trees and, somewhere not far off, the sound of a jet engine in the sky. As foolish as the description might appear, it is as if something has brushed over or passed through me.

I take a right onto the Avenue Carette, where Oscar Wilde's grave impresses me in a lonely, solemn way. A flying angel headstone, reminiscent of Egyptian sculpture such as a sphinx, lies atop his grey stone tomb. There are flowers, both fresh and decaying, left for him. I feel an awful sense of having failed to bring a gift, some sign of affection, till I notice the pebbles left by similarly bereft mourners. So I lean down to pluck a stone from the ground, brushing off the damp soil, and place it neatly on a marble ridge beside the other small stones.

Behind the tomb (designed by Jacob Epstein) is a last testament: 'OSCAR WILDE, author of *Salome* and other beautiful works was born at 21 Westland Row, Dublin, October 16, 1854.' There are brief details of schooling, academic medals, literary prizes, and that's it, as if a life can be summed up in that promising edge between adolescence and the blush of adulthood when the world is first recognising us.

'He died fortified by the Sacraments of the Church on November 30, 1900 at the Hotel D'Alsace, 13 Rue des Beaux Arts, Paris. R.I.P.'

This reclamation by the Church sits uneasily with Wilde's reputation. Somehow his own words from *The Ballad of Reading Goal*, also inscribed here, ring out truer and more painfully for the close of his life.

And alien tears will fill for him,
Pity's long broken urn
For his mourners shall be outcast men
And outcasts always mourn.

A boy not quite a man sits in the gutter of the cobbled road, pale and visibly overwhelmed. Some American tourists comment on Wilde as being English. 'Irish,' the boy says, correcting them flatly.

And then, funnily enough, a young Irish couple arrives, taking snaps of themselves by the grave. They look at the birth-and-death dates. Then the Irishman says to his love, 'He didn't live long. Genius, eh?' It's an equation.

The pale boy just sits. And waits to be alone again.

On the next avenue, according to my map at least, is Silvia Monfort, 'comedienne.' But I can't find her. Instead I look at tombs with beautiful stained glass and feel a sense of violation and loss when I see that one stained glass window has been broken and ripped from its wire moorings. Why would you want to hurt something like that?

Around the corner is a monument to a DC–10 air crash:

A LA MEMOIRE DES VICTIMES DE L'ATTENTAT CONTRE LE DC–10
SURVENUE AU NIGER LE 19 SEPTEMBRE 1989.

An iron rose sits on the silverwhite granite wall. With the words, 'A *notre père*.' Then a few smaller tributes, one for an '*enfant*,' another for 'papa' with his picture, strong and stocky with a dark receding hairline. The wind, as if on cue, picks up intensity in the trees. I think I can hear it carrying voices from not far away, but as I daydream, almost melt into my surroundings, into this queer serenity, a bee buzzes in close to my ear. I am terrified, ducking my face away from its orbit, almost losing my balance, before moving off again shaken and embarrassed, still feeling the sound of it like a mark in my ear.

The next site:

BUNA-MANOWITZ-AUSCHWITZ 111 ET SES KOMMANDOS

39 CAMPS

N'OUBLIONS JAMAIS!

It's a 1992 sculptural monument by Louis Mitelberg, Gilbert Clementi and Marcel Schmit. Strands of steel, like flaps of clay, make up the trudging bodies of a group of men. One body is in a wheelbarrow. The men surround the barrow in a terrible cortege. All of them are hunched forward. The sculptures have a shredded, beaten quality. All faces are turned downward in pain, or perhaps prayer. Only one face looks to the sky. And oh how you love that man's face.

Diagonally opposite is a gigantic bronze structure, oxidized into a lime colour. A man, an Adonis really, is held in its umbilical metal grip.

Further down in this corner of Père Lachaise there's a jumble of gaunt human sculptures, angled and tangled together in sombre agony. It twists the heart just to look at it. This is for 'Buchenwald-Dora.' The first Nazi concentration camp the Allies saw after the War. In General Eisenhower's autobiography there's a recollection of US troops vomiting over what they witnessed at Buchenwald: 'bodies stacked in obscene anonymity.' It's echoed here in art.

More austerely, there is a beautiful rough stone slate with a single green bush growing in front of it to commemorate the martyrs of the Resistance 'assassinated' by the Nazis.

Last but not least in this quarter of war memories, another sculpture for 'AUSCHWITZ BIRKENAU CAMP NAZI D'EXTERMINATION.'

A foetal being, like an alien, is morphing out of the stone, blank-faced, smooth, innocent, not accusing – it's more like the figure is posing a question as it looks down at you. It could be a woman, a baby, a boy.

Now we move back to people, to accountable identities. The Surrealist poet Paul Eluard 1895 – 1952, his name written in blood red on grey marble, a mound of earth with a single small bush. Beside him, Maurice Thorez, 1900–1964, *Secrétaire Général du Parti Communist Français*, or, as my leaflet map puts it, *homme politique*. His grave is considerably grander, black marble reflecting back the gold lettering on the tombstone, the sky itself, the blacker shapes of leaves and branches just above. In the middle of this hard black pool of reflections, a stone black flower and a single fresh red rose.

A little further down the Avenue Circulaire, two huge sandstone hands are tightly bound with sandstone rope before a sandstone wall. Above them is the word 'RAVENSBRUCK.' Only one thought can follow such an image: execution. (Ravensbruck was a concentration camp for women. Like at the infamous 'Black Wall' of Auschwitz, an early and popular form of murder there involved lining up for a bullet in the back of the neck.)

As I begin looking for the graves of the singer Edith Piaf and the painter Amedeo Modigliani, it feels odd to find myself immersed in searching for the dead. A little map in my hand. A sunlit afternoon turning moody. The ordered avenues of Père Lachaise beckoning you into the side alleys and shady walkways that turn twisty and quiet – for this is really a town with street names and by-ways and pockets of character, a necropolis with major buildings and slums, parks and forgotten places.

Piaf's grave is a family tomb, small and humble, with Christ-on-the-Cross above her. Modigliani's is even plainer, with a stone pot and some old flowers drooping. On his tombstone the words, 'COMPAGNA DEVOTA FINO ALL ESTREMO SACRIFIZIO' and another name, 'Jeanne Hébuterne.' A Dutch woman who has walked up beside me translates it hesitantly: 'His fine and devoted companion until the last sacrifice.' A pregnant Hébuterne committed suicide by leaping out a window two days after Modigliani died of meningitis.

On the Avenue des Acacias a large seed falls from a tree and almost hits me. Birds are feeding above, breaking them open in the trees. The seeds are spiky, with flesh like an apple. Not far off this path is a section of sunken ground, wet looking, where a broken and erased grave site is cordoned off by leaning cast iron rails.

There are sepulchres here as big as small churches. Inside one, a photo of a princess, her hair cut in a black fringe, her eyes marked in black kohl. A 1920s girl, a lady of the world.

After some snaking around, finally, the grave of James Douglas Morrison 1943–1971. And beneath his name, '*Kata Ton Daimona Eaytok*.' It's a Greek epitaph: 'To the divine spirit within himself.' But I am told that the interpretations of it can vary. In Old Greek it means 'the demon within himself.' In Modern Greek it can also mean 'the genius in his mind' or 'he caused his own demons.'

Morrison's resting place is a small, even inconsequential grave, pushed into a corner between bigger monuments to other more forgotten deaths. People crowd around and into it. One feels pressured to not linger. To grab your moment.

On the grave are notes to 'Dear Jim…' from Gavin, Jude, Chlöe, Paulo and Said. There's a broken watch strap, cheap candles burning, cigarette butts and fresh cigarettes for that heavenly puff, the words 'no one gets out of here alive' scrawled on and torn from a diary, a grotty mess of flowers and pulped notes and foil, a poem from Paula that begins 'Your flesh has gone…,' a blue stained piece of paper where another poem has not survived the last rain, a red trail of old wax, two large seeds like testicles, and all around a crowd – old, middle-aged, young, leather-jacketted, suited, grungey, absurd, beautiful, fat, stunned, indifferent, all taking photos, all posing beside the head stone.

As I move on and further into Père Lachaise, I realize how many people are here tracking, in death, a love of their own. That the love is not just love of a person now dead. It is also a love of rock 'n' roll or philosophy or the piano or sculpture or politics or literature, and somehow we are all here in an attempt to find a little of ourselves in what these great figures did and what is left in their memory.

Chopin's grave is the most impressive for the love that it inspires. A sculpture of a woman guarding the grave is overcome by many, many, many flowers, the brightest, the healthiest, the most alive flowers in any part of Cimetière du Père Lachaise. Chopin's grave sings with their colour and their slender, temporary life.

Further along, Bizet's grave is marked purely by purple flowers. A bust of his head, noble, soft in expression, gives a skyward glance. He rests with Madeleine Jacques Adolphe. Such details matter as you visit more and more graves. The sense not of a life lived, but of more than one life involved. That even a great life has its partners, its family, its seemingly anonymous, necessary, real love.

An old couple suddenly walk out onto the cobbled pathway from a grove of trees and grave stones. The woman is wearing all black and crying, and the man, dressed in counterpoint grey, puts his arm around her shoulders. He tries to help her forwards even though he is so old and infirm he can hardly carry his own weight. Their grief does not seem fresh. More like something revived, as if they have visited an old friend. I leave them behind me, wondering who they were and who they were crying for.

Up ahead is a basalt-coloured monument to Eugène Delacroix, unfurling like a curved black bed or an ancient scroll. A cool tomb, indeed, for the painter of *Orphan Girl in a Cemetery*, which mixed sanctity and terror in the gaze of a young woman and whatever it is she sees that we cannot see.

I begin to go in circles as I search for the grave of the poet Apollinaire. Till I cross paths with the old couple again. Which is when I see the old woman walk up to a headstone and touch it with the back of her hand. The gesture is unspeakably delicate and I look away from its intimacy, moving off hurriedly to give them both a privacy I have somehow invaded with my eyes.

A little further on, I pass by a small white square stone in the dirt. It's for 'Paulo and Isabell.' On it are two white birds flying towards the sun. Despite the kitsch illustration, and in some ways because of it, I feel a pang of sad happiness for their ideal of love – and for whoever remembered them in such an adolescent way.

Finally I find Guillaume Apollinaire 1880 – 1918 and Jacqueline 1891 – 1967. His gravestone is a rough oblong with the vaguest impression of a cross, and some French words I can't read at the centre of a heart. Not far away, in fact just across the path, is Marcel Proust 1871 – 1922, with Adrien and Robert, indeed a whole family of Prousts remembered. The grave is very plain black marble, and a single vase of fresh flowers sits upon it.

By now bad weather has moved in and I should go. I am also tired by walking, heavy and exhilarated and worn by everything I have witnessed. But I want to see the Colombarium Crematorium, to have seen as much as I can see, to feel I have completed something. It's a daunting set of buildings with thousands of small metal plates marking the remains of the cremated, yet another world of the dead, another universe all over again within Père Lachaise. Where to start?

I wanted to find Maria Callas, but I never do. Instead I meet the Surrealist painter 'Max Ernst 1891 – 1976,' his name and dates inscribed sober as a judge. I see 'Achille Zavatta 1915 – 1995,' apparently a famous clown. On his door are a white tree and a sky with birds, and a gypsy's gold house on wheels. On another door is a set of handwritten names, 'Aldo and Clarissa Machetti,' he 1907 – 1968, she 1913 – 1992. There's a picture of them inside a hand-drawn heart, all peasant-like and in love, like an image from some sentimental Hollywood movie. On yet another door is a photo of Leilah Mahi, who died in 1932, a seductress wearing a beaded headdress of jewels and what looks like nothing else but shadows.

As I walk around I stop for some reason and look directly above me. There I see 'Armand and Jeanette Morel,' he 1914 – 1966, she 1915 – 1997. I mark the gaps in their deaths, the time she must have spent alone. The doors to each of their places of internment are distinguished by life-size casts of beautiful bronze hands. Their hands, a man's and a woman's, side by side. They are reaching out towards each other.

But I cannot see if their hands are actually touching. My view is obscured by a bunch of fresh flowers in their honour. An ocean of feelings rushes into me and all the air rushes out and I suddenly feel like sobbing as I start to move, gasping and fighting back tears as it becomes desperately important for me to see those hands touch.

Green Light

European lights are seen
from a departing flight east:
sprays of white lanes, a gilded coast,
and great patches of black
between the sprinkled gold,
one green star alone
in the low firmament,
my last anchor, but not my home.

How upside down the world is tonight
as I pass through the darkness.
My face in the window
coming back at me, haggardly bright,
the last city long gone,
extinguished by speed.

This journey alone
to a broken love affair
in a foreign city –
I was summoned, not beckoned,
and it threatens me.

I am lost like that city in the night.
I am lost in flight.

Below me after a time
Istanbul begins to pulse,
so many green gems
on the floor of this new world
spilling wariness and nausea
upwards, clawing me down,
igniting the earth of my lover:
the end of my journey?

Sorrows are the rags of old clothes.

RUMI

Turkey Old Clothes

Whom Do I Meet?

WHOM DO I MEET?
A sweet girl happy to see me.
An intimacy I thought I'd lost.
The smell of her hair as we hold each other. Her hip joining mine as we walk. How stunning that is when you find it: a lover you can walk with. How stunning to forget it and find it again.

A white hotel to sleep softly in. The bathroom flooding every time we use it, a perfect bad joke on us because it is a mild misfortune and shared happily.

A rooftop view of the Marmara Sea. Honey for breakfast and light off the water.

The call of the muezzin to prayer. Orange and grey clouds of pollution floating across the minarets of the city.

Days spent reading day-old copies of the *Guardian* over cups of Turkish coffee. That shop with great shish kebabs where we got food poisoning and didn't care. Sipping shot glasses of *raki* at night in a room full of raucous men watching football on a hazy television set. Waking up hungover with the taste of aniseed in our mouths.

Four entertaining hours of Bill Clinton answering questions very, very carefully on CNN. The guy may be a liar, but by god isn't he smart?

A night out to see the Rolling Stones do 'Gimme Shelter,' 'Can't Get No Satisfaction,' 'Sympathy For The Devil,' 'Honky Tonk Woman,' 'Start Me Up,' a million shards of silver confetti raining over the crowd.

You have to watch yourself in Istanbul, I know.

All those taxi drivers trying to run their meters at the night-time rate to double their fare. The shadows on the faces of men. The market where they charmed, then bullied, then threatened us.

But I feel like a bird relaxing into gravity here. My old resistance has turned to air.

Istanbul, City of Cats

ISTANBUL IS A CITY OF SKINNY CATS. SLINKING DOWN A stairwell at the bazaar, slipping by a sea of blind human legs. Feasting on bones under a truck with a sick, skinless dog. Lapping milk in the company of old men at card tables. Crossing your path in the night.

Revenge on François

WE ARE AT A SMALL CAFÉ ON THE EUROPEAN SIDE OF Istanbul when we hear her talking. An Irish journalist happily accepting some tickets from a middle-aged Turkish businessman wearing a suit and running shoes. The tickets are VIP passes to the Rolling Stones, 'For you – and François of course.'

'Oh, thank you,' she says, genuinely grateful. The tickets are of the no-strings-attached kind, but you can see this guy would love to fuck her.

That's why he is acting so generously. And so unlike those other sleazy guys. He is not even asking her on a date.

You see, 'I cannot attend this evening. Business,' he says, shrugging his shoulders wearily. Begging her secretly to imagine just how important that business might be.

'So now these – I wish them for you and for your friend – from me.'

He presses her ticket-holding hands in his, smiles, looks into her eyes, holds on for just that fraction longer than perhaps an apparently disinterested fellow should.

She smiles back at him, oblivious to the carnal ambitions beneath his generosity. But that's not true. It's just her way of negotiating the world because she is still young enough to pretend. In her mid-twenties she can 'play the girl,' willingly flirting along, not letting the left side of her brain know what the right side is really doing. Her naiveté is neatly compartmentalized, diplomatically effective.

We strike up a conversation across the tables when I hear she is a journalist. I tell her I am a writer too. Ask who she works for. What kind of pieces she does.

That she is going to the Rolling Stones show tonight is another happy coincidence. Lisa and I have tickets too, a quest that has successfully taken us through every clothing shop, record store and z-grade radio station in Istanbul. It is the final concert of the Bridges Over Babylon World Tour and a large crowd is expected.

Her business friend 'must be leaving,' their *tête-à-tête* shattered. So she joins us for a while, all Irish brightness and British ambition, pale skin, lovely smile, red lips. To tell the truth, she reminds me a lot of an old girlfriend. Her name is Sarah.

After chatting for half an hour about Istanbul, the media, and the show tonight, she tells us she must get back to work – but she invites us to share a taxi this evening to the stadium with her and her 'partner' François. He is back at the hotel completing the research on a story that must be filed for the paper in London today.

'I'm actually new in town,' she admits. 'François knows just everybody. He's technically my boss, although we don't work like that. It's much more democratic because it has to be in a job like this,' she says pragmatically. 'It's so exciting to work with someone so experienced, who really knows the country,' she adds with such admiring disbelief I'm not even sure she really believes it herself. 'Six months ago I was just a cadet in Dublin. Now I'm here. It's just too wild.'

We make arrangements to meet her later in the day at their hotel apartment. We are right on time, over-conscious of the unpredictability of an unknown city in another country. Instead of Sarah greeting us, though, it is François who opens the door – and who is openly unimpressed.

French to the core, he exhibits a prissy politeness that seems like a slap to the face with every act of hospitality. A drink? Ice? Anything else I can get you? Please, do not put your glass there, that table is not for glasses. He looks down at me. *Sacré bleu!* I am the instant barbarian he needs to affirm his own sophistication.

'So you have been in Istanbul long?' he asks listlessly.

'No,' we say, 'just in from Paris, before that London and India. We're from Sydney originally.' Even if it wasn't clear before, that snippet of our itinerary confirms his worst fears. We are backpacking scum lucky to have hitched onto a shaker and mover like him.

'Do you like the underground here?' he asks me pointedly.

'I didn't know there was an underground,' I reply.

'Oh yes, it is very exciting. I am surprised you have not noticed.'

'Wow, an underground city. I'd love to see it. How fantastic! I didn't know Istanbul had an underground city.'

François rolls his eyes. 'I meant the underground culture. The music and the art.'

Sacré bleu!

At this point Sarah walks in and saves us all. It feels like it is going to be a long night. François fetches her a drink, but their older brother/younger sister act has a weary tone, and its own covert power plays, mostly in his favour.

In the taxi on the way to the show François insists on sitting in the front seat, largely to avoid sitting with us and communicating at all. When he does speak he does not turn around to address us, preferring instead to address the windscreen.

He tells us he knows 'Mick' and 'Keith' from when he played pool with them in Bangkok. Does not like going to stadium shows as a general rule, nor rock 'n' roll either. 'I much prefer a comfortable seat. It is so much better for the music and the show to be close. The best concert I have ever seen – ever seen – is Diana Ross at the Hilton in Paris. This is a real show. Diana is just wonderful. The greatest. I met her after the show, a delight.'

François hopes to catch up with Mick and Keith later if he can. We've heard there's a rooftop party at an exclusive hotel we know of, and mention it to François. He knows nothing of this. 'Perhaps the invitation will become clear,' he says in his barbed French accent. Such a honeyish venom.

When we get to the show a predictable state of organized chaos is underway. Something like 80,000 Turkish fans are being shepherded through alphabetized, colour-coded gates. François moves on quickly ahead of us, while Sarah tags along, looking back at us a little helplessly. He moves through gate after gate, exclusive zone after exclusive zone. Years as a rock journalist have inured me to such obstacles – Lisa and I simply march through like royalty daring to be challenged. As Europeans who look like we know where we are going, no such resistance occurs. François is simply livid we have made it into the VIP area beside the stage. His efforts to shake us have not been strong enough. In the meantime I'm insulted he thinks he has had anything to do with it. As if my rock 'n' roll smarts have not had a part in things. But the concert is about to begin, so who cares anymore? We're here, let's relax and enjoy ourselves.

Sarah, Lisa and I all sit happily down in the front row seats, ready for a great show. Through the storm wire we can see huge clouds of smoke hovering above the crowd, the incredible results of an intense Turkish predilection for tobacco not yet tempered by the slightest anti-smoking campaign. Red-tipped embers dot the night-time like a low rent light show. You'd think it was a smoky club out there – not an open air stadium.

Unfortunately for Sarah, François has opted to sit quite a few rows back. She is clearly embarrassed about this, so she goes up to him and invites him to come down and join us – but he will have none of it. 'Non.' The view up the back is better for his eyes, he claims. 'Myopia.'

I can see the strain on Sarah's face when she returns, caught between her boss and two people who are her guests. The poor thing goes back and forth between us during the Stones' performance, finally accepting defeat and sitting with François, a man not given to dancing or uncouth displays of pleasure.

No matter, let the nonce have his evening tantrum.

As we leave the show afterwards it is even more chaotic. People swirl and bulge out onto the streets. And as if God was a jester at heart, who should we have to share a taxi ride back into the city with but François and Sarah.

'It seems we are destined to be friends,' I say to François.

No reply.

'So what about the Stones party? Do you think it's at the hotel? Maybe we should try and gate-crash it?'

Once again François makes no comment, but his disgust with us is palpable. Sarah is excited by the idea and has heard rumours of a party there too. The taxi seems to be headed towards the hotel anyway, so as we chatter it's more or less decided without any final agreement from anyone. At the driveway the stretch limousines and taxis indicate something big is going on. We're in such a long line of vehicles Lisa and I suggest getting out and walking down to the hotel entrance to save waiting around. As we all climb out, François stays seated inside the taxi.

Sarah is confused and aghast and half climbs back in. We can see him say something very heated to her as she slowly shuts the door and sits there with him.

'Are they coming?' Lisa asks me.

'I don't think so,' I say, and we walk on down to the hotel leaving them stuck in traffic. In the lobby we find a sign declaring a rooftop garden bar has been closed for a private function. This is obviously where it is happening. We begin climbing a spiral staircase. A couple with VIP passes swinging on their necks comes charging down. 'It's up there,' they say helpfully.

At this point François and Sarah enter the lobby. Lisa and I call to them from the stairwell, 'It's up here!'

François lifts up his nose like an irritated giraffe and pulls on Sarah's arm, ignoring us completely. She looks back at us then away again without saying a word. They head towards the main desk inquiring about the party. I can hear François and Sarah saying what newspaper they are from, trying to sound important. We call out to them again but we may as well be dead.

'Forget them,' I say to Lisa and we move on up. I know that by asking to be let in to the party François and Sarah are almost certainly asking to be excluded.

A bouncer puts his palm out as we arrive upstairs and says, 'Where are you going?'

'The Rolling Stones after show party.'

'Certainly – sir and madam, this way please.' He bows and makes a sweeping gesture with his hands.

Inside the room is decked out with lit glass partitions patterned with multi-coloured peacocks, beautiful satin pillows on the floor, large round tables filled with pistachio nuts and fine food and wine. A traditional Turkish band plays in between video clips of the latest Lenny Kravitz and Rolling Stones songs. All of Turkey's elite are here to meet the band.

We're tempted to go back downstairs to try and get Sarah in if we can. But we don't trust our luck to go out and get back in again, so we kick back and enjoy the party. I am returning from the toilets when I am accidentally caught up in the arrival of the Stones, with Mick Jagger just in front of me in a bright purple jacket and Charlie Watts beside me. Charlie and I chat briefly about whatever two men might chat about while walking quickly over pistachios and satin cushions at 3 a.m. in Istanbul. But our ways soon part again.

I start to go back to where Lisa is sitting, though not before a gentlemen grabs me by the hand and starts shaking it vigorously, saying 'Thank you, thank you, thank you!'

I say I did nothing, and he says 'No, thank you!' and shakes my hand again. What can I do but say thanks back? I'm only 38 years old, though. Do I really look road weary enough to be a Rolling Stone? I touch my face and wonder.

We of course get staggeringly drunk. And become certain that François and Sarah have not been allowed in. It really is the most terrific party: Mick, Jerry, Charlie, the whole gang. Look, there's Ahmet Ertegun, the Turkish-born founder of Atlantic Records, too. Hey, Jerry is smoking! Oh, we have a splendid star-fucking time.

I call François and Sarah late the next morning to make a point of asking where they were and to let them know we got into the party without a problem. 'We wondered where you went,' I say. 'We were looking for you everywhere!'

Sarah says, 'No way!' over the phone, like she can't believe it.

'Yes way!' I say back to her. 'You should have stuck with us. I'm pretty experienced at getting into events like that back in Australia, you know. I was a music journalist, very involved with the underground.'

Olympus Presleyiad

HE WALKS INTO THE WATERS OF OLYMPUS WITH HIS BLUE jeans on and a black belt with strips of silver metal. His hair is styled in a black pompadour like a 1950s rock 'n' roll star.

He wears black sneakers, drags a branch of wood behind him, the same colour as his skin. He begins beating the water with it, white lashes shattering the Mediterranean surface like a 1000 ropes of tearing glass. The stick lands with a sodden thud one last time, sucked quickly into the weight of the sea.

Two girls are laughing near him.

They move tentatively out in deeper water. They try to protect their long wavy hair from the sea. Parting a way forward in a clumsy butterfly stroke, breasts rising and submerging.

The boy drags the stick behind him and moves out deeper towards them. He arches his brown back and pulls the stick in a wide, heavy circle, taking in the wet glitter of the sea with it. Slams it down near the girls.

He's chewing gum. White gum flashing as he draws his jaw out and smiles.

I lie on the only decent beach left free of shithouse tourist development on the entire coast of Turkey and watch the birth and rebirth of unpleasant gods and myths. An old volcano can be seen quite far away, a pencil sketch on a dream horizon. Turtles cross a sea to fuck each other here. An old kingdom is buried in the vines – just back there – amid tumbling stones. These randy children of the ancients are an annoying vanity with their stick, their gum, their laughter. But I'm envious about this life that passes me by. Their dumb splashing pulse amid it all.

Town Hall One (A True Story)

THE MAYOR'S BEEN STABBED IN THE ARSE!

This 'hit,' so to speak, is rumoured to have been organized by a gathering of Goreme residents unhappy with their mayor's extravagant and ill-considered community projects. Of which there are too many to list here in their entirety.

You will have to take my word that there is serious ill-feeling in Goreme towards the mayor. Enough to want to see the man dead – or at least unable to sit down for a lifetime.

For your tourist information, I will tell you that Goreme is at the heart of Turkey's eerily beautiful Cappadocia region, justly famous the world over for its 'fairy chimneys,' phallic-shaped rock formations that have been eroded out of the volcanic tufa landscape.

In the hills and valleys around Goreme, ancient Christian communities once lived inside these rock penises, weaving tunnels between them, cutting through the powdery earth to create underground homes and churches that escaped the wrath of passing invaders. They just rolled a stone over their doorways and waited till they were gone.

In Goreme today it's still possible to stay at local hotels built out of these 'fairy chimneys' and the more typical concrete and timber we are so familiar with. One can sleep in a cave or a room, double bed inclusive, at a reasonable price.

But our man in Town Hall does not entirely respect tradition.

He is a modernizing force, perhaps a misunderstood visionary. At the centre of Goreme, for instance, right atop the tallest fairy chimney in town, he has planted a glittering disco ball to jazz things up. An outdoor invitation to 'doof' the night away, baby, dancing in the street.

Not far off, he also built a glass pyramid modelled on that grand architectural achievement, the Pompidou Centre in Paris. It was thought to be a rather ostentatious structure for a Turkish desert town of some 3,000 people, even if it is a popular tourist spot. A somewhat, shall we say, self-aggrandizing gesture. Besides, he hadn't even bothered to get the planning permits! So the locals tore it down in a fury once the judge said it did not conform to specifications. That should have taught him.

Meanwhile the disco ball remains there. Once every blue moon a tiny piece of mirror flakes away in the sun and drops to earth, a tinkling you might think you are imagining if you happen to be nearby and the time is right. Mostly though the disco ball does nothing, out of reach, barely noticed, unless you bother to look skyward against the bleaching sun. Like some sad refuse left behind after a particularly wild party, a Christmas decoration hangover that no one bothers to remove.

Despite these failures and tensions, the mayor maintains his sense of importance, his enthusiasm for innovation. He currently struts around Goreme with two cell phones crackling and beeping, calling out loud messages of great import from 'Town Hall One'!

That's him by the way – 'Town Hall One' – a victim of too many American television shows. He is much excited by communications technology, is even rumoured to be getting an IT feeling in his blood. On the phone – either one, sometimes both at the same time – he instructs his secretary to make announcements that are then broadcast over a public address system dotting the town. Power will be cut off between 2 p.m. and 4 p.m., trash will be collected earlier this Tuesday and such like matters. You know how administrative inspiration works.

Since the assassination attempt on his mayoral arse, Town Hall One also carries a handgun conspicuously slung on his hip. You don't wanna mess with the mayor, baby. You don't wanna make his day.

Some people say this is an overreaction on his part. Paranoia. Besides, he doesn't even have a limp, so what's his problem? And this talk of an 'assassination attempt' – bah, it's just hysterical gossip. After all, the man who stabbed the mayor is mad. Quite mad.

So mad, he is officially recognized, certified, loved and avoided as the community's local mad man. Every town and neighbourhood has someone like this walking around. Only a fool gets tangled up with them in the wrong way. He's harmless, really.

Because of this local agreement that he is quite mad – almost a people's contract, a protectorate you might say – and the fact he only got the mayor in the arse anyway, 'the assassin' was sentenced to a mere six weeks jail.

When you consider that the proprietor of our hotel did eight months in jail for building eight steps up to a fairy chimney without a proper building permit – that is, one month in jail for each step he made – you could rightly say six weeks for a stabbing is a very light sentence indeed.

It's a quirk of Turkish legal statutes that stabbing someone below the hips is also not regarded as attempted murder. Lucky for the mad man it wasn't serious. So now he is out again and back in Goreme, a free agent wandering the streets.

Perhaps the sentencing also reflects the fact that the judge just didn't like the mayor. It's been said, you know.

Then again, perhaps the judge had not heard of the deep, dark depths to which this conspiracy theory sinks in Goreme: that the mad man had been put up to the attack simply because he was mad, and that the angry locals knew he would therefore not be punished severely for his crime. He was the perfect foil, the entirely innocent assassin. Local politics in Goreme is indeed a devious business, eternally below the belt.

C'mon, folks. There's got to be a better way. Spin that disco ball, baby, let Town Hall One take you higher.

Kayseri, 20 October 1998

...THAT STRANGE SENSE OF WANTING TO NOT FINISH A story came to me while reading the obituary of a writer in the Kayseri Octogar, a bus station in the middle of Turkey. A local comedy was playing loudly over the television, wired into speakers directly above our heads. It made no sense at all to me and no one was laughing or even watching. It was coming on to dusk, and as the silver movement of night approached a hazing passed through the windows from the outside world until there was no light at all but that of the moon and the stars. The bus station was full of men's voices – sometimes contained in a murmuring wave, sometimes broken by a cough or a boy's clearer voice. But here I was reading the obituary of an East Side New York American writer I'd never heard of and my eyes were tired and I wondered if, just for a moment, I had stepped outside of time and could somehow float away from meaning and death, float into those voices and disappear painlessly forever. A small piece of news that someone else might notice somewhere else in the world.

Double Cross

IN THE MORNING THE HOTEL OWNER CLEANS A .38 PISTOL at the desk, spinning the barrel then clicking it shut with a heavy fast slap. Gun-mad like so many Turks, he slumps it by the registry, don't-fuck-with-me-style. An encouragement, if any were needed, to pay the bill. Two other men, barely more than boys really, laugh as it catches my eye.

The man behind the counter is podgy and moustached – maybe ten years older than the look-alike teenagers but a universe beyond them. His pupils are brown and blank as tiny blocks of hash. Morally dead. I get the awful feeling the boys will catch up with him soon. That this is what manhood means around here. A slob at a counter, a spinning barrel, a price for everything and nothing of value.

The hotel is deserted, a few permanent rooms for 'the Natashas' (Russian whores), most others as vacant as the hallways, all darkness and mouldering red carpet from fresher if not better days. The downstairs lobby feels the same.

People don't stay here. They pass through. It's a smell, this continuing 'absence' that people add to. Made up of cigarette smoke, body odour, decayed fruit (orange peels? apple cores?), the dull waft of hairspray and something earthy and a little frightening. There are also sounds here, not the noises of rowdy guests, but old sounds, faraway sounds in muffled rooms, like the echoes of something that has already happened.

Outside the streets are muddy, bustling. It reminds me of a mining town in a cowboy movie where everything is built to fall down again, as if the energy of this place is about to burst its badly concreted seams.

The social glue appears to be cash and entrepreneurial adrenaline. Underneath the carnival of opportunity and mud something else endures: old customs I can't quite put a finger on, the mere sight of a man's knitted cap and the slowness of his walk, as dusty and blown about as the street on a dry day. This sense that culture and earth feel bound together is the only encouragement I have against the rapacious surface life gnarling its way forward: lire, rials, pounds, dollars, guns, heroin, blackmarket goods, just name your denomination, this place is alive.

Dogubeyazit is about 35 kilometres from the Iranian border, on the Turkish side. Not too far north is the Armenian border as well. Pronounced 'Doh-oo-bey-yah-zut,' most English-speaking backpackers refer to the town as 'Dog Biscuit.' The guide books say it is an affectionate nickname.

Established as recently as 1937 when Kurdish pastoral nomads were first forced out of the hills by the Turkish army to live on the plains more permanently, Dogubeyazit claims a population of 36,000. I'd hazard such robust numbers take in recalcitrant outlying villages and army encampments as well, varying greatly with the seasons and the boom-and-bust blackmarket character of the town itself. For those adventurers moving east, it's simply the end of the line, a point from which you drop off the face of the world.

The territorial frontiers nearby constitute a hot zone where tight military control has failed to stem the heroin trade making its way overland from Afghanistan via Iran. To give you some idea of the intensity of that trade, local authorities claim they seized 70 per cent of the heroin meant for Europe in 1999. If you don't want to fully include us in the European Union (EU), the Turkish government threatened surreptitiously, we can always let our vigilance on your behalf slide away.

Turkey's role in NATO as an armed bulwark against Arab nationalism, Iran's unpredictable brand of Shia Islam and the nearby unstable ex-Soviet republics (once a focal point for Cold War jousting), all coalesce into a strategically vital identity as the West's enforcer. That this predominantly Islamic nation also has strong military connections with Israel is just one more curious aspect to its Eurocentric – and aggressively ethnocentric – self-image as a superior country in the region. Something the EU has yet to acknowledge by granting full membership credentials. In short, we need you – but we don't want you. Like the Turks and Kurds who serve in some of Germany's lowest paid jobs, there's still some confusion about the dirty work that needs to be done in the world.

DRUG SMUGGLING ON THE TURKISH BORDER WITH IRAN IS cynically tied up with ethnic divisions in the east of the country. In the past it has helped finance Kurdish dissent against the rule of Ankara, the Turkish capital located westwards on the Central Anatolian plateau.

Back even further west is Istanbul. I recall seeing a gun shop on the cold shores of the Bosphorus, that thin grey channel between Europe and Asia Minor on which the great Byzantine city rests. Above a dense display of well-patronized hardware, there was a huge billboard of a man with shooting gallery glasses and ear protectors, eyes glaring down the barrel of his big, big gun. As I headed across the country towards Iran, I would find this advertisement a telling metaphor for Turkey and how it defines itself today.

Out here in the so-called 'Wild East,' the army does more than patrol the borders. It is the law. The army has always played a central, if troublesome, role in the progress of democracy in Turkey, instigating coups, acting as the primary source of power or a volatile alternative force. Yet it enjoys a higher standard of public approval than the parliament, the judiciary, the media, or any other organ of civil society. Pride in the military is a strong characteristic of Turkish life, an extension of the local emphasis on machismo and an older lust to restore the nation to the grand old days of the Ottoman Empire. Inevitably this militarized sense of nationhood, along with compulsory national service, has extended to a love of guns, and a surprising respect for the rule of law despite its draconian nature. Those who have most felt the weight of this rough justice and its backing by the military are the Armenian and Kurdish peoples who have predominantly occupied the east. Why these ethnic groups should rebel so strongly against a central Turkish authority has a long history.

After years of persecution, Armenians suffered what they call 'the Genocide' after an uprising on 24 April 1915 in the city of Van (still remembered as Armenian Martyrs Day) in support of invading World War One Russian forces. Their massacre by the Turkish military, along with cruel forced-march expulsions into Syria and reprisal purges in many other cities, saw one and a half million Armenians across the nation killed, almost wiping them off the face of the earth. It was viciously repaid in the northeast of Anatolia when Russia was briefly able to proclaim an 'Armenian Republic' there, slaughtering a few thousand Turkish Muslims into the bargain before they were routed in 1916. These crimes remain part of continuing nationalist struggles that saw a spate of Turkish diplomats assassinated in the 1970s by Armenian terrorists. Nowadays the struggles are more cultural, with a strong desire from Armenians to see the dark side of Turkish history acknowledged and apologized for. You don't see Armenians any more in eastern Turkey, nor much talk of their cause anywhere. If you want some history of the scorched earth civil war that raged, it's not in local books. You're more likely to find it elsewhere in the poetic thoughts of an Armenian-American playwright like William Saroyan, who once said through one of his characters, 'Life is on fire; caught in a hurricane; submerged in deep and blind water.'

A more contemporary and volatile debate revolves around the Kurds, who constitute a surprising one-sixth of the entire Turkish population (that is, 12 million out of 60 million total). These mostly devout Sunni Islamic nomads were disenfranchised when the redefined borders of Turkey, Iran, Iraq, Syria and the Soviet Caucasus cut right through their homelands in the wake of the post-World War One break-up of the decaying Ottoman Empire.

Much like the Palestinians (who have given them support), the Kurds found themselves a people without a country, their misfortunes exacerbated by the brutal, competing governments they were forced to live under and their own fractious tribal divisions. That their traditional living areas are rich in oil and river headwaters has never helped their claims for a homeland – then or now. In Robert D. Kaplan's book *The Ends of the Earth: A Journey to the Frontiers of Anarchy* the author quotes Erduhan Bayindir, a site manager for the Ataturk Dam: 'Water is a weapon. We can stop the flow of water into Syria and Iraq for up to eight months without overflowing our dams, in order to regulate the Arabs' political behaviour.'

Since 1984 the Kurdistan Workers Party (PKK), a Marxist-inspired group led by Abdullah Öcalan (pronounced 'Oj-hah-lan'), have indulged in terrorism and drug smuggling in their quest for a national state of Kurdistan. They've also profited from protection money extorted from labs in eastern Turkey which refine the raw poppy substance colloquially known as 'base' into powdered brick heroin that is shipped on to Europe. Every now and then tourists have also been kidnapped. Turkish teachers, especially, found themselves on the receiving end of PKK liberation bullets – 'better illiteracy than indoctrination,' it was said, an extreme position that did not endear the Kurdish cause to the wider population. Some 6,000 Turkish soldiers have gone home in body bags as this ugly guerilla war finally peters out. Another 27,000 Kurds have also been killed.

Turkey has come under international censure from both the United Nations and Amnesty International for its sanctioned use of torture and murder to combat the PKK, along with excessive judicial prejudice in the arrest and prosecution of so-called anti-terrorist cases. The PKK for its part has killed substantial numbers of Kurds accused of collaboration, and has continued its involvement with drugs and crime right across Europe. In the meanwhile the very word 'Kurdistan' is banned from public life in Turkey today while the Kurdish language is not allowed in schools.

The sensational arrest of Abdullah Öcalan in February 1999 and his trial were the flash points for a new crisis – as well as the first signs of a possible resolution. Carrying out a death sentence would have transformed Öcalan into a martyr, spreading word of his revolutionary mix of Islam and Maoism, as well as damaging Turkey's chances of possible entry into an EU that no longer tolerated capital punishment. In an act of strategic diplomacy, the Turkish prime minister suspended the death sentence, for which there is massive popular support, while appeals continue.

A violent egomaniac who should not be romanticized, Öcalan is nonetheless a key to resolution. After his arrest he immediately began to reconstruct himself as a peacemaker and instructed the PKK to withdraw its forces from the east and into the mountains of Iraq. The Turkish army meanwhile claimed the PKK was already all but broken well before the Öcalan arrest, and continued shelling across the border, pounding Kurdish villages full of guilty and innocent alike.

As in previous years, the Turkish army sent its forces across the border in spring 2000 as the snows melted to clash with recalcitrant Kurdish guerillas, claiming 'hot pursuit' while executing manoeuvres at a division level that would have taken months of planning. A warring anti-PKK Kurdish clan from the area supported them. Meanwhile the PKK is attempting to shift itself away from leading an armed and seemingly hopeless struggle for a homeland to becoming a political party pursuing cultural identity within the Turkish state. These efforts are at best in their infancy and mostly in disarray.

Through it all, Iraq remains a shadowland of violence. It was in this high, rugged landscape that Saddam Hussein began testing chemical warfare while the West idly sat by in the 'Anfal' campaign that killed up to 100,000 Kurdish civilians in 1987 and 1988. British and American air cover now shields the Kurds from such Iraqi atrocities, though not the Turkish ground campaign. With or without Öcalan and the PKK, a tribally divided, fractious nomadic people with nowhere to go will not become invisible. Their wounds and they are part of the land itself, just as the smells of 'garlic, rotten apples, roses, mint, sweet melons, cucumbers and perfume' belong forever in Kurdish collective memory to the evil chemical scent of Iraqi gas, gas, gas ...

QUIETLY STANDING BY ON THE GREY VOLCANIC ANATOLIAN plains of the Wild East is Dogubeyazit. Most of Turkey's 'dirty war' lays further to the south near Iraq, but more than close enough to affect the atmosphere of the town. And yet not all the locals here – be they Turks, Iranians or predominantly Kurds – seethe with hate and corruption. For some goat herders, farmers and border dwellers, life goes on as it always has: slowly, steadily, *inshallah* (God willing).

Making your way across Turkey to Dogubeyazit by bus is a straining business. Otogar (transport terminal) after otogar, with hours, sometimes a whole day, waiting listlessly for the next connection. The buses getting ever more crowded as peasants bring back a cornucopia of supplies and gifts from large western cities like Erzurum: bags and bags of clothes, electric heaters, bird cages, plumbing, the cries of a newborn child ...

The further east you go across the Anatolian plateau, the less touristy it feels. There is a dramatic shift, too, from the nationalism championed by the Republic's founder, Mustafa Kemal Ataturk ('Father Turk') to a more Islamic world-view resistant to a twentieth century culture of Westernization and 'Kemalism,' a secular process sometimes naively portrayed as democratizing. When Ataturk banned the fez as a backward item in 1935, men out here opted to wear woollen caps rather than hats: the brim was regarded as un-Islamic, an obstacle to bowing one's head to the ground, an affront to Allah! People who kept a fez on their heads were sometimes hung or shot. A woollen cap was a subtle, even sarcastic form of protest.

At a roadside café somewhere past the city of Kars, Lisa and I are forced to wait while repairs are conducted on our bus, which has broken down for the second time on this leg of the journey. It's 2 a.m. and about a dozen local men sit bedrazzled by the light flickering from the television, a roll of video clips from Turkey's late night equivalent to MTV.

Like the stranded passengers who are so accepting of the delay, the locals sip *çay* (tea) slowly, smoke cigarettes stoically – except that we are here because of a breakdown, and they – well, they seem to have made a choice: to sit in cruel plastic chairs at empty tables and sit and sit till time itself is a fluorescent hole in their heads. The idea of a village square appears to have collapsed in on a small electronic tube receiving signals from other places.

Typically, the news bulletin features gangs of men pursuing some miscreant or other down streets or across fields to deliver vigilante justice, an assembly of stones, fists and clubs. Police are usually just trying to get some guy or other into custody without the crap being beaten out of him by a mob. These kinds of scenes are put on high rotation at prime time, played every fifteen minutes or so for the pleasure of family audiences.

The favoured news article of the moment features a distraught woman in panties and bra, click-clacking in her high heels across a road, weeping madly. The whole thing seems like a lewd set-up to boost ratings in this partially secular, mostly conservative Islamic country. But it emerges as a genuine story: a woman fleeing her nightclub-owning fiancé who wants to sell her into prostitution in Istanbul. Men surround her, someone throws a coat over her body. It's an unusually chivalrous act for Turkish men, who seem to know more about ogling and manhandling women than any other males on the planet. In my eyes they are the kings of unwanted attention, masters of revulsion. At least when it comes to how they treat foreign women.

At the café, one man continually stares at Lisa, even though she has now taken to wearing a head cover as we move east into the increasingly Islamic countryside. She moves chairs to avoid his gaze. I start to stare back at him, but it is still quite some time before he ceases his almost anaesthetized lusting. I have an overwhelming desire to hurt him badly. A cheesy love song is playing again on the TV now that the news is over. A sexy, middle-class Turkish girl in designer clothes looking sadly out a window for the lover that will never arrive. Her heart is broken. It makes me pity both the women and men here: what they are; what they can never be.

The bus returns to pick us up and we all straggle aboard. It must be about 4 a.m. now. It's particularly cold outside, but the air conditioning is roaring with heat, slapping us with an enervating rush of air as we take our places. A young man walks down the aisle, spraying sickly smelling, lemon-scented water onto the grateful passengers who refresh their hands and faces with it. The men and women sit separately, but for married couples and their children. Through the window before we leave, I can see the café television droning on, previewing another world, inciting desire, drowning in stale smoke, the men not moving at all before its light.

IN THE MORNING WE DON'T KNOW WHERE WE ARE. SOMEONE says Agrì, but that seems wrong. There are no mountains in sight, only clouds. All that we know is that everyone is getting off the vehicle.

We haven't been told anything about changing buses and are under the impression we are travelling straight through to Dogubeyazit as our ticket declares. 'Are we here? Are we here?' Our sleep-tangled question is useless. 'Dogubeyazit? Dogubeyazit?' People shake their heads, rushing to get by us. So we clutch at our own bags, throwing things together unexpectedly, rushing to get off and grab our backpacks as they are unloaded into a frenzy of passengers now taking what is hopefully theirs (and not ours). Pumping through us is that awful feeling of uncertainty and mistrust.

We are completely off-balance. But a man in a brown suit suddenly puts his hand on my shoulder. He lifts the hand up to me, open palmed in a soft, pushing motion: a calming gesture. Then he waves us to a few old school chairs placed beneath some plastic sheeting in a corner of the *otogar*. Someone is cooking *doner* kebabs there. Tea is boiling. An open air café. Sit, sit, please. So we follow his directions, placid as lambs.

The rest of the passengers splinter off into waiting cars and trucks or the *otogar*'s main terminal, a cinder block headquarters for whatever 'travel agents' may be there. I say 'Dog Biscuit' to the man who seems to be helping us. He makes the same hand gesture to me, lifting his head to the vendor making tea. Three tulip-shaped cups are brought for us on the basis of a nod. He pays before we can offer a single note of lire. Holds a cube of sugar between his teeth, sips the steaming tea through his lips, letting it dissolve in his mouth.

We grip onto our packs. Still waking up. It is early morning, cold, with a strong sun that burns the skin. As we drink our tea and calm down, going with the flow, we move our chairs to avoid the sun's rays. He seems unaffected by the light.

Our new friend nods at me. He is curious about a hand-carved walking stick I purchased back in Goreme for my father, who has recently suffered a stroke. He takes the walking stick from me and lightly stamps it on the ground, raising dust. Then he runs his thumb and forefinger down the silver snake-like threads carved into it and nods to me appreciatively. I mimic his gesture, nodding back towards the large cardboard box he is nursing. He opens it for us to reveal a giant wall clock, like the face of a grandfather clock, wrapped badly in voluminous amounts of plastic. He also has some small gifts poking out of his airbag, the zip half-broken: a pretty piece of material, a few toys – for his wife and children we assume. He lifts the material out, a deep blue, and rubs it in his fingers, inviting us to do the same. It's as smooth and cool as water. I realize he appears older than he actually is, all salt and peppery hair, face lined and weathered and dry like the land. His squint is permanent, a glimmer of life in a body that looks hard and tired.

Another bus arrives, with a broken window and plenty of dings in the bodywork. He stands up and again we follow him. In front of us people start pulling out different bus tickets just as I try to offer our old ones, thinking they still carry us on into Dogubeyazit. Again that firm hand on the shoulder comes to me before I can start asking questions. He says something to the collector at the door, guides us on board. I realize he has paid for us already, but he refuses any money from us – once, twice, three times we try, enough! It would be an insult to try again.

Why he has smiled upon us I do not know. But the bus rocks wildly down the potholed road at an indecently fast pace, and we all grasp to maintain our balance. A trail of giant pipes follows beside us along the road, disconnected segments that lay on the land like a long string of beads. To sit sideways and engage with us, our friend has to lean with one hand on a seat to stabilize himself, the other wrapped tight around his great clock, his bag of gifts safely between his feet.

We are the only Westerners. There are about a dozen people aboard, all men but for Lisa. Our friend points to a snow-capped mountain, then calls out to another man who appears to speak a little English. He shouts out back over the rush and roar of the engine, 'Mount Ararat! Noah's ark!' Our friend nods in agreement and quickly rocks his clock like a baby, bringing it to rest and pointing to the mountaintop again. He says the Turkish word for Ararat, 'Agrì.'

We've already heard of the famous mountain where Noah's ark is reputed to rest. We signal that we understand him and look meaningfully at its ice-capped heights. There is something forbidding about it as it towers over the flat lands, a profound coldness. I'm told that the Israeli and Turkish military use if for group training manoeuvres, making their soldiers run up and down it to test fitness and will power. It was also a popular hiking trail till PKK activity in the region closed it to tourism. Scientists, archaeologists and myth seekers still come here to dig for the beginnings of mankind, or some part of mankind's story, real or imagined.

I notice a long, thin trail of paper beginning to litter the road, condensing into a sea of white leaflets floating and turning carelessly across the bitumen. A head-on collision has occurred between a car and an overturned truck, everything twisted, pulped together, spangling in the sun. Glass is everywhere. The door of the car is ripped completely away, open to our gaze. No one is around. No movement but the sheets of paper, rising and rolling in the wind. We pass by the scene in a matter of seconds, possessed by the same floating sensation and the great emptiness around us.

Men gradually get off at deserted spots along the road. Turn-offs to villages where they choose to sit and smoke and wait for someone, or places where they simply start walking off into the landscape.

Soon enough our friend yells to the driver, says something inexplicable to us like a good wish over our heads. He staggers down the aisle as the bus careers to a lunatic stop. We barely have time to try and express our gratitude, silenced by our lack of language, reduced to gestures and what brightness we can give our faces, the tone of our words. We hope he understands the sounds we make. He waves again to us once he is outside and turns away. The bus cranks up and begins moving. As we look back, we see him striding out jauntily across the harsh, dun-coloured plain, the wind filling his suit with air, his greased hair blowing loosely into tufts and strands, a long thin cloud racing to claim him, the dusty plume of a distant car from somewhere we will never know.

DOGUBEYAZIT REMINDS ME OF THE TOWN MACHINE IN THE film *Dead Man* when Johnny Depp's character, William Blake, finally arrives there: a mired hallucination, busy as hell. Buses, trucks, vans and carts clog the major entry points. Dirt roads are wheel-rutted and churned completely to mud. In this flattened world, civilization appears to rise crudely from clay paste and dissipate into drifting coal smoke and diesel fumes.

The bus driver keeps looking for a way to get into town, unsuccessfully. We try a few roads before all hope is abandoned of reaching the central otogar. Eventually we're dropped off somewhere nearby that's deemed appropriate. Left to our own devices we load up our backpacks and begin walking into the heart of 'Dog Biscuit,' following everyone else. We trudge past a tourist information office, a one-door shack with multiple nationalities all jammed around it babbling hopelessly. We decide not to bother with inquiries there.

We try a few hotels and make the fatal mistake of booking into a mid-price joint that instantly appears shady. It has all the ambience of a violent, deserted pool hall. Neither poor enough to be humble, or expensive enough to protect us from the rough edges of the street, it is the worst of both worlds – overpriced and seedy, a place without character or peasant honour of any kind. And yet we find ourselves gridlocked into a decision to stay.

Exhausted and somehow hustled, we rationalize that 'It's only one night.' Check the bolt on the door, try the hot water (none of course), hide or lock what we can, carry anything else of value with us. If we could nail our packs to the floor we would.

Apart from Mount Ararat, there is only one other major tourist attraction in this neck of the woods: an old seventeenth century Kurdish castle called the Ishak Pasa Sarayi, which is visible in the hills nearby. It was once a grand place indeed, with large courtyards, viaducts for running water, banquet rooms, imperial bedrooms, and gigantic entrance doors of emerald-studded gold (stolen by invading World War One Russian forces and now stored in a museum in St Petersburg). All that's left now is the dry, flaking yellow stone, and deep silences from room to room.

Despite the centuries-old ambience and unfinished restoration work, it's not hard to imagine people still living here. Maybe it is the grandness of the place in such an apparently inhospitable world. Maybe it's the sound of the wind blowing through – but you sense an old richness, something ghostly amid the rooms. Time is a presence here. Through the windows, the wind-carved hills appear like an ocean set in stone, a landscape paralyzed in the midst of sudden, even violent movement. It is a dramatic illusion. I imagine a young and beautiful princess gazing out at the same, unchanged earth hundreds of years ago, drawing her strength and identity from a place where we find only sheets of loneliness. Further up the hill from the castle is another fortress, centuries older again, so decayed and brittle and shot with heat the earth and sun have finally reclaimed it as their own.

Our taxi driver waits outside for us impatiently, estimating how much more he should charge us for taking so much time. All the while a tourist tout tries to conscript us into joining a small group he is taking across the border into Iran. He gives us his card – the proud sign of the self-made businessman in Turkey. Lisa consults him on the respectability of her outfit for the crossing: a scarf for her head, a loose green leather jacket, a shapeless long skirt to her ankles, socks and walking boots, with only her face and hands visible. He says it is fine for Iran, 'Fine, yes, this is good.'

'Otherwise …' he laughs, and makes a rough stone-throwing gesture at her. 'And that is not so good.'

We lie to the tourist guide about catching up with him for dinner, and say we are staying at a different hotel to the one we are actually booked into. I don't feel comfortable about doing this but he already has a few customers for 'the crossing,' as he keeps calling it, and I get the impression he has followed us here to manufacture an accidental encounter. For the rest of the day and the following morning I dread we will see him again and our white lie will be revealed. Why I should care about my word I don't know, but it seems to matter to me here, even in the fast patter of bullshit between us.

Back in town we go to an open-air bazaar, full of trolleys and carts and wooden trays loaded with carrots, cabbages, cheap clothing, cigarette lighters ... We look for a *chador* for Lisa to wear, but they only have manteaus, ugly raincoat-like creations with padded shoulders and hideous buttons. Better a crow-like *chador*, Lisa feels, than these fashion insults. Her own makeshift outfit will have to do till we get to Tehran.

I want a suit like the men out here, but no matter what I try I can't seem to get the right balance of exhaustion and grace that has inspired me as a fashion statement. On me the suits simply look what they are: bad, cheap and uncomfortable. I am unable to fill them.

WE DECIDE ON AN EARLY START, BUT AS ALWAYS IT TAKES longer than expected to wake, to pack, to determine those last minute, essential constituents for a long journey: chocolate, a pocket knife, a pen, toilet paper, a torch, available cash and hidden resources, something warm just in case ... We have unpredictable bus travel down to an art form by now, but the thought of crossing the Iranian border still makes us nervous. I have already torn stories from my diary that might implicate me as a journalist. Doubly paranoid, I burn the pages and wash the ash away in a sink rather than throw them into a bin for someone to read. We are about to enter another world. I feel as if we are opening a door like no other, and that we have no idea what is really behind it.

Downstairs I deal with the Three Stooges act and the big gun that they play with at the lobby desk. That spinning barrel, those cold eyes. It is my last encounter with a Turkey that demands I define my masculinity in equally strong terms. I feel exhausted by the challenge, resentful at the start of our great adventure into Iran. I want to curse Turkey and the way it swings so sharply into virulence. But maybe all I curse is being a tourist.

We know that a *dolmush* (mini bus) leaves regularly every hour from somewhere near the bazaar. So we have breakfast in the main street, beautiful local honey with bread, then a thick grain soup that is too heavy for me to finish. Lisa encourages me to take my time. So I continue to eat greedily against my lighter morning habits because we do not know what is ahead. Like a camel, stocking up my internal provisions. But I get a sick weight in me, a bad feeling. Like I could shit myself. The worst kind of meal: it's not the food, it's me.

In the restaurant a young girl on her way to work eats alone, but she seems to know all the men who run this establishment. She is curiously modern and fresh in this hole of a place, rising with her leather briefcase as if on her way to do business in downtown Istanbul. The men like her very much, and openly care for her, and I wonder if she is their daughter, niece, sister? Such slender shards of feminine sweetness are water in the desert for me right now. To be a man in a world like this is to feel that the world could bruise and overwhelm you at any moment. You know that you are just not hard enough, tough enough to meet it at its worst.

Out on the street we barely walk more than a few metres before an empty, well-kept *dolmush* stops beside us. The driver gestures frantically for us to jump aboard, touting for business to take us to the Turkey-Iran border station at Gürbulak. We start haggling over the money, having established exactly what the costs were yesterday by talking with various traders at the markets. He agrees hurriedly and we climb aboard. We go about two blocks before he makes us unload again in order to get onto another *dolmush* – this one absolutely packed with men and goods. In his book *A Fez of the Heart*, the English writer Jeremy Seal explains that, 'Dolmush derives from the word to stuff, most vividly expressive in its frequent use to describe peppers or vine leaves stuffed with rice.' Now I understand what he means.

I do not like the idea of not sitting with Lisa on a bus crowded with men, but it is not a problem. There is some commotion as the crowd inside half shout and grunt at each other in what passes for a conversation. Finally an old man up the back pushes another man by the elbow – he hops up, climbs over the top of some men, and plonks himself down towards the front of the *dolmush* in a place where there had been no sitting space before.

It's a miracle of rearranged seating. We are then required to crawl through to our seats at the back. One man outside keeps offering to hold my walking stick while I climb over everybody. I get this stupid feeling he will run away with it, so I do my best to act confused, holding onto it with all my might as he tugs away at it too, wrenching the walking stick free of him as I bound aboard. Lisa is not far behind me. In the meanwhile our backpacks are thrown on the roof, and while we barge through the scrum of male bodies to our seats, the door is slammed shut and we are on our way.

Once again, we are the only Western tourists aboard, something we have become very used to. But in this situation, the closeness of everybody adds to an even greater intimacy. Once we hit the road, an old tape is pushed into the cassette player and a long wail sets up, Arabic-sounding music as big as the spaces around us, climbing and spiralling. The old man next to me smiles, holding a set of green beads in his harsh hands, rubbing them one by one and letting them drop like seeds. They swing in his hand as the *dolmush* rocks along, picking up a few more passengers along the way, disgorging others, mostly at inexplicable, nowhere points where they set off into oblivion, just as yesterday. In the distance I can see what look like small villages or ruins, collections of single clay shacks, so grey as to meld into the landscape altogether.

We are deep into the borderlands between Turkey and Iran. The singing climbs higher and higher. Someone says 'Sivan Perwer' and turns up the volume. The speakers distort at times but no one seems to mind. We see hills and mountains, an infinite open sky. Beside us is the same never-ending pipeline we saw yesterday, part of postponed plans for transporting gas from Iran and oil from the Caspian Sea. The pipes lie waiting to be joined together as various strategic negotiations continue with Iran, Turkmenistan, Azerbaijan, Georgia and American corporate and political interests. All they know for sure in Turkey is that somewhere near here one pipeline or another must meet.

Army troops at a roadblock flag us down. The music is cut dead as the bus slows and everyone starts reaching for their passports and what look like work permits. I wonder what they do in this nether region between the two countries, whether these men are Turkish, as I took for granted, or Kurdish? One man in front seems wealthier than the others. He is dressed in a smooth green suit that gives him all the brightness of a mint sweet. He has a gold watch and strong cologne. I get the feeling he is the boss of something, but none of the other men discriminate against him.

As I reach for my passport, the old man beside me signals to wait first and see if we are requested to hand anything over. Be still. After thoroughly inspecting everyone else's papers aboard, an inquiry is barked our way. The Turkish soldier is not in the least friendly, his dark brown eyes hard as beetle shells upon us. He looks at our photos on the passports, then at us. I feel guilty or in danger somehow, as if I am not who I am at all. Outside the *dolmush,* half a dozen soldiers stand with automatic weapons at the ready. Their leader hands our passports back cursorily, has a joke with one of the men on the bus, and slams the door shut. As we take off again someone says something and we all laugh. The tape is turned back on. The old man next to me keeps rubbing his prayer beads, nodding his head to the music, half-dozing for the whole journey, content with his world. Only a few of us are left by the time we get to a much larger and final checkpoint. Here the bus can go no further. The old man climbs off and signals for us to head to a gate where soldiers again look at our passports and glance at our packs suspiciously. By this time the old man has gone on ahead of us, a frequent traveller to and fro.

The walk through to the border zone should feel interminably long with our heavy backpacks on. But it is rather like wading through a dream. Trucks of all kinds, oil tankers, semitrailers, goods vehicles, large, small, new, old, broken down, silent and rumbling, are all lined up for what seems like miles. To give you some idea of the time they have to wait at the border, I see that some of the drivers are conducting extensive repairs on their vehicles. A few have portable stoves out and are boiling up tea. They look like they are very used to delays. Opposite this long line of vehicles are disused shacks, storage places, guardhouses, graffitied brick walls. It reminds me of a huge railway siding, the same dull grind of industry and transport, clanking, greasy, rusting.

Finally we get to a group of buildings where we must fill in forms declaring our departure from Turkey, showing our passports yet again. They are sucked in through a hole-in-the-wall service counter about the size of a small fruit box, into a small office where I can see someone running them through a computer check. Some time later they are handed back to us, stamped with permission to leave. We are then invited to walk through a small door into a room that looks like a large farm shed.

The scene before is one of boredom. Peasant women sit on large cotton sacks filled with clothes. Others deal with their children. A few men play chess and suck on pipes. Behind us as we enter is a thumpingly large portrait of Mustafa Ataturk. Directly opposite by a doorway that leads us into Iran is a giant picture of the Ayatollah Khomeini, the brimstone hero of Shia Islam. I am surprised that the portrait of Khomeini is slightly smaller than the picture of Ataturk the secularist. I can't imagine such a thing goes unnoticed here. But it interests me that the two face off so obviously, so radically opposed, one against the other. I take a good look at their eyes, their mouths: these are not men given to making easy compromises. There is nothing soft about them.

A brassy entourage of a dozen Russian women also enters, talking loudly, rattling with fake gold jewellery. At least I assume it's fake. The heads and bodies of the women are covered, but their volume blows their false modesty away. Every now and then a man comes to a gate entrance and passes out forms for people to fill in as the room gets more and more crowded. His assistant tries to help us fill ours out, but he gets everything wrong. At first I am too nervous to change his botched clerical job in case it is easier to just go with whatever he thinks. But I see that these forms are being passed on to another, more senior figure in the production line, so I think better of his assistance and get another form after some extra jostling. Thank god I have a pen of my own. One could pay with many stranded hours here for the lack of a pen.

Groups are let through a small gate, single file into Iran. People are also coming through the opposite way, rather like cattle in grids. In our confusion we almost join the line about to re-enter Turkey – as one does nothing in this world but line up somewhere, it's an understandable mistake, a habit. Eventually we get to a customs area where we are confronted with the grim sight of about a hundred women with two or three sacks each the size of swollen rubbish bags. We are in for a long wait it seems. But an Iranian customs officer sees us and flags us forward. No one seems to mind or care and we're happy to be the privileged Westerners under these circumstances. That is if we are being 'privileged' by his attention.

He eyes me curiously. 'No sexy magazines, sir?'

'What?'

'No sexy magazines, sir?'

The second time he speaks I take in what he is saying and laugh. 'No.' He looks at our passports. 'Australia,' he says smiling. 'Very good. Azizzi. Harry Kewell, 2 – 2.' The customs officer is talking about a famous soccer match between Australia and Iran. It led to Australia's elimination from the 1998 World Cup and Iran's advance onto Paris – and their much celebrated defeat of the US football team.

'Yes,' I say, smiling.

'Very good. Very good, sir! Welcome to Iran, sir.'

He waves us through heartily. Our being Australian clearly pleases him. It's a nice feeling. And so we pass through what we think is the last obstacle. Outside, money changers are everywhere. You have to push by them to get into the bank. I go to exchange American dollars for some local *rials* there, but a hapless clerk looks at me mystified. The bank is utterly deserted. I cannot speak Farsi (Persian), so he writes down the money he will give me in the bank, pointing to the counter in front of him. Then he writes down a substantially superior exchange rate and points outside to the waiting money changers. It is obvious what we should be doing.

Out we go. Into the arms of a guy who short-changes us about 20,000 rials, or about US$10 on what he promised us once we count out what we have received. We almost miss the bus as we haggle with him for the rest of the money. The driver toots the horn furiously, so we kiss the few dollars goodbye and curse him roundly under our breaths as we rush aboard. It's a routine our Iranian money changer has obviously pulled before. As we climb on the bus with all our bags, I've got money stuffed in my pockets all over the place, a mix of US dollars, English pounds, Turkish lire and a brick-thick wad of fresh Iranian rials. It's a messy look: rich stupid Westerner here, please rob soon.

We are sent to the back of the packed bus where a man with a sharp thin moustache has been observing us with some amusement. He is dressed in a dark blue, pin-striped suit and eating a large bag of sunflower seeds, cracking them in his teeth and spitting the shells out. He offers us some. I take two, an obscurely tiny number that makes him laugh. It feels like I am eating parrot food but I do my best to seem grateful.

He signals for us to sit beside him. Later we will realize that he too has paid for our bus tickets as a gesture of friendship, just as the man did yesterday. That he has kept some seats for us while we struggled ineptly with the moneychanger. 'Welcome to my country,' he says, crunching and spitting more seed shells out around us on the floor, creating a brittle carpet beneath our boots.

And so we arrive: with yet another border check to pass through when the bus stops. But this time it's a mere formality, a last glance at our passports. We are in a new country now and a siege of taxi drivers awaits us beyond the barriers to take us wherever we like. Having travelled through Turkey into the Wild East and finally Iran, sensing danger and uncertainty, past the spinning gun barrel, the hard and dubious men, the swirl of strange music and space, we have been delivered again and again into kindness, always kindness, around the arabesques and edges of our path across the borderlands.

No vision can grasp Him,
but His grasp is over all vision.

QU'RAN, 6:103

Iran Over All Vision

Dream

IN ESFAHAN, 'THE CITY OF GLASS,' I WAKE UP AFTER A NIGHT
pursued by assassins in my dreams. They come for me without a clear reason, but I know I have done something, broken some covenant, and damned
myself. The dream is not hot with panic, however. It is cool, detached,
watched like a distant movie. I seem to be befriended by loyal men and passionate, beautiful women, but their lives are lost as I continue to move on
and the assassins follow. Some sacrifice themselves to block the way of my
pursuers; others try to accompany me but are eventually caught. I may kill
some of these assassins, but they continue to track me, and to grow stronger,
bigger, more dangerous in quality the longer I elude them. There is therefore a sense of time running out, of things moving faster. There now seems
to be only one route of escape. To jump off a high mountain into a shaft
of snow and ice, to disappear into a great whiteness and perhaps survive
to begin a new life elsewhere. Publicly it is suicide. Privately it is a chance.
There is another loyal friend with me, and another passionate, beautiful
woman. I feel inklings of a weariness and a guilt for the lives that have
been lost. I have eaten up people as I ran. Their deaths were not always my
fault, but just by being attached to me they have become lost. I want these
two people in my present to survive, but I don't know if they will. Before
we jump, we strap on special watches that emit an electronic heartbeat.
The jump may take us anywhere in the world. These devices will help us
find each other. We are close to leaving. It is cool and now another woman
seems to be helping us too. It feels as if we are somewhere in Tibet, and
there is a calm, religious air to the proceedings. Finally, an assassin arrives
just as we are about to jump. But he is more like a superman, an 'Adonis
of assassins' I remember thinking. He is a giant, muscular, perhaps twice
my height. He has an assistant who helps him disrobe until he is naked. It
is as if he has done this before. It is a ritual. He is more than an assassin.
He is an executioner. And his manner is cool and indifferent and assured.

WHEN I WAKE I AM LEFT WITH THIS DREAM, INCOMPLETE.
I do not know if I die, if I escape, if my friend and my lover live, or for that

matter anything about the woman who was helping us.

It does not feel ominous. But as I shower I find myself thinking about the nature of love. Of passion versus affection. Of all the friends and lovers I have known, the way their faces disappear in my mind. It is hard for me to remember much of detail about anyone. I feel cruelly forgetful. The present has become a remnant experience of my collected history, ghosted, broken. I wish I was clearer on this, more coherent. But it's all a mess. I'm not good at remembering. I've lost my hold.

And yet lately I have been thinking about the idea of oblivion. Of the tabula rasa. The clean slate. The white field of snow. Of beginning anew.

This idea of disappearing into the world is very attractive and very frightening.

There is something of a reincarnation fantasy at root below these daydreams. But I know it's not as simple as that. You can't get born again from running.

I recall a story Lisa has told me. An example of dream analysis from the works of Jung. Of numerous people in a mining region who dreamed of black horses running down a hill. This dream came to many people over a period of days. Till a great landslide came and destroyed a mining village in their region in one great black weight of stone and dirt.

Waiting for a Chance

HE LAUGHS AND SAYS 'KHAMENEI' IN A LOW VOICE. THEN HE makes a slicing motion with his thumb all the way across his throat along with a quick, hacking sound. Then he looks at me.

'I don't think so,' I say back to him.

But I hardly understand what I am saying at all. Just the sounds of confidence these automatic words somehow conjure, a droll white noise in place of language.

I keep walking. And let the door swing shut behind me as we leave the restaurant. Still tingling with the tracheal gesture. Still feeling as if he means me. Me who will lose my head in Iran.

Oddly enough, there is no particular menace to the moment.

It all happens so quickly I barely take in the interchange. It almost seems humorous: the bland smile, the smell of baking food, his weary gesturing.

For some time afterwards I still try to take it as a joke. A joke for Westerners fresh to the 'madness' of Iran.

Then I wonder again if it is what he wishes. If he wants to see a jihad, a 'holy war' or 'a struggle in the way of God,' continued against the infidels now beginning to infiltrate his country as tourists for the first time since the Revolution. If he would really like to see my head roll.

Lisa and I have sat eating rice with fish, a bowl of salad with a vinegar and yogurt dressing, and a plate of mint with two halved onions. A typical Iranian meal in a clean, basement level restaurant in Esfahan, the city of merchants and glass, a place renowned for its crafts and craftiness, its skilful liars.

I talk to the men who work in the restaurant, making self-effacing fun of my guidebook Farsi phrases: where are you from? hello, goodbye, I'm sorry I don't speak Persian (*bebakshid farsi balad nistam*). One man on his lunch-break smiles at me from across the room. The others look on bluntly, staring slowly from the fluorescent, middle-aged weight that seems to colour the whole room and drag at the heels of their boots. Moving like men in some invisibly thick soup.

We stand. Go to the cashier. '*Chand–e?*' An enquiry about the cost. He holds up a 10,000 rial note to our eyes. The money changers on Ferdosi Avenue call this 'a Khomeini' after the dead Ayatollah whose stern face stares out from it. I leave an extra 1,000 rials tip (about US$0.50). And we start to walk out the door.

That's when the moustached 40-something man in the washed-out khaki uniform of a cleaner or a dishwasher looks at me and makes his little cutting motion to the throat.

It's not because I'm a lousy tipper.

I'd already heard about this gesture yesterday from a Frenchman who had just visited Tehran. He wasn't clear on the meaning of it either – if it was a joke, or something very nasty indeed.

In Tehran people had done the same thing to him, but they had made a brief whirling about their head as well, to signify the turbans of the mullahs (Islamic clerics), before they too slashed at their throats with their thumbs and laughed.

At first I don't tell Lisa about all this symbolic throat-cutting. But eventually I have to mention my goodbye message at the restaurant as we walk off into the silence of the city's 10 p.m. streets. It troubles her, then she says, 'Perhaps they mean death to Khamenei?'

Well, do they?

People say there is much unhappiness with the rule of the mullahs in Iran. In the 1998 parliamentary elections for the Assembly of Experts, clerics ensured that the candidates who could run were predominantly conservative. Only 46 per cent of the population bothered to vote. It had already been decided behind closed doors by the mullahs. What was the point?

The Assembly selects and appoints Iran's Surpreme Leader – currently Ayatollah Ali Khamenei, the like-named successor to Ayatollah Ruhollah Khomeini – who controls both the military and the security forces as well as the judiciary. This is Khomeini's vision of the world's first Islamic theocracy, an indisputable leader who can interpret God's will with an iron fist wherever and whenever necessary.

The President, Muhammad Khatami, is an anomaly in this scene, a freak victory in a landslide people's vote that saw 76 per cent of the voting population, mostly women and the young, turn out to elect him in 1997. But the conservative mullahs aren't so impressed with a man who studied philosophy in Germany for two years, nor the Western 'liberal decadence' he is encouraging.

Khatami lacks real power, yet he has popular support. He balances himself delicately on this edge. As one local told us, 'Khatami says such beautiful words. Such beautiful words. But what is really happening in Iran? What is really going on?'

A strange tension underlines Iranian daily life. As if the opening up of the country is contained by a firm vice that will only allow it to expand so far. The question seems to be: when will the unstoppable force meet the immovable object?

THE WORD 'MULLAH' SWINGS IN THE MOUTH LIKE A CLUB. It carries weight when you say it.

Walking around the streets of Esfahan, we get very used to being stared at by people curious about Westerners in their midst. Whenever the turbaned shape of a cleric approaches, however, there is not a flicker of interest or recognition in their eyes. We do not exist. We are not there.

One feels the mullahs' neutralizing power, the sheer stoicism of how they refuse you through the mere act of not looking and looking right through us at the same time. They simply erase us from the scenery.

This oppressive weight, this power of erasure, has an effect on far more than tourists. It extends into all aspects of Iranian life. The mullahs are always 'there,' through the secret police and informers, through faith itself and the constantly inflamed values of the devout. In this way the mullahs invisibly penetrate and purge the world with their presence, possessing their streets – when they do appear – like fearsome and radioactive stones.

The result is a country silently divided. And a pressure that creates an even greater longing for freedom.

You sense this most when you talk to the young. At first there's pride, of course, in their country. The initial images that they paint of Iran are almost Disneyesque, 1950s-pure. They're also very aware of Western stereotypes of them as screaming, crazed religious fanatics. Most people hate this global media cartoon of them and their country and their faith. As if to counter it, people are ridiculously friendly – strangers literally invite you home for dinner, take you on personal tours of their city, give you small gifts. It's actually quite difficult to deal with this overwhelming enthusiasm and courtesy wherever you go.

But like the 1950s there's a lock on the mind and the spirit. As we talk more and more to young people and they open up to us, they admit to being 'stuck' in their lives, often speaking of their desire for change, or of simply wanting to leave Iran altogether. They also tend to idolize the West with a naive enthusiasm. As a dream of freedom, with all the forbidden fruits that go with it. As a total fantasy.

Within six months of the Ayatollah Khomeini coming to power in

1979, he made a speech declaring that, 'There is no fun in Islam. There can be no fun or enjoyment in whatever is serious.'

It's hard to maintain that sour reverence when over half of your population is under 25. Iran is witnessing a youthquake, and it can't cope with the energy. The strange thing about its youth is how commonly they refer to the time of the Shah with yearning and nostalgia – yet they have no memory of his brutal and exploitative reign or the Revolution that deposed him. It is as if they yearn for a past that never existed.

In Tehran we read a newspaper article warning that the clerics in parliament have voted to send a paramilitary group known as the *Basij* into the universities, to help police and suppress 'liberal Western influences.' Their goal involves more than just intellectual oppression – it means intimidating young people to stop them holding hands in public, and preventing women from wearing lipstick or pulling their chadors back provocatively onto their heads to reveal a little of their hair. These acts of 'Westoxification' that hark back to the days of the Shah, these relatively mild gestures of public affection and decoration, constitute the pagan rebellions of Persian youth today. In the extreme and early years of the Islamic Revolution, the Basij were renowned for their opposing fervour, taking the lipstick off women with razor blades. Drafted from the ranks of a massive peasant underclass, they are devout enough to still serve the darkest commands of hardline mullahs, to be thugs in the name of Allah.

'What will they do?' asks one Tehranian man benignly of yet another bout of oppression from the mullahs and their henchmen. 'This is nature. A boy and a girl. It is like trying to stop running water.'

We talk to a tour guide about it all. He tells us how he wants to escape. Maybe through India. Maybe through Hungary. He can hardly go anywhere in the world, he complains, as very, very few countries will give him a visa, with exceptions like India, Pakistan, Nepal and Japan. It is hard to get out. It is hard to travel at all.

'I am 26. Two years ago I fall in love with a German girl,' he tells us. 'I could not go to see her. They would not let me leave here. And Germany would not give me a visa either.

'I was very angry. Very crazy.' He shows us pictures. Two shots of a blonde, one of her sitting on a beach, another of the two of them in his car. The photos look creased and old.

'Many times I have been arrested for mixing with tourists too much. They put me in prison one week, two weeks. I say, "Why do you do this to me? I am representing Iran to tourists in a good way. I am working hard for my country. I am contributing to my country."'

He looks at us with a salesman's eye. 'Okay, of course I do for myself as well. But I work hard. It is good for Iran too.

'And they arrest me! So I tell them, "Send me away. You arrest me. You don't like me, you don't want me. You don't want hard working people. You would rather I did nothing. So let me leave this country. This is a crap government that wants crap people."

'They tell me, "You talk a lot" and put me in jail,' he smiles. Then laughs. 'But I am not political. I don't care about that.

'I am 26. I just want to live. I meet tourists. Sometimes I go to Goa. They tell me things,' he nods childishly, conspiratorially, alluding to the rave capital of India's reputation for partying and drug-fueled abandon. He wants us to understand that he knows what real pleasure is. 'If you have tasted an orange and an apple, and you want the orange, you want the orange. If you do not ever taste it, then maybe you don't know.

'I know my country is very beautiful. But it is no good for me. I am 26,' he repeats as if it is something to be astounded and depressed by. His mantra. 'How can I meet girls? I am not allowed to wear a bracelet even,' he says, looking at mine as it sits heavily on my wrist, 'it is too Western.

'No!' he cries out. 'What sort of life is this? To get up early to work all day, to come home at night quietly and sleep like a cat. There is nowhere to go at night.

'My friend tells me I should stay. Iran is changing. Sure, maybe in five years. Maybe in ten years. He is 35 and married. It is okay for him. But what about me now? I am 26.'

And with that outburst over he shares his simple plans of escape, how he will sell his car, his motorbike and his rare Persian carpet. How he will go to see the girl in Germany. How he doesn't like the cold, however, and he will wait till spring before he escapes to Europe. How Western girls on tours often flirt with him and try to kiss him even when they have husbands or boyfriends. 'Why they do this? I think sometimes they want to punish their men.'

We explain to him that sometimes Western girls play games and that it doesn't mean they are really interested in him or love him. He lights up with recognition – this is a suspicion confirmed.

'Now I understand,' he nods. 'Now I understand.'

He considers himself a man of the world. Didn't live with his family as a boy. Was brought up in the snake turns of the local bazaar, 'working very hard. Very hard. Very hard like you cannot understand.'

Now life is good. He is a man on the move – or on the make, at least. But he has no freedom. He cannot fall in love. He cannot go anywhere. He cannot wear a bracelet. And there is that burning experience of two years ago, and these two photos of the girl he loves, both pictures marked with sticky tape where he has pulled them from his bedroom wall to show us. Marks that show he has pulled them from the wall a dozen times or more and told this same story to other travellers, whoever listens.

He unfurls his carpet, with its myriad patterns and silky blues and royal reds. He shows us where the makers wove an error into the carpet on purpose, so as not to affront Allah, since the Creator is the only one who can make a perfect thing. This is his magic carpet ride out of Iran. 'I think if I sell it I can make much money. It's beautiful,' he says a little sadly.

I try to warn him that he could be jumping into a deep hole if he becomes an illegal immigrant in Germany. For some reason his fears about the winter cold quietly depress me about his hopes. But he thinks he could just as easily fall down a hole in Iran, he says. 'Anything could happen here. Anything.'

So we talk about love again. And another painful experience as a teenager, when an older married Iranian woman had an affair with him. He didn't know she was married until after the affair had begun and she finally told him the truth.

'I told her to leave me alone. Sometimes now a married woman here in Iran will try to give me her phone number,' he says, disgusted. 'This is dirty. I tell her go away, you bastard. I don't want this. You are dirty bastard woman, leave me alone.'

He is 26 years old, going on 14. It seems to be a part of Iran's 1950s moral atmosphere to reduce people to adolescents. For him, Iran is frustrated desire and perpetual lies behind the backs of people. He wants the girl in Germany. The dream life. The dream love. But thoughts of freedom lead him back to the emotional prison of Iran, and Iran leads him back to questions and plans and schemes to escape. Running his fingers over the carpet, thinking, looking for the error.

We talk about him over dinner that night. In that sullen, slow-moving fluorescent restaurant where everything feels becalmed and exposed. Me twisting my bracelet round and round as I worry about him, till I'm given something else to keep me thoughtful.

Later still as we lie in bed, I think about the gesture at the restaurant. Whether it was friendly or aggressive, or even subversive as quite a few people have quietly suggested. The end of Khomeini and Khamenei, the death of the mullahs? Or a deepening and darkening of the Revolution as they fight to preserve their rule?

I'm really not sure. But this to me is the hidden Iran: a thumb at the throat, a girl who can't be loved. All blurred, hard to see, waiting for a chance.

The Car that Killed Elvis

A MAN IS WALKING DOWN A DESERT HIGHWAY SOUTHWEST of Esfahan. The Dasht-É Lut stretches out around him, a plateau of salt and stone all the way to the horizon. Diesel fumes and car-stirred dust blow by in stuporing clouds. An oil refinery in the distance mimics the polluting sting of the traffic, a bad oasis belching smoke into the blue sky.

The man keeps walking steadily into the sun, long used to the roadside grit and glare of the desert. He holds a giant trout above his head, a whole fist disappearing into its gut. Some handwritten Farsi declares *Fish for sale* in cursive script on a piece of cardboard hanging from his wrist.

What a strange sight he is here in the Dasht-É Lut – a freakish, sweaty looking thing halfway between the human and aquatic. His own hallucination.

Elsewhere racks of bananas on trucks. Carrots piled high in baskets, carrots hung in rows, carrot jam, so many carrots and uses for them. Fruits, nuts, sweets… all for sale. Petroleum tankers parked askew and at rest. Military jeeps and Iranian soldiers in khaki green at the turnoff to the refinery. A car broken down, spewing steam. The arterial busyness thinning into nothingness the further we get from town.

Way up ahead, a group of men in suits is smoking pipes at a T-intersection in the middle of nowhere, waiting for what? The dark flecks of a few hungry kestrels scratching the sky. Then a lone overtaking vehicle reflecting hot light, the driver tooting the horn and everyone waving at us like friends – ironically enough it's a huge purple Chevy, the paintwork ridden in hand-brushed blotches. 'The Great Satan' makes a hell of a car; these locals do their best to keep her pretty.

We're careening down the road in a 1959 Buick Le Sabre. It's black and battered, with a badly cracked windscreen, as if a spider has brutally worked a web in thick lines across the glass. Another image that comes to mind is of looking through the veined translucence of a dusty moth's wing. Either way, it's a fuckup.

Towards the driver's side, towards the left of this American dream machine, there is a single bolt at eye level, holding broken plates of glass together, making the windscreen hum with each tick of the speedometer above 40 kilometres. A leftover from the era of the Shah, US imperialism and petrodollars, 'the car that killed Elvis' (as I've taken to calling our vehicle) won't be stopped. I like the idea that this pop culture icon of the 1950s is not just a weary machine. That it symbolizes, somewhat contradictorily, an America shut out of the Iranian oil game and an America frozen in time, still rocking and rolling down the highway.

Most American automobiles have died here for want of spare parts since the Ayatollah Khomeini's Revolution twenty years ago and the US trade embargoes that followed Iranian complicity in global terrorism. But those still moving are accorded a rebellious, romantic status among the young – typical of a resilient Persian attitude I'd define as 'prestige in decay,' a furious holding on to what some Islamicists regard as the vestiges of Western decadence.

I reflect back on the Ayatollah Khomeini's return to Iran in 1979. Walking off an Air France flight to kiss the earth and travel through a fervid crowd of people in their hundreds of thousands chanting 'Allahu Akbar' ('God Is Great'). He waved to them from the back of a Chevrolet Blazer station wagon, an unlikely brand promo. Amid the fever of his return, the car would accidentally run over an old man who had thrust himself at the vehicle. Khomeini demanded that they stop, but the old man just asked how much he need 'pay for the honour of being run over by the Imam's car?' An extreme example of the ecstasy which possessed popular imagination at the time.

What do you feel, Khomeini was asked, upon such a mighty return from your enforced exile? 'I feel nothing,' he said. And that was that. A stoic response for a stoic future, as dry as the desert we travel through today.

A Persian *dastgah* seems the only appropriate sound to fill this arid space. So we put a tape of Shajarian into the cassette player: his latest recording, *The Secrets of Existence*. Its cover shows the singer's brooding profile against a black background, looking not unlike an Iranian Leonard Cohen on a heavy day. His voice cascades out of the cheap speakers, crying out in a hashish-like reverie for a love that is all-vanquishing in its obsession: 'I have fallen into your dark eyes. And I am drowning.'

His tremulous wail and buffetting winds dominate the car. At the wheel, our driver Ali tries to keep our spirits high. An improvisational tour guide, quasi-carpet salesman and motor-mouthing 'friend of tourist,' he tells us, 'I like to help. Show people my country. Tonight maybe we sleep in cave or with tribes in mountain. Or we can go to hotel if you want?'

We don't want. But Ali throws in the thought of a hotel as a legalistic sub-clause, a small aside beneath the conversation. They say Iranians hate to disappoint you, so they would rather confuse you than tell you something directly that you don't want to hear. Perhaps that's why Ali tries to bamboozle us with options and possibilities. But we don't need much choice. Just what he'd originally promised: a road trip into the

Zagros Mountains where we will camp out with 'some nomad peoples. In cave or tent. Maybe Bakhtiari, like your music tape and postcard I sell you.'

Ali has been out this way before. With 'many tourists.' And a Polish girlfriend or a German girlfriend, we're not sure. His stories get a little blurred: European girls seem to be perpetually trying to grab his hand or kiss him or look at him 'in a funny way,' usually while their boyfriends aren't there or 'even when they are just around the corner'! He is ripe for a tell-all book of naive erotic flirtations, *Adventures of an Iranian Tour Guide*, perhaps, 'as told by the Tom Jones of the Middle Eastern travel industry,' I joke with him.

'This Tom Jones, women like him?' he asks. 'I think I am not so attractive as him if he so popular. But not so bad as some. What do you say?' He laughs, but I get the feeling he'd like a flattering opinion, nonetheless. 'Do you think I would do well in the West?' he says, striking a strong pose in profile.

'You could be a very dangerous man, Ali. A very dangerous man.'

We all laugh. He appreciates the joke. But with his sharply cut black hair and equally sharp Persian eyebrows, Ali exudes a bright yet baffled air. His whole mind caught somewhere between a trick and a question, part-entrepreneur, part-child at sea in an uncertain era.

He has dealt with tourists for a long time, speaks excellent English and yearns for a greater taste of the West. In his car we can listen to Iranian music like Shajarian, or maybe something Western and illegal, he says naughtily, 'like The Spice Girls.' Western pop music and recorded female singing voices of all kinds are banned in Iran lest they incite corrupting passions. The Spice Girls are akin to protest music at its height. Ali sees the irony of this and can make fun of it. 'I know this is ridiculous, but it is true,' he says incredulously. In spite of that awareness, the risqué quality to his Western flirtations is imbued with something desperate. An uncomfortable mix of the truly kitsch and a feeling that amounts to exclusion, even exile, from both the world at large and his own country, from what he is supposed to be and what he yearns for.

'I love my car,' he says proudly, hitting the steering wheel for emphasis as it hovers on down the road. It's a beast, no doubt about it, a gargantuan look-at-me mess of a machine. Touring Iran in a clapped-out Batmobile hadn't come into our tourist plans before this. But here we are, nonetheless.

Not so surprisingly, we have to stop in the middle of the desert when noxious smoke starts coming up through the back seat. Ali explains that the exhaust has broken off underneath between the seat and the boot area. 'This can make problem. I have been wanting to fix it but we can get no spare parts in Iran! Like my windscreen. It is impossible. This is an American car. But so many things we can not get in Iran. It drives me craaaaazy!'

We unpack the boot, which now stinks of rubber. And find the carpet floor has been badly singed in the back corner – and also that the spare tyre has been melting as well. A terrific amount of heat is being generated from the truncated exhaust pipe up through the car's metal base. We have to douse the smouldering carpet and tyre with water, then reload the now sodden boot, moving anything valuable away from the hot spot. It's a discouraging sign so early into our trip.

'Last time I drive to Tehran, my bag was burnt,' laughs Ali with a touch of happy curiosity. 'I wonder – how this happen? These marks,' he says, holding up his lightly scorched satchel with a smile. 'Now I know.'

Before we'd started on this journey or seen his shitheap of a car, Ali had told us back in Esfahan that, 'We will cruise on down the highway like a sheep.'

'A sheep?!'

'Not a sheep. A ship,' Ali had said, clarifying his pronunciation. 'Like the *Titanic*!'

How apt. And so it was that Ali's prophecy began to take shape: a mix of human comedy, sacrifice and disaster, with us as his co-stars in Iran.

Our cast is an interesting one. There is Ali, of course, our self-appointed tour guide and driver of the most dubious credentials, doing his best to keep us happy as his promises fall to pieces with every kilometre we drive deeper and deeper into the desert and the mountains.

Then there is Robert, the English ethnomusicologist working on his

MA in Middle Eastern music. Robert thinks Ali's Buick is 'the ultimate joke. It really is like Chitty Chitty Bang Bang. But without all the special gadgets. So when you drive it off a cliff, wings don't sprout out, nothing happens – it just plummets to earth and we're all smashed to pieces.'

Then there is Paul. A South African who'd fled the family farm for a bit of fun elsewhere. He tells us how his mother became a born-again Christian, 'putting her head under water, the whole bit.' She tried to have him exorcised when he was about thirteen. He had 'escaped,' but got into a lot of trouble on the streets and was eventually given the choice of going to prison or joining the army. Proof perhaps of his demonic inclinations as a youth. Which was how he found himself fighting in Angola at age sixteen, driving a tank.

'It was great! Just like a really good video game, yah,' Paul says in that peculiar gulping way Afrikaans is released from the mouth. 'I saw very heavy fighting, as heavy as you can see, but it never really affected me. Some guys had really bad crackups – they just couldn't handle it. It was usually the older guys, yah. Some of my friends now suffer from post-traumatic stress syndrome, have really bad dreams. But not me.'

Paul has a nose ring, a pierced lower lip and a goatee beard. His body is covered all over with warrior tattoos of his own design. A bit of a show-stopper in Iran, even when modestly dressed. It is hard to tell his age, maybe mid-twenties, a little older perhaps. He is now a leathermaker of some ability, and like so many craftsmen has assumed the qualities of his own raw materials, in this case a sundried, tough fleshiness. Paul usually lives on a farm north of Johannesburg where he smokes copious amounts of pot and opium, 'yah,' and drinks 'a litre of beer and a litre of cider every night.' His home is set up in the back of a truck, he tells us; his younger brother prefers living in a tent nearby. They run the farm together along with their own alternative businesses. Paul makes it sound all very happy and hippie, if feral. But the idea that he is 'not affected' by his war experiences is laughable in the face of the tight energy barrelling out of him.

Carsten is our youngest traveller. A mostly silent 20-year-old Dane on a journey of self-discovery. With his fair-skinned looks, blond hair and blue eyes, he is something of the ideal Western prince to local Persian and Turkic girls. They want their photos taken with him, even boldly invite him to sit with them, or make eye-gestures towards him that he nervously deflects.

One look into a Persian woman's eyes can be a dangerous act in this country. Twice is a deadly temptation. Under *sharia* law the modesty of women is protected by the chador. They are described in this way as 'pearls in their shell.' All they are left to flirt with are their *chesm ciah* ('black eyes') and the swift movement of their hands. They make the most of this in public: glancing directly at you, then shielding their gaze as if you are an intruder, pulling back the folds of their chador to let you into their eyes one more time, before quickly covering their faces and walking on. Oh the gravity of that second look!

Robert informs Carsten that 'the girls in Shiraz are real goers' when it comes to this kind of flirting. A nerve-wracking thought. There are still fresh news reports about a German man being held before an Iranian court on a possible death sentence for the crime of sexual relations with an Islamic woman. Carsten is not about to cross that line lightly, however much he wants to. There is also a youthful ungainliness to his six foot five inch bulk, a stocky lack of certainty. As he moved overland to India from Europe, that was possibly changing. In some ways the process of his adulthood was already distilling itself before us.

Last of all, there was Lisa and I, postponing all thoughts of the near-future when we would both leave Iran and head off in different directions across the globe. She home to Australia in time for Christmas with her family, me back to Paris to play at being Henry Miller for a few months. What would happen to us then? I tried not to think about it. And yet my conception of our place on the road was as a couple together. I saw us as a unit rather than two separated forces. Most other people took us as one creature. It was hard to imagine losing that unity. But once again it was me who was breathing this 'space' in and out, albeit gently; we who were trying to ignore it.

'I really don't like it,' Robert says, interrupting my thoughts. He is looking out at the great emptiness of the desert landscape. I don't agree with him. I feel thrilled, even liberated, by the hugeness of it all.

'It just gives me the creeps,' Robert goes on, 'like it's not right to be here.'

He explains how he is used to the city, to things being closer to him – buildings, people, cars, activity, signs, lights – and that this limitless terrain is disturbing. As a London intellectual, it makes perfect sense that this isn't his environment. But I am still surprised by the chill it puts into him. As Australians, I realize Lisa and I enjoy this landscape because of our familiarity with big skies and similarly barren, open vistas. But it's odd to understand from his repulsion that a desert can somehow be 'native' to our eye, our spirit.

'It's very much like central Australia,' I say back to Robert – and for Ali's benefit as well – looking out over the pasty, greyish severity. 'Except the mountains back home are red. The earth is more oxidized, more a rusty colour.'

'Yah,' Paul pipes up. 'It reminds me very much of parts of South Africa too. Except our landscape has more of a dirty green colour.'

Robert just shakes his head and mock shivers. Carsten laughs and says nothing. I can't imagine Denmark is much like this either.

Out front of us the afternoon sun is sending down sharper, steeper rays of light, making it harder and harder to see anything. The glare does not slow Ali down one bit. If anything he lets the weight of the car eat up speed with a grateful momentum, carrying us further into god knows where.

'Hey Ali, we're not in a hurry you know,' Robert says. 'How fast do these nomads travel anyway? Or are they all in cars like this?'

Ali laughs. 'I know. I know. I just want to get up into mountains before it gets dark. It's okay. I know what I'm doing. I am good driver. Very good.' He smiles unconvincingly across to me, a road accident face if ever I've seen one. Then turns around to everyone in the back seat without watching the road, nodding positively. 'Just watch the road! And take it easy Ali,' Robert says a little more forcefully, with a new note of fear in his voice. 'We like being alive.'

Despite his reassurances, Ali's eyes are straining to negotiate our climb into the Zagros Mountains as we keep getting the full blast of the sun in our faces. I eventually have to hang my head out the side of the passenger window and scream out to Ali where the side of the road is as he blindly manages the steering wheel back and forth on the sweeping turns. Robert is beside himself with nerves, as are Carsten and Lisa. Paul loves it. I must admit I am enjoying the wild ride as well, my head out the window, face burning in the sun, ears freezing in the wind.

'Turn more to the left,' I say sharply. But Ali's wheels keep rolling forward. I start shouting, 'Left, left, left!' till I'm screaming and Ali breaks hard, hitting the gravel and skidding to a stop a bare few metres from a cliff edge. 'Fucking left, I said. Left! Left! Christ!'

We all pile out of the car, laughing and trembling with nerves. Robert mutters under his breath, shakes his head again and again like something is inside it that he can't get out. I look at our skid marks – just a bit too close to the edge for comfort. Then I slowly wonder about my cursing the name of Jesus just a few minutes ago: what does that mean in a Moslem country where he is recognized as one of the prophets, though not the son of God. How sacrilegious was I?

Behind us a full moon sits high in the still-bright daytime sky. Meanwhile night approaches from over the mountains in an early gloom. The highway we've been travelling on peels back away in a great downward arc towards the moon, and there is that peculiar sense of being on a planet, of gravity holding us all to the great curve of the landscape. From our vantage point we can look down to the desert plateau we've climbed away from, its emptiness serene or vile depending on who you are.

Ali laughs off the near-accident. 'I know you think I'm crazy. But it's okay. We must *keep* going as it will be dark soon. So we can find hotel or nomad peoples. Maybe it is too late for us to find Bakhtiari. If we stay in hotel tonight we can look tomorrow now we are in mountains. I think this is better plan.'

At this suggestion there is much grumbling and a few sarcastic retorts. I can see Ali feels pressured, but unable to do much about it. And also, finally, that Ali is making this up as he goes along. He has no plan, no contacts, no arrangements with anyone. If we happen to crash into a tribe of nomad peoples as they cross the road, well then, he will have succeeded in his promises to us. Otherwise we are in the hands of Allah. Or Ali and his car. Which sounds *almost* the same.

We pack ourselves back into the hulking Buick, our spirit of adventure and our joy for the journey fading with the day. It's getting hellishly cold, and everyone begins putting on jumpers, coats, even raincoats, anything to keep out the mountain chill and the cut of the wind as it drafts into the vehicle. As evening descends in heavier veils of darkness, the likelihood of a night by the fire with some Bakhtiari musicians slips beyond our hopes. Now we just wonder where we might be going, and if Ali has any idea at all of what he is doing.

He stops by a road sign and debates whether to drive into a small town well off the highway, but decides it is better we push on just a little further. We catch a few lights in the distance, gone again in seconds. It is hard to know how welcome a village will make us anyway. How friendly or otherwise people will be. And with night enveloping us ever more coldly, the idea of any welcome takes on more malevolent shapes. We know Ali has no real licence to act as a tour guide, and that in all likelihood this whole journey is illegal. We've gone way beyond the strictly controlled tourist pathways in Iran. And contact with nomad people is not something the government encourages, that's for sure.

Ali's sad and groaning Batmobile begins to make the climb higher up into the Zagros Mountains. But his headlights get dimmer and dimmer as the engine strains to meet the incline of the road. 'My lights are not good,' he confesses uselessly. 'Maybe I should turn back to village and see if they will put us up for night. Real Iranian village …'

People just say yes, yes, wearily and nervously. They don't need the sales pitch, like it's all part of some great plan he has pre-arranged. And so we turn back, looking for the sign again – and a gravel road that chews off into the darkness and some chance of life beyond it. The further we go off the road along the dirt track the rougher it gets, more fit for donkeys and goats than an American gas-guzzler of this size. We barely fit on the gravel and feel dangerously close to the edge of certain turns, not a good feeling in Ali's hands. But some fifteen minutes later the road comes to an end and we are driving into a cluster of mud-walled houses. Ali instructs us to wait by the car while he goes off to make enquiries, but he doesn't have to go far as a man and his family are already looking down at us from the roof wall of their home. Ali and he converse in brief and busy shouts, before the man clambers down and starts gesturing for us to bring our things up. The outlines of the women and children have already left him, to clear the way, it emerges, because by the time we climb up a small pathway and walk around into his courtyard they are taking their own things out of one building and moving them across to another.

The man gestures for us to enter, pushing open some grey wooden doors. It is a mudbrick single-room home with a dirt floor. Sheets of crocheted material cover the ground, blankets and some pillows. We are required to take off our shoes as a matter of course before entering. On the walls photos of the family are kept in handmade frames assembled from scrap wood, flowers and cotton, almost anything appealing that has come to hand – one is built and sown in the shape of a purple star around the face of the man's youngest son, who now clings to his leg, eyeing us all curiously.

There are also fine examples of needlework hanging from the walls. And a small picture of the Iranian soccer player Azizzi, housed like a little god in a tiny open wardrobe. Soccer being the one thing that unites all Iranians, whatever their faith or ethnic affiliation – it even competes, in some secular way, with religion itself as a release for more usually suppressed passions and energy, a chance for Iranians to feel a part of the world again after years of being an excluded pariah state.

The man whose home we have entered is very interested to discover we are Australian. 'Harry Kewell. 2–2. Good,' he says, words we are becoming very used to hearing everywhere in Iran. Relations between Australia and Iran are 'very good,' we are repeatedly told, because of the drawn Australia vs Iran game that allowed the Iranians to go through to the World Cup and defeat the US. As a taxi driver informed us with gusto, 'Australia and Iran are very great friends.'

It's interesting that because of the soccer most Iranians make a very clear distinction between us as Australians, once we've identified ourselves, and the Americans or the English. They have some empathy with us as if we are in a similar bind, squeezed under imperialist histories. They also appear to nurse a bigger grudge, if such a thing is possible, against the English than even the Great Satan – the US is the enemy of the last few decades, but many Iranians blame the English for the colonial circumstances that have led to their country's demise as a great nation in the twentieth century. Robert gets rather sick of this – his 'What?! You bastards still trying to blame us for everything?' not endearing him to one person in particular back in Esfahan. We, of course, appreciate our football-bred popularity.

As Robert is the only person who can speak Farsi, I ask him to tell the man whose home it is how friendly people are in Iran, and how much we appreciate their hospitality. Robert says something to him, he responds, and they both laugh.

'What did he say?'

'He says don't be fooled. They're a bunch of assholes here. But I'm glad you're at my home.'

This translation from Robert is at best a modified Western version of the conversation for my ears. 'Why does he say people in Iran are assholes?'

Robert explains that the man and his family and indeed most of the village are of the Baha'i faith. Even the Jews are better off in Iran than the Baha'i. Beginning in the nineteenth century, the Baha'i religion was started by Baha' Allah, who claimed to be a gatekeeper for the sacred Twelfth Imam. He preached modernization, equality of women and pacifism – not entirely popular beliefs with the Shi'ite mullahs now, let alone a century ago. Worst of all, by claiming divine visions, Baha' and those who followed him were guilty of apostasy for not accepting the view that Mohammed was the final prophet to have received such messages. Salman Rushdie was the last well-known man to be accused of apostasy in recent times, so you can imagine how the Baha'is have suffered for their faith. The coming of the Ayatollah Khomeini was not a happy day for them.

Not all the people here are of the Baha'i faith. Christianity, Zoroastrianism and the impact of Sunni Islam throughout the more Arabic south of Iran have their followers too. But like other nomadic and semi-nomadic tribes, these people have had to adapt Shia Islamic beliefs and *sharia* law to their own needs. Most noticeably in the way their women dress, modestly as ever in Iran, but unlike the dark crows of the city. Here in this small village the women wear bold greens and pinks and reds, covering their hair with multi-patterned and polka-dotted scarves, bursts of colour that would scandalize a city dweller and be looked down upon as a sign of their peasant status.

The women quickly take Lisa away with them to the kitchen, where they reside with the children. The family have sacrificed their bedroom for us. In the kitchen Lisa starts showing them her digital video camera, playing back footage to their great amazement – though she can never quite overcome their tendency to freeze when the camera is upon them, their inability to understand that the video can catch moving images. Lisa is also confused by a curiosity on the women's part about her breasts, which leads her at one point to think they want to see them, an amusing misconception. The women all laugh and shake their heads. Only later does she understand that they were wondering if she had any children. A woman and a man over twenty without a child is cause for much sympathy in Iran – people look at you as if a terrible tragedy must be hanging over your sad head. At times we pretend to have children in order to prevent this mood of popular depression on our behalf.

Back in the bunkhouse the boys are getting down to serious men's business – the football and glasses of *sabok* (weak tea). We wonder if there is a shop in the village where we can get food, so the man leads us down a long alley, creating a village parade as people stand on their roofs and children follow us. The shop owner opens up specially for us and we buy a frenetic, confused selection of fruit, potatoes, biscuits, tea, crisps, bread and toys, including a soccer ball, what looks to be the only one in the shop.

People follow us back to the house, and it looks as if we might be in danger of causing a mini-riot. I realize this small village would rarely receive visitors, let alone people like us. Our local friend is getting irritated by all this fuss, and by now has employed a number of his family as bodyguards to protect both us and his home grounds.

Lisa rejoins us for *sabok*. A neighbour begins insisting that as a married couple we should stay at his house. We politely refuse and state that we want to stay with our friends, but he remakes his offer. This happens a few times, with some intensity. He obviously feels it is not right for a woman to be sleeping in a room full of men, even if we are Westerners. More than that, though, I realize our friend has gained a lot of status by putting us up, and this other fellow simply wants a piece of the action. But his pushiness is unattractive, and at the risk of offending him we refuse one last and absolute time. He seems angry, an attitude infinitely less appealing than the gentle sweetness of the man who has been helping us.

Robert asks Ali to explain to everyone he is studying music, and to tell our host he has some recording gear with him. Would there be anyone in the village who likes to sing?

Ali says something and the man quickly sends off a young messenger. 'There is one young boy here who is very good. So he has sent someone to fetch him for us.'

Before long a frightened and rather snotty boy is pushed through the re-gathered tribe of onlookers outside the door. He comes into the room shaking with nerves, like a young puppy. Hair shaved short, eyes wide as saucers, with a distinct hacking cough.

'This one is not well,' explains Ali. It seems that the children who learn the traditional songs are often the most sickly. Any able-bodied person must work in the fields, male or female. There is little time for music. So it is often the sick who are given songs by the old people, who become the voices of the village if they endure into adulthood. The blind, the weak, they must do something to support themselves. No one here can afford to be useless or idle.

The boy is positioned in the middle of the room. Robert sets up his small microphone and mini-disk equipment as gently as he can in front of him, and tries to smile at the boy to alleviate his fears.

We all nod and smile. Do our best to be welcoming and warm. The room itself is now quite crowded – the man and his extended family, wife and children, some neighbours and their boys, as well as all of us, making up a small crowd of some twenty or more people in a space used to a quarter of that many. Outside we can hear muttering and talking – the doors strain with pressure as the crowd try to see over the closed shutters into the room.

Robert presses some buttons on the recorder and nods to the boy. Our village friend touches him on the shoulder and lets him know he should start to sing. At first the boy's voice is throaty with illness. He shivers a little in the night air and is in faltering form. A few verses in he unself-consciously snorts and swallows some phlegm back down his throat to clear himself.

As the spirals of his song build and build, a more trance-like sweetness and loneliness begin to fill the air. The boy pumps each verse out like a single long note, a call beseeching god or the sky, it's hard to know.

When it's over a brief silence ensues. We applaud, while the locals prefer to nod their approval. We ask what the song was about – something to do with a goat-herder thinking of his beloved, we are told.

An argument then ensues between Ali and Robert about giving the boy some money. Robert feels this is a bad idea. He would rather offer a gift because he thinks giving money might set up bad interchanges for the future when other people try to make field recordings and study songs. So a motley set of gifts is assembled – a pen, a packet of crisps and a chocolate. I ask if the boy has a tape player? He does not, but his neighbour does. So I give him the tape of Bakhtiari music I bought back in Esfahan from Ali. Songs he might learn, or know and sing along to. His eyes are overwhelmed, as if by some great event. He can barely believe his luck.

Some village boys have come into the room, and while people start looking at the tape and the gifts there is a small scuffle. All of a sudden the tape is gone, the cassette cover sitting disconsolate and empty on the floor. The boy singer looks crestfallen.

Our friend assures us the tape will be found and returned to the boy. But the boy does not look so sure or so happy as he is being hustled out of the room. By good fortune I actually have two copies of the Bakhtiari recording, so I offer him another tape, and tell our host if he finds the stolen tape it is rightfully his – a belated gift from me. In the boy's eyes as he leaves, half-escorted, half-surrounded by other village boys, there is a mix of happiness and fear. I get this feeling everything we have given will be taken from him, so I ask if he will be all right. The neighbour I spurned sends one of his sons to walk home with the boy and nods and raises both his hands as if to say the matter is now finished.

Ali says it is very tough in the village. 'That is how life is here.' The strongest survive best, he explains, while the weak descend to the bottom of the pecking order or simply perish. 'He is not well, that one,' he sighs. 'We should try to send him a coat or something when we get to city. Winter here is very cold. I do not think he will live many winters at all.'

The singing now over, we will soon bed down for the night. The villagers disperse easily, the entertainment complete for them as well. Ali has excited plans for bringing tour buses to the village now that he has discovered it, but it's doubtful he will ever pull such pipe dreams together. While we sleep Carsten will rise in a burst of nervous energy in the middle of the night and sit outside on the roof smoking a cigarette, determining, he tells Lisa later, 'not to go back to Denmark for a long time. I will keep travelling!' She loves the honesty of his enthusiasm, the way he is not jaded or too cool. That he is young enough to let himself be openly carried away.

In the early morning we climb a low hillside near the village. Fields of wheat blow in the sun below. A small school yard empties of children in a neat marching line. We hear bells ring from the necks of goats in a small flock climbing towards us, an old herder leaning hard on his walking stick, examining us. I can see Lisa photographing the women and children down on the valley floor, their colours blossoming between the clay roofs.

It's time to leave, so we descend to pack the car – and hope that in the daylight it will have the strength to make it up over the mountains. A small farewell party gathers for us. We leave painkillers for a grandmother whose knee aches in the cold. The family waves us off like royalty.

Barely a few miles from the village Ali's car fails to make the first steep incline. We try getting a run-up, to no avail. The engine is in too pitiful a state to climb any further. Ali says he is going back to get another car, for us to 'please wait.' About an hour or so later he arrives on the back of a small utility truck. This is how we will make it into the city of Shiraz.

Here we must part ways with him. 'Pay me what you like later. I am sorry for my car. What I will do I don't know! Give the money to Mark and Lisa, they can pass it on to me when they return to Esfahan,' he says trustingly.

We stream through the mountains on the back of the truck, down a wild road with the wind blasting us. No one knows where we are. There is that tremendous feeling of free space. Of having disappeared into the world. But things start to sour once the ride is over. Paul says he feels ripped-off, despite the adventure, and he refuses to pay the full sum we agreed on because 'Ali did not take us to our final destination.' Carsten feels the same, which is even more of a surprise. Only Robert will grudgingly pay the full amount – US$10 each for the whole trip. Lisa and I feel that despite all the bumbling, Ali has delivered on his promise. But now he has gone and has no way to argue his rights and this is how the tide has turned.

In Shiraz we still act as a group, but at heart we only feel a kinship with Robert. Paul is tight now, not wild; Carsten penny-pinching, not free-spirited. Their new definitions set in my mind. Paul is nonetheless app-roached on the street because of his wild looks by someone selling opium. I notice men on the nod around us from time to time, street junkies.

That night in a hotel room we all decide to try the opium he has bought. 'It smells like great stuff, yah.' Paul cuts a large plastic juice bottle in half to use as a smoking cone. We lean over the chocolate lumps sitting on a hand-held sheet of aluminium foil heated by a candle flame and suck in the smoke through the torn bottle. In the background Robert plays his recording of the village boy singing, his raspy breath, his snotty gasps. The opium is of poor quality, and no matter how much we smoke there is little effect on us beyond a sickly warmth across our bodies and the stronger feeling that our throats are being burnt by the metallic oxides coming off the constantly reheated foil. We trade stories of our childhood and adolescence, the aftermath of the closeness we briefly felt along the road. The boy's voice climbs around us, longing for his imaginary lover as we try to daze ourselves. But it is useless. The next morning we go our separate ways and do not ever send him a winter coat. Only Lisa will per-sist with finding an address for the village, with sending copies of the photos that she took.

Opium Poem

Just listen to the conversation in a room:
drum 'n' bass, hawkwind, palace –
musical names and drugs
like hashish and opium.
The candle burns
and the gatherers suck half
a plastic bottle full of smoke.
Spines disappear, skin warms,
techniques get developed.
Stories of the self
can now begin:

The first one is pulled from a river
after an escape through toys
pursued by police in a supermarket.
Another crawls in the dirt
for a committee of childhood
in a secret place among the bushes.
She remembers her hair
in the black world
and bones that held it high.
While the boy wants Nirvana,
a band not a place,
pale and young
on his last cigarette outta here.
All this while the leathermaker
repairs a money belt
and recalls vegetable names
from the farm of his experience.

This is a room in Shiraz,
a travellers' place.

Familiarity is a light cord
around each voice.
Some shared slowness
to the evening's tales
enveloping them all.
Just listen to the conversation
Listen, listen to it disappear.

Is Terry Venables Evil?

IT HAS BEEN A BUSY DAY, AN INTENSE DAY, AS ALL DAYS
are for visitors in Iran.

A morning spent at the Aramgah-é Sa'di, the tomb of the great Persian
poet Sa'di, sees Lisa talking to a string of Iranian women, a veritable line-
up of hooded female fans.

'Where are you from?'

'Welcome to our country.'

'What makes you choose our home?'

Again and again their questions and greetings are offered up to her
as we sit relaxing with cups of *chai* (strangely enough made from instant
tea bags rather than brewed – for Iran an unusual concession to modernity,
and somewhat untraditional in so reverent a place as this).

The women settle around Lisa, reserved, happy to just smile with her
even when the conversation peters out and their limited English is not
enough to take things further. It is peculiarly gentle, if a touch uncomfortable.

I fade away beside her, a man suddenly in a woman's world. For some
reason I feel an obligation to look away and not let my eyes dwell in their
space.

We are deep down inside an underground chamber, children's voices
bounding off the domed ceiling. The chamber itself is built around a
circular fish pool sunk another twelve feet into the ground below us. It
bubbles and thrashes with activity as visitors toss in broken biscuits and
what look like cheese Twisties to a hungry school of large goldfish darting

and eddying across the face of an underwater mosaic praising Allah's name.

It feels as if we are at the centre of a similar, if somewhat subtler, feeding frenzy. People in Iran are so curious about us, so eager to make contact we are overwhelmed wherever we go. Today is no different.

The women always speak to Lisa, the men to me. At times it is clear we are having two different journeys, masculine and feminine, through this elaborate nation. Rather than finding it oppressive behind the cover of her *hejab* Lisa is now enjoying what she calls 'an unexpected sisterhood' as the women embrace her with their eyes and sometimes their conversation. A sense of feminine society and common feeling she says she has not experienced to the same intensity in the West. She is finding it hard to put this 'understanding through eyes' into words.

There's also something childlike about the attention we receive from people – in the same way that a child will invade your boundaries or not recognize a limit unless it is enforced. Tourists are a rarity here, exotic things. We often feel pushed and pulled at, exhausted of all polite conversation when polite conversation is required every five minutes from yet another aspiring new friend, let alone that most dreaded breed of local, the practising English student.

Despite Lisa's popularity, we leave the fish pool for the serenity of the extensive gardens outside. Sa'di's poems are being broadcast over loudspeakers. It is a nice change of pace, a beautiful notion, his words winding among the boughs and shadows, floating around us. If only we could understand Farsi.

A cranky-looking mullah not far from us snaps our moment of peace like a twig. It is a pure gesture. An ugly gesture. As he pulls his hand away from a woman who has seized it to kiss lovingly. She is on her knees; he is seated on a bench. He rises and strides off, black cape swinging. She flinches, then chases after him – or is he really making her follow him? Perhaps they are husband and wife, the latter duty-bound to his irritable brand of godliness.

Some soldiers sit on another seat, oblivious or wisely blind. They tease one another boyishly, comparing the quality of their blackmarket wristwatches. In the West they might be getting drunk or going to prostitutes in their time off; here in Shiraz they are visiting the marble tombs of great poets like Sa'di and Hafez – whose resting place is across town – looking for prophetic guidance in their verses and words. These men from the past occupy a monumental place in the Iranian consciousness, poets who are revered and remembered, their words rote-learnt and recited by the young as if they were the lyrics to a pop song. It's mind-blowing to see poets given such serious and mainstream stature in a culture.

Ironically enough their words encourage the pleasures of wine, sensuality, women, boys and song (Sa'di in particular was quite the bisexual swinger). Along with Rumi and Omar Khayyam, these poets lie at the roots of a lush Persian culture that refuses to surrender to Islamic aridity. There's a curious femininity to this culture, partly understood through reading *The Gulistan* or *The Rose Garden of Sa'di*, wherein Sa'di cites passionate love affairs and bonds between men. A stealthy homoeroticism paralleled by a desert austerity and a generosity that can also flair, it feels, into the wildest of tempers given a reason. Passion here is dark and deep as a well.

In another part of town, the faithful are taking their Friday prayers at one of the great pilgrimage sites of Shi'ite Islam: the Shrine of Shâh-é Cherâgh.

To enter this grand building is to be overwhelmed by light. Bejewelled glass and mirrored fragments line the domed interior and create the impression of walking into the guts of an intense kaleidoscope: this is the wonder of Allah made physical, the rule of light over man.

Islam's architectural greatness is at both a philosophical and a structural peak here. Form and function perfectly married. A billion glass angles reflecting all those who pass and bow down to prayer, exalting them into a glittering oneness at the same time as they are individually disintegrated by each tiny mirrored tile.

Inside this hushed space the self explodes into a reflected and refracted realm like nothing I have seen before. You are nothing, nothing but light and a part of light. Bow your head.

Here lies the tomb of Emam Reza's brother, Sayed Mir Ahmad, 'the

King of the Lamp' who died in the year 835 A D. This grand shrine was erected over his burial place in the fourteenth century. It has been an important Shi'ite pilgrimage site ever since.

You do not need a warning sign to tell you it is best to tread this place in all humility.

To enter the huge courtyard area around the mosque, Lisa, who is already dressed adequately for the street, must cover herself up even further with a large grey-striped blanket, a *hejab* so voluminous it is hard to see if she is a woman at all. These 'human tents,' as Lisa calls them, are thoughtfully provided for free at a religious souvenir shop just outside the entrance.

The shop also sells exquisitely bound Qu'rans and fine cards with extracts printed in beautiful calligraphy. There are also large photographic books about Iran's culture and landscape, prints of Ayatollahs Khomeini, Khamenei and Khatami all smiling together (and unlikely event crafted into life by montage techniques), various poetry books by Sa'di and Hafez and the odd copy of Adolf Hitler's *Mein Kampf*.

Mein Kampf is a creepily popular text in Iran with its mix of Aryan superiority and anti-Semitic (read anti-Israeli) proselytizing. Its evil consequences disregarded, even dismissed, as if it were some obscure but interesting philosophical manifesto with no historical association worth commenting on, a blank contemporaneity that has its own dark messages for the crumbling rule of the mullahs happy to service it to the population. After their senile theocracy what will come? If not democracy as we might hope through Khatami's extraodinary guidance, then maybe Persian fascism. One only need look over the border to Iraq to see that kind of virulent nationalism is not so far from reality. It only needs a face to help it grow.

School children line up beside us to look at the Ayatollah Khomeini stickers (he rarely smiles in any of them) and the Qu'ran cards as children in another nation might stop to look at football or Pokémon heroes.

I stand by them, yearning to buy a blood red hardback copy of *Mein Kampf* with Adolf Hitler standing in a *zieg-heil* pose, arm outstretched before the book's title, written in the sloping cursive script of Persia. The very look of the book, its beauty, burns me with lust. My attraction to it as an art object is unnerving. A little corrupt. Lisa discourages me strongly.

Once swathed in her blanket, she and I leave the shop and enter the main courtyard to the mosque and shrine. It is as if we have suddenly found ourselves at the very heart of Islam – as if we have indeed journeyed back a few hundred years. The muezzin is calling and his cry loops out over the square, over the city, occupying the sky itself, belting out through endless loud hailers wired over the rooftops.

People have been here all day. Families are finishing picnic lunches, children play, men smoke and talk. A society condensing happily around the outside of the mosque as much as the devotional rigour inside it.

A dark cluster of women is already squeezing back into the shrine for midday prayers. There is a totally separate entrance for the women, so Lisa must join this throng of black chadors, an odd giant walking in their company. I go round a corner where I have to take off my shoes and hand them over to a man who seems to know exactly where mine will be among the hundreds he has stacked on shelves behind him.

Men kiss the doors before even entering the building. At the tomb itself, encased in glass and a hand-carved wooden cage, people caress the walls, kiss the barriers, touch their faces against it all as a lover would brush his cheeks adoringly against his most beloved. Men on one side of the shrine; women on the other. All looking for sanctification as they slowly move by. The intensity of this affection has a terrifying quality: overflowing with self-abnegation. It is hard for me to give in to and yet I mimic it lest anyone be offended.

Prayers are now beginning in earnest and the mosque fills rapidly in a final rush. The activity is feverish and solemn at once – and yet not so extreme it verges on some radical 'otherness' I cannot comprehend. No, foreign as it all is to me, the exotic clichés one associates with Islam do not quite hold. If anything it is a relief to see the mundane regularity of their worship after the passions which were incited by physical proximity to the tomb.

I begin to register the workaday reverence of a church experience: the half-hearted and sloppy bowing, the slightly unruly disorder before prayers begin, the jostling for positions on the mats, the blue and green chink of worry beads as they are dropped lazily to people's sides, the quick chit-chat before people get down to the business at hand, even the rushed distribution of Qu'rans and prayer stones as they are noisily, softly yet noisily, pulled from a communal box dusty with their accumulated grit.

Is a Catholic Sunday service so different from this?

A mullah begins the prayers, pronouncing strongly over the microphone, standing to one side of the congregation as they all face Mecca: its direction sign-posted by gold lettering on a large piece of silver, a script that translates into the single word 'Allah.' This is their road sign to God. All prayers must face this way.

You see this script and the associated phrase, '*Inshallah*' ('God willing') everywhere in Iran. The word is inscribed over and over on walls and mosaics around mosques, in blue tangles of calligraphy that tear at the mind's sense of beginnings and endings.

The prayers increase in intensity as the body of worshippers assumes a greater unity of response to the mullah's words. I feel an approach of energy among the congregation, a more purposeful mindset bearing down on them all as they pray and chant. Two open palms are held out before each face, as if they are reading an open prayer book, holding an imaginary Qu'ran. A thousand lips run with the whisperings of God and the divine recitations he has inscribed on their minds since childhood. Allah is written into their eyes.

Knees bend. Men kiss their prayer stone, then touch their forehead to it as they bow down to the ground. Their prostrate whisperings run into the floor, down into the earth, creating a deep, powerful drone through the building. They rise again. They repeat the actions. They rise again…

One of the mosque's attendants, dressed in a dust-coat like some lab assistant, plucks a stone from the distribution box. He hands it to me. 'This is called "*ma*",' he says, popping the word out so deeply it is more like a sound than a word. Every piece of stone has been quarried from Mecca, he tells me, so that the faithful may feel they are touching some small part of this holy place.

I am fascinated to recall a conversation with a taxi driver from only the night before, who had pointed at the night sky and told me that the Persian word for moon was 'ma.'

Are the word for this prayer stone and the word for the moon the same I wonder? Why?

I suspect it is because of the combination of Arabic and Persian words now in common usage in Iran, words that become even more mixed when it comes to the practice of Shi'ite Islam. Over centuries of war and invasion, the tidal movements of culture and faith, the words for moon and Allah have come to resemble one another.

My mosque attendant can't understand what I am asking him about, but he is happy for me to hold the stone, to feel its wonderful, slightly chalky coolness. I kiss the prayer stone and touch it to my forehead, and nod to the attendant, handing it back, saying 'tashakor' (Arabic for 'thank you'). Of course I do this awkwardly, finding myself becoming self-conscious all over again, clinging to a collection of signs to show my respect, my appreciation – my understanding I hope.

There's a sense of being afloat on the surface of events inside the mosque, of being carried along by them and becoming a part of them, yet still, obviously, watching and being outside of them. Inevitably I feel out of place. No matter what I see as common to my Christian experiences.

Somewhere towards the back, over a dividing screen among hundreds of women in black, I can see Lisa, her head bowed inside that heavy striped shawl. We had not expected to be caught up in prayer. Least of all Friday's prayers, the most important of the week. But caught we are.

I fear a hidden rage or contempt for our gawking presence in some part of the congregation. This spurs me further to conduct myself with the utmost respect. What brewing animosities lie here?

But as the prayers end, a man comes up to me quickly and shakes my hand by way of welcome. Then another man, then another. The mosque attendant remains by my side, acting more like my personal guide, not someone with other duties to do in support of the faithful.

I glance back to the segregated area of women worshippers, a sea of black chadors: old women, young women, tiny girls. These glances are tentative, stolen – at the same time a gravity, and a curiosity, emboldens me. I remember being a teenage boy at church in my old hometown, looking across the congregation for girls that I liked, and I wonder about the young men here today, how daring they might be, how sharp their eyes are?

As I start to bounce off the mass of worshippers leaving, I find myself pushed back through the entrance chamber to the shrine itself. Those who are leaving the mosque do so without ever turning away from it – head bowed towards it as they walk out backwards. I comply in my clumsy Western way, crab walking the last few metres to the door and out into the blazing Shiraz sun.

Where I am immediately accosted by a young soldier in a clearly intense mood.

He tries to speak English to me, but I can't grasp what he is trying to say. Another dozen soldiers quickly gather. One can speak English 'a little,' and certainly better than his compatriot, so he translates for my military interrogator. By now there are at least 50 soldiers surrounding me, some smiling, others craning their heads with curiosity, others very serious indeed.

'He wants to know why you bowed when you left the mosque?'

'To show respect,' I say, half-bowing again nervously.

Words are exchanged between my translator and the interrogator.

More questions. 'But why you respect? What you respect? You are not Moslem. What is your religion?'

'No, I am Catholic,' I say rather quietly. I don't quite know why I say this, but I don't feel like being faithless or pretending to be faithless before them. I want somehow to state that I too am a believer. But the very word 'Catholic' creates an uncertain ripple in the ranks. I sigh. Try to answer the rest of the question: why show respect then?

'It is hard for me to explain. I do not speak Farsi,' I go on slowly. 'But I believe when I am in your father's house, I should respect your father.'

This seems to go down pretty well, much better than confessing I am a Catholic. And I am mightily impressed with myself for coming up with such a neat metaphorical explanation. But before I can rest on my laurels, another young officer barges into the fray and says something to the translator, who hits me with yet one more question, this one from way out of left field.

'So is Terry Venables a good man or a bad man? Is he good or evil?'

Oh my god, a football question. About the former coaching genius of the English soccer team. In Iran the popularity of soccer is at fever pitch. It is as if a foreign concept called 'fun' has somehow snuck into the country and run riot.

But this is still hardly a question I could have expected.

They have obviously detected I am an Australian. And they certainly know Venables recently coached the Australian team after being forced out of his English position by a series of scandals and his own ego. Under Venables the Australians had become a more formidable playing unit, though not strong enough to resist Iran's march to the 1998 World Cup.

Terry Venables: a good man or a bad man?

What to say? The man was a sporting svengali with a few smudges in his copybook. In Iran that could also mean he was Darth Vader, part of the Evil Empire. Half the country hated the British more than even the US, I'd learnt, blaming Great Britain for a colonial carve-up that had screwed their country for most of the century.

Terry Venables: good or evil?

The soldiers pack in around me, awaiting an answer. I need to get this right. 'Oh, he's a great coach. But,' I say, shrugging my shoulders for effect, 'he is English.' Then I wave my hand equivocally, like I could take him or leave him on that count.

This is a very satisfactory response indeed – particularly the idea that someone British was, well, not necessarily bad in soccer terms, but perhaps not so good generally. The soldiers cluster in even closer again, asking questions I cannot understand because they are so excited. They now want me to come with them to visit the ruins of Persepolis. They also want their photos taken with me. More than anything, they want my friendship on a battalion scale. I am a popular guy.

But I raise my hands up gently in a defensive gesture and say, 'I have to go,' poking my hands out further in a mock pushing motion towards them – then pointing back at myself and shaking my head vigorously, as if this is all too much. Which it is. They laugh. And when I say 'khoda-hafez' (goodbye) they cheer me goodbye and with their 'khoda-hafezs' ringing in my ears I slip off to get my shoes and make my run for freedom.

Taksi God

TWO COUNTRY MEN, IN WORN BLACK SUITS WITH THREE-day growths shadowing their faces, stand at a busy intersection in bustling Shiraz, the city of poets, holding their sheep as tightly as possible. They've moored the beast to a traffic sign, and are holding their hands over its head and eyes, looking around as though they themselves need similar protection from the furious honk of the city, all glarey and polluted and loud in the early morning sun. Later in the day their sheep will no doubt be slaughtered for some occasion or other.

We sit in a *taksi* watching them as we weave our own way through trucks, buses and cars. There do not appear to be any particular lanes of traffic – just pump your horn and push your way through, or hit the brakes and let a bully or someone crazier than you take the path *mostaghim* (straight ahead).

Our cab driver has a kind face and a carefree demeanour. Perhaps because the boot of his vehicle hangs open loosely on our pile of baggage and he wants to make us feel confident that it won't bounce out and all over the road.

'Will the backpacks stay in there?' we had asked. 'Will we make it to the airport in time for our flight to Tehran?' He nodded meaninglessly, patted the boot with a wink, then took off at a bruising clip.

Now I see that our driver has what looks like a lava lamp on his gear-stick. Orange, black and white patterns swim inside a radiant globe. There's a universe in there. I comment on its beauty and he points back to it and shouts over the roar of the engine, 'God! Farsi God!'

I see even better now. It's calligraphic writing – the name of Allah is at his finger-tips in a psychedelic swirl every time he shifts up or down a gear. No one can touch him out here on the road but Allah, the traffic warden of the soul, sending us all to a four-on-the-floor heaven sooner or later. Metamorphosing gridlock into a freeway with one wild turn of the wheel.

The plane to Tehran? Bah! It's open sky in front of us already. We're free as birds. '*Inshallah!*'

Dead Flowers

THE NEWS FROM TEHRAN IS ALL BAD. RAMPANT POLLUTION. Major heroin problems. Overcrowding. Poverty. Rising inflation that money traders fear will be 'brought down with the gun,' all the while fistfuls of Iranian rials are handed over for blackmarket American dollars on Ferdosi Street ($100 denominations, 1996 issue preferred). And nothing else but a vast 600 square kilometre blur of chaotic urban development to negotiate your way through.

Upon arrival, it all seems true. Tehran is madness itself. Ugly and out of control.

But after spending only a little time in the city, we begin to notice something else about the place that is hard to define: its energy.

Unstoppable, mercantile, dreaming, struggling, seething energy, bubbling to the surface like the labyrinthine Main Bazaar that snakes for miles underground, bursting the earth and spilling its way onto central Tehran's streets.

Tehran is a city of thirteen million that literally teems with life. A beggar weeps while shaving himself on the street. Another reconstructs computer hardware beside him with nothing else but a screwdriver and a cardboard box to rest on. Women clothed head-to-toe in black chadors sweep by like flocks of crows, the young ones flirting with an erotic glance at you before wrapping their faces up quickly again in the folds of their material.

Along with the commerce, pain and mystery, a sense of casual disorder and coping mechanisms that spring from the Islamic belief in '*Inshallah*' – that 'God willing' everything will work out as planned, a fatalistic outlook most radically manifest in the attitudes of local drivers.

Towering above it all – and usually unremarked on by locals who treat it as part of the same old scenery or 'just more propaganda' – is some of the most dominating street art since the heyday of Soviet Realism and Mexico's Diego Rivera. Gigantic murals on the sides of inner city office blocks, billboards and suburban units, praising dead soldiers from a war with Iraq that lasted eight scarifying years from 1980 to 1988.

The murals provide Tehran with its most distinctive landmarks, along with the Head Telegraph Office's satellite tower just to the south of the Mediun-é Emam Khomeini (the main square) and the smog-shrouded pencil lines of the Alborz Mountains to the north.

Many Iranians who fled this city in the wake of the Shah's 1978 down-fall and the Ayatollah Khomeini's hideous purges ended up creating a refugee community of artists, aristocrats and business people in Los Angeles. With brilliant humour, Tehranian locals now refer to these ref-ugees as the inhabitants of Tehrangeles.

Some things never change.

Back home in Iran the pollution is so bad it begins to burn your sinuses and sting your eyes within a few hours of arriving. Tehran is currently rated the fourth most polluted city in the world after Delhi, Beijing and Calcutta. Having been to Delhi and Calcutta in the past year, I would say that the pollution of Tehran is less leadenly visible but more immediately noxious. Oil accounts for 80 per cent of Iran's economy, and with prices down internationally fuel within the country is dirt cheap, solace for a population that is predominantly dirt poor.

Beyond the panic of city traffic, the chaos of people and pollution, is the sprinting thoroughfare of Bozorgrah-é Modarres, a highway dramat-ically marked by some of the most haunting war murals in all of Iran:

A bearded young soldier in a halo of colour, looking forward into the future, face filling a billboard-size painting, a bunch of blue flowers – bright and painful, funereal, and quiet – just to his left.

Another depicting a cascade of history – the Ayatollah Khomeini, his successor the Ayatollah Khamenei, between them a dove, signs of war, the Islamic Revolution and its holy visions like a psychedelic 1960s album cover.

A child kneeling, placing with cupped hands an open rose by the covered head of a soldier, his eyes closed in eternal peace. Her father? Her brother?

As you begin to look around, you see that Tehran's urban world is painted with an ever-growing collection of beautiful if sombre portraits, rising out of the smog to give this bustling city a genuine sense of awe.

It's interesting to reflect on the greater absence of advertising. A sign for Panasonic, that's all I can remember. Local ads for nuts and bolts, heaters, sweets. It's hardly Times Square. No, the images here are very different.

The cold-eyed stare of Khomeini, stern as a hanging judge, is everywhere of course. Along with the similarly implacable Khamenei. And an inevitably softer President Khatami, who manages to exude smiling tolerance next to their brimstone stares. In some places near the Main Bazaar there's even a daring criss-cross hatched over Khamenei's face where it adorns fading political posters from the last election to the Assembly of Experts.

It is these faces that are determining Iranian destiny.

And with them the mythologising art of the 'martyrs' from the Iran-Iraq War. These acts of praise in tribute to the dead are all over Iran. An exorcism of the profoundest significance.

A VISIT TO THE TREASURY OF THE NATIONAL JEWELS BELOW Bank Melli's head office on Ferdosi Avenue in Tehran reveals one of the most nauseous displays of wealth and bad taste the world has ever seen. A residue of the Shah and the Pahlavi dynasty.

When the Shah fell in 1978, there were five million people in Tehran. His ill-planned programs of urbanization and industrialization were well under way, fuelled by the 1974 boom in oil prices and appalling rural deprivation. But the petrodollars would only line the pockets of a select few. The inequities of American and British economic interests in tandem with the Shah's extravagance and increasingly oppressive regime were impossible to sustain. He killed hundreds of student demonstrators on the streets before fleeing the country to Egypt, entirely baffled by the rejection, ignominious.

A triumphant Ayatollah Khomeini returned in 1979 as people were basking in the euphoria of a glorious Revolution. The corrupt and indulgent Shah had been deposed – and his brutal security force, Savak, which made a salt lake famous outside Tehran for the bodies it dropped into it, was gone with him.

This was a revolution against something – not necessarily for what was to come in its wake. Leftists, Islamic fundamentalists, nationalists, opportunists: the wave of protest against the Shah and his Western supporters was at best a loose coalition.

Khomeini charismatically overshadowed them all and provided a symbolic focus as he returned from exile. Hundreds of thousands of people chanted '*Allahu Akbar*' as Khomeini passed through the streets. His arrival is still celebrated each February as The Ten Days of Dawn.

Before long his supposedly symbolic leadership began taking ferocious root. Disappearances. Show trials. Secret trials. Executions. Orders for women to start wearing the veil again, the banning of alcohol and music, the stoning to death of adulterers. As one Jewish man told me, 'they put black into the faces of the people, it was a disgusting thing.'

Only Khomeini's mix of nationalism and fundamentalism would be allowed to flourish as he sought to establish the world's first Islamic theocracy, the rule of the mullahs or Islamic clerics. It was a fearsome and oppressive world to be in, particularly after the intense Westernizing push that had characterized the previous 50 years of the so-called Pahlavi dynasty. Civil war appeared ready to break out in Iran as dissent reached an early peak in the wake of Khomeini's purges.

In the meantime students and militant elements invaded the US Embassy in Tehran in November 1979. Fifty-two Americans were held prisoner. An unsuccessful attempt to free them precipitated the end of Jimmy Carter's presidency and prolonged a 444–day hostage crisis that would turn Iran into an international pariah. Khomeini maintained a duplicitous distance from the crisis, stating only that he had no control over the 'students,' a patent absurdity.

In Iraq, Saddam Hussein was watching. He saw an opportunity to exploit a politically weak, internationally isolated and unstable Iran – and quickly invaded in 1980. Hussein wanted control of the long contested Shatt-al-Arab River Estuary as well as the oil-rich southwest Iranian province of Khuzistan, where he hoped to capitalize on the support of a large Arab minority.

The West happily armed Hussein against what they saw as a dangerous Islamic leader in Iran. Hussein had presented himself to the world as a 'moderate' and made great play in the Middle East of Persian imperial arrogance and the anti-Arab racism that sometimes underlined it.

Whereas most Arab countries are of the Sunni Islamic faith, Iran is ethnically Persian and predominantly Shi'ite, a strand of Islam that regards itself as more truthfully in line with Muhammad's teachings, its proper influence usurped by schemers and betrayers in the line of ascendancy that followed the prophet. Hussein was deeply worried that the extremist fervour being propagated by Khomeini would spread to Shi'ites in Iraq, who made up over half the Iraqi Arabic population in spite of the ruling Sunni-dominated Baa'th Party, whose dictatorship under Saddam Hussein depended more on secular nationalism – and the fist – than religious passions.

Ironically enough, Kuwait was one of Hussein's major financial supporters, while the US provided him with crucial satellite information about Iranian troop movements late in the Iran-Iraq War. Iran could well view the US's prosecution of the first Gulf War against Iraq in the 1990s with a jaundiced eye.

GO TO THE SOUTH OF TEHRAN, TO THE CITY OF SHIRAZ, AND there is a long hand-woven banner hanging from a second-floor roof all the way to the pavement. At top a fiercely ethereal Khomeini, at middle the saintly, clear face of a teenage boy in an army shirt, at base a tank. The colours are those of the heavenly sky, the desert and a bloody red.

I pause and take a picture of this banner. Without any knowledge of its meaning. A Westerner devouring some Middle Eastern kitsch with my camera. Wow.

An Iranian man stops me in the street. An old man.

'Do you know what this is about?' he says, pointing firmly toward it. He looks at me. I can't tell if the intensity is friendly or angry, and I quickly push my camera out of sight. It's only then I realize that this building is the Main Police Headquarters, and that taking a photo anywhere near it is liable to get me into very serious trouble.

The old man won't let me go, however, and I am frozen to the spot while he speaks. 'This is Muhammad Fahmedi,' he instructs me slowly, making me write the boy's name down. Making me accept an image which has a relationship with a life and a history. 'In the Iran-Iraq War, he took a bomb with him and rolled under that tank.'

This is the 'human wave' technique that the Iranian military and the mullahs devised, making use of the jihad to sanctify death in the minds of their troops.

This was how Iran pushed back Saddam Hussein's vastly superior forces. With sheer numbers. With men, and when necessary, boys, grandfathers, whomever could help. Blessed in death.

This was how Iran pushed on into Iraq with useless expansionary hopes of its own. This was how a generation and much more were destroyed over eight years of fighting – some 500,000 Iraqis, over 700,000 young Iranians, dead. And then there were the damaged, the crippled, the psychologically destroyed, the immeasurable social and human costs.

Saddam Hussein indulged in his first experiments with chemical warfare: mustard gas, sarin nerve gas, all manner of deadly and banned cruelties. The world turned its eyes away. But the impact was unforgettable. They say the fighting was like World War One trench warfare all over again.

The Iranian people didn't like this war. Nor the way the mullahs ran it. Dismissing good officers and replacing them with more devout ones. Letting so many die in the name of Allah. Using up the idea of a jihad to excuse incompetence, even blind arrogance, in their judgements. Iraq had been the aggressor, the invader, but after eight years the Iranian people developed a profound distaste for this prolonged battle and the intransigent leadership of the mullahs. Conscription was tearing at the country's heart. Draft dodging was widespread.

The war would end without gain to either side. After being pushed back out of Iraq and put on the defensive again, Iran was forced to sign a ceasefire agreement thanks to the intervention of the United Nations. 'I'll drink this bitter cup of poison,' said a seriously ill Khomeini. He could count himself lucky.

Resentment over Western support of Iraq was compounded when a US man-of-war, the *Vincennes*, mistakenly shot down an Iran Air passenger plane with 290 innocent people aboard in July 1988. Beyond Iran's chauvinistic posturing in the wake of this disaster was something much deeper – a psychic wounding of the country. It was followed by the death of Ayatollah Khomeini the next year and the rising contention that he was in fact the Twelfth Emam, a Christ-like figure in Shi'ite Islamic teachings, whose earthly return was meant to set everything right with the world.

DESPITE THE TRADE EMBARGOES INSTITUTED BY THE US immediately after the embassy seizure in 1979 and still in place today as I write, Khomeini and the hardline mullahs who followed him would continue to support fear tactics and terrorism, internationally and at home. The Basij, a militia made up of zealous working-class youth, were often used for the 'human wave' assaults during the Iran-Iraq War. After being blooded in this way, they were later called upon to assist the Pasdaran (Revolutionary Guards) to restore order within Iran whenever necessary.

It is the Basij and the Pasdaran that continue to provide the regime with its most dedicated and hardline supporters. Soon after President Khatami's election in 1997, a new young commander called Yahia Rahim Safavi was appointed. It was not a progressive sign. Responding to liberalizing trends, he threatened to 'cut off the heads of some and cut out the tongues of others.'

The behind-the-scenes executions of dissident intellectuals in late 1998 further intensified a dark mood in Iranian politics, though Khatami insisted on bringing the perpetrators – 'rogue security elements' – to justice. One of the accused, a senior government intelligence figure, would eventually commit suicide in his jail cell, bringing the enquiry to a dead-end. Progressive newspapers were meanwhile shut down, their editors imprisoned for various affronts to Islam. At each and every point, the hardline mullahs continue to stop or suppress any significant changes. Everything feels bottled up. Tight.

Just before we arrived, the whole country was in the grip of its first televised trial, a case involving Gholamhussein Karbaschi, the popular mayor of Tehran at the time. Karbaschi was a progressive who had supported the rise of the liberalizing President Khatami in the elections of May 1997. In what was widely considered to be a political trial, he was accused in 1998 by a conservative-dominated judiciary of corruption.

The twists and turns of the trial paralleled Iran's fortunes in the lead-up to their victory against the US in the World Cup soccer preliminaries during 1998. Clerics feared protests as millions entered the streets to celebrate victory. Despite Karbaschi's conviction (one of the interesting vagaries of Iranian law includes a judge who also acts as prosecutor, deciding if he has proved his own case) there was no such trouble. Nonetheless, it is one of the strange by-products of governmental repression in Iran that pleasure – in this case the ever-widening appeal of soccer – can threaten to become such a destabilizing force politically. Joy is dangerous.

Demographics tell the story here. The population of Tehran has more than doubled in the last twenty years. This is not just a matter of declining rural conditions and a peasant migration to the cities – the boom is mirrored nationally over the same period with a growth in numbers from 35 to 65 million. A public awareness program advertises the family planning virtues of 'two is enough.' You can find the slogan on cigarette packs and the back of chocolate boxes (to the great amusement of Iranians, who have few opportunities to joke about, let alone discuss, sex).

Once you turn fifteen you are legally eligible to vote. With half the country's population now under 25, restlessness is the emotional currency of the day. The culture and the freedoms of the West – rock 'n' roll, fast food, short skirts, free love, democracy – are all mixed up in an exciting dream.

President Khatami and more politically sophisticated political elements have no desire to see a McPersia take shape. They are trying to turn a theocracy into an Islamic democracy, not pave the way for a capitalist rampage. Much of what they argue for is done on devoutly religious grounds and fought over in fine theological debates about how the Qu'ran should be interpreted. Khatami's moves towards 'a civil society' – including the first local council elections in twenty years, an attempt to slowly decentralise the power structure – remain a tightwire act between these competing sensibilities, perhaps the finest political act in the world today: an attempt to bring democracy peacefully to a dictatorship without forsaking Iran's cultural and religious integrity.

Khatami continues to debate the concept of 'a righteous path' with his fellow mullahs, and says unspeakable things correctly. The hardliners hate him for this devout intellect and the acute way he exercises it to argue for political openness. Then they do as they please anyway, no longer serving Allah and the Qu'ran as they pretend, but taking Allah's breath as their very own. Khatami is an irritating reminder of another way. His former closeness as a young student and protégé of the Ayatollah Khomeini is just one more thorn in their side. Below the surface one senses the age-old Shi'ite archetypes of struggle, sacrifice and martyrdom, the battle over teaching and who rightfully carries the heritage of faith as well as nation.

IF SOMEONE ASKED ME TO SAY WHAT IRAN'S FAVOURITE COLOUR is, I would say 'blood.' You see it depicted in images everywhere from postage stamps to paintings and, of course, the war murals.

These murals were first painted during the Iran-Iraq War by the *Bonyad-é Shahid* (Foundation for Martyrs). The controlling organization for all the murals was and still is an advertising agency called the *Ebtekaré Nour* (Invention of Light). Since the *Bonyad* began working, *Sepah* (the Revolutionary Guards Forces) have also been commissioned to paint martyrs' stories. But they lack the artistic richness and commitment of the work from *Bonyad*. The families of dead soldiers are sometimes disappointed, says a representative from *Ebtekaré Nour*, 'that it is only a portrayal job with not much artistic value.'

Abbas Ganji, aged 41, is one of Iran's leading war mural artists. He works directly with all these groups. For him it is important to create something that 'has a message' as well as 'aesthetic value.' More than that, Ganji wants to stimulate in the families 'something spiritual where memories come alive.'

A tall man with curly, grey-dark hair, glasses and white whiskers, Ganji looks older, more authoritative than his age might suggest. Though he has had no formal training, he admires the contemporary Iranian oil painter Khosro Jerdi who also pursues a strong interest in the martyrs, his fellow war-mural artist Iraj Eskandari and the sixteenth century miniaturist Reza Abbasi.

Ganji actually graduated as an auto-mechanic from a technical school in Tehran. He explains, 'I liked painting when I was a child and I served at the war front,' as if it's a casual observation. 'I had friends in Sepah. There was a day when they asked me, "Why don't you use your creativity to paint murals?" and that is how I started.'

He harbours no bad feelings about the war and the increased use of conscription as Iran at first repelled the invasion, then continued on into Iraq with futile expansionary hopes of its own. 'We had to resist the enemy against the imposed war,' he states faithfully, 'so that they could not come to our territories. And as Emam Khomeini says, this was a war between Islam and the impious. I want the murals to help people to always remember the desires of the martyrs and keep the Islamic ideology alive.'

Ganji talks about the way the murals 'reinforce the good breeding of being a martyr.' His favourite colours are blue for infinity, green for fertilization and red for blood, he says. His favourite stories expound the martyrs' desire to 'sacrifice themselves in order to fertilize the ground with the blood of their Islamic generosity.'

To Ganji, his proudest moments are when the families see the mural depictions of their lost sons, husbands and brothers. 'They say to me, "He is alive and we are in connection with him. He talked to us."'

There's no doubt that the Iran-Iraq War is still deeply felt in this country. That it still speaks to the people in a variety of ways.

In Tehran, the Revolutionary City. In Shiraz. In Esfahan. In all of Iran. Through giant murals adoring those who were lost and how the Revolution was sanctified in blood. With posters and banners. With poems and stories. With graveyards infinite with the photographic tombstones of the boys who went to die. Behind each photo, a picture of Khomeini, blessing them in their brave death. Like the artists who bless these young martyrs with their murals.

In Tehran more than any other city, though, the dead look down upon you everywhere.

How people look back at these pictures is another thing. As a glorious sign of Khomeini's Revolution? As mere propaganda? As a source of grief and shame? As a bitter cup of poison? As a sign of repression and waste? As brave soldiers, or Pasdaran and Basiji stooges?

Just what do these war saints remind people of?

These men looking directly out to the future. From a bloody past. Receiving offerings of flowers. Holding guns. Standing proudly on crutches with a leg blown away. Bearded, uniformed, visionary. Lying dead and solemn with a child beside them. In Tehran, where roses grow a metre high on once-sad buildings. And dark eyes pierce the smog.

Moses Baba and His Brother

MOSES BABA AND HIS BROTHER HAVE A SMALL SHOP ON THE Avenue Ferdosi, near the corner of Manuchehri Street, just opposite the old British Embassy in Tehran. It is well worth a visit if you happen to be in town.

Their window is crowded with miniatures torn from old books, equally old looking pottery with blue fish painted on the sides, handmade silver teapots and mirrors, papier mâché Pahlavi-era pencil boxes, rusty locks in the shapes of animals with strange keys that never turn easily, water pipes that would baffle the spine of a snake… one thing after another, all stacked one on top of the other: an Iranian jigsaw for the eyes.

Try putting this together in your mind – just how the hell does it all stay upright! – and you will most likely see a bargain, an item ready to be plucked from the window as neatly as an egg from a nest.

Some poetry by Hafez in a lovely script, or a set of old postage stamps perhaps? It's there if you look. A little something you might like, yes?

Go inside and you'll probably catch the two elderly brothers sleeping in the middle of the day. They snooze listening to a loud radio while a pot of *chai* bubbles quietly in anticipation of the next customer. When they prefer the radio to be silent, they clank a fat cup of coins violently on top of the machine. It's the only way they can turn it off.

There is no rush hour here. A young lad sits at the door and watches out for visitors. He has a solid, nervous build, and is aged about twelve. There is something over-obedient about him and he moves in a permanently bent-shouldered manner, as if living under a loud noise only he can hear.

Moses sleeps on a pile of carpets and newspapers behind the main glass counter, with his leather jacket for a pillow. His face betrays blotches of skin cancer and a nose that seems to be missing its tip, leaving what is almost a cavity in the middle of his bright face.

His somewhat fatter brother Simon drowses heavily in a battered desk chair, feet up on a high stool, his bulk resting all over whatever places and things he can find to support it. A pillow here, a box there, the bric-a-brac marshalled in support of his precarious comfort.

Not far from Moses' snoring is a picture of their grandfather dressed in a white robe tied with rope at the waist. He has a black oval hat on, and a long white beard, a Biblical man from another world. Moses' and Simon's father is dressed in a suit in a smaller black-and-white photo tucked in the right hand corner of the same large frame – he is much stockier than their grandfather, physically more like Simon, but his face is like Moses,' blazing away chirpily. He is holding an unlit Hanukkah candle.

Out front of the shop, some curved Farsi script and block gold English lettering announce 'MOSES BABA' to the street.

A Jewish merchant doing proud business at the heart of the Islamic world. Not so strange in Iran, where the Jews are probably more accepted than any other religious minority. Here the tradition is one of happy co-existence despite recent rumblings of persecution and talk of 'Zionist spies.' Most Iranian Jews speak Farsi and don't seem too obsessed with Israel or ideas of a homeland. They already are home. They don't want to go anywhere.

Inside the sleepy shop, the boy continues his lookout while Moses and Simon dream away. Sometimes even his head slips a little to his chest.

The boy wakes Moses first when we enter. This is a matter of seniority. Moses goes off like a jolly alarm clock: 'Hello, how are you, do you want *chai*?, here is papier mâché, very beautiful, good luck, here is mirror, 100 years old, see birds, see them, very beautiful, *coo-coo-coo*...'

His automatic sales pitch, reported here verbatim, with the cooing of painted birds thrown in for free, pours out like a stream-of-consciousness poem. It wakes his brother Simon, who smiles sedately, privately, even-handedly – he has seen the world awake and asleep and can let it all pass by either way.

'Come upstairs, ceramics, Chinese, look at book, miniature, very pretty, pencil case is good, here is plate, look, look…'

We are in a swirl of Moses' proffered objects as we move up the stairs, into a room you can't stand up straight in. Samples of this and that are pulled from behind paintings, off the top of vases, out from in-between the crevices and cracks of everything else you might want to consider. 'Here, look, look…'

This is more of a hunchbacked archeological dig than a shopping expedition. With Moses making great play of all the discoveries and unearthings. Loving to nudge a new object into sight.

Another mirror leaning face down against the wall seduces us more than the one he has just shown us downstairs. We wipe away the dust. It has enamelled blue and red diamonds patterning the borders and more of those painted birds that first made Moses sing. A hundred years old, you say?

'Yes, yes…'

Moses is most enthusiastic. We sit on some small stools and quickly get down to bargaining. Our chai is now beside us in thin, hot drinking glasses, placed down softly by the boy.

This mirror will bring us luck, Moses insists – like a couple in a photo from the 1950s that he has. He presents us the photo out of nowhere, framed somewhat heavily in gold. Compares Lisa to the woman with the black hair who is in the shot. They look nothing alike. 'Yes. Yes,' Moses insists, doing a bad job of flattery. 'You.'

We decline the photo and the concept that goes with it (another sale). As for the mirror we like best, well – Moses wants US$80 for the mirror. And that is too much.

'$50,' we say as bluntly as we can.

'$65!' he booms. 'Let's shake hands. Good luck. This is very good.' Moses is pitching his conversation at us like the bargaining is all over.

'$50,' we say again emphatically. Adding that, 'We bought another mirror here yesterday off your brother. C'mon!'

'Last ones, from my grandfather,' Moses says, pointing sadly back downstairs to the image of the be-robed disciplinarian who built the family business. 'After this, no more,' he declares in the same wheezy, sing-songy voice he says everything in. It's a voice fit for weeping.

'$50,' we say once more, completely unmoved.

'All right!' he roars. '$50. For you. I like you! This will bring you good luck. *Cooo, cooo…*' he burbles away, pointing to the blue birds, then claps his hands, barking affably downstairs for the boy to get up here now – a deal has been sealed, it's time to pack the goods.

Simon smiles his sad frog's smile as we come back downstairs with our prize. Moses is so delighted he practically does a jig around the room.

'Did you have a good day yesterday?' I say to Simon slyly, alluding to our previous buy: the same kind of mirror – for $60! Two of them at that price, actually. Ten dollars more than his brother squeezed from us today, *for each mirror.* Simon chuckles and shrugs his shoulders at me. 'Not bad.' We both laugh. Everybody is happy.

I notice then that Simon is a little sweaty and heavy of breath. Not from effort, but obvious illness. He trembles and grimaces when he moves even slightly, like a man who should be in hospital. I think I smell shit.

Moses is busy, rattling on about luck, birds, his grandfather, rope, paper, and the rest of his shop still for sale. 'You like papier mâché, coin, plate…?'

'No, no. *Tashakor,*' we laugh. 'Three mirrors is enough for us from Moses Baba.'

'Then give 200 toman to the boy,' Moses urges. 'Tip him. He is poor. Only 200 toman. All his family are dead in Afghanistan. They kill them,' he laughs.

Then he starts waving an imaginary machine gun around. '*Tick, tick, tick,*' he says slowly, making a noise more like the turning of an old wooden cog. 'Kill them: *tick, tick, tick.* Yes, all of them! The Taliban. *Tick, tick, tick…*'

We just wish he would shut the hell up with all that ticking. But we get the message. And give the boy some money. He accepts it with such cowering gratitude I feel ashamed and sad for having offered him so little.

Simon smiles his unwell smile towards us. Moses' eyes glitter and his mouth pours yet more of that mercantile telegram he calls a conversation. The boy hands us our package wrapped in a truly reckless style. And we leave with our mirror, patterned in diamonds and birds, secured in old Tehran newspapers and a mad tangle of bright yellow rope, with Moses singing after us, '*coo-coo-coo.*'

Songbird (Flower of the Night)

SHE'S YOUNG AND VERY, VERY BEAUTIFUL IN PROFILE AND wears large dark sunglasses like Jackie O. With her *hejab* covering her head, she could even be grieving, but her words are too fresh and bell-like, too knowing and in control for grief or doubt to enter into them.

She is Maryam.

Or so everybody in the hotel lobby tells us when she flickers into view on a large television set. 'Maryam.' They say the word with pride and awe. A single name, like a flower, a leader, a pop star.

Maryam Heydarzadeh is Iran's most popular poet. In a country where poetry matters intensely, where thousands visit shrines to Sa'di and Hafez, and people know their verses off by heart. Centuries-old Persian verses which still have the ability to make an Islamic universe quake. Words of sensual wisdom and wit that invite an alternative way of thinking to the law of the mullahs.

In Iran, it is a relief to know aestheticism has not yet been conquered by asceticism. Much as the clerics have tried.

Maryam's latest book and accompanying CD, *Like No One*, are in all the stores. You can hear her girlish voice pronouncing the verses, accompanied by an orchestra and tinkling piano and new age pop, with men crooning and yearning songs in between her spoken-word reflections. That child's voice of hers broadcast out into the open streets, a strangely cool and disembodied consciousness.

Yes, Maryam is everywhere.

Perhaps because it is illegal to buy or sell or record or listen to a woman singing in Iran since the Revolution, Maryam has become the focus for what is lost. All those missing women's voices.

Replaced by the sound of a girl talking.

Tonight she faithfully addresses the leaders of Iran, Khamenei the intransigent and Khatami the progressive alike, reciting from the Qu'ran in her clear, girlish way. People rush to television sets to see her, hear her. Stand as quiet as can be.

Maryam Heydarzadeh is blind.

On the cover of *Like No One* she looks down from her impenetrable sunglasses, her profile afloat in a night sky, her *hejab* part of the night itself. Beneath her gaze sunflowers rise up in a sucking rush to become skybound yellow birds.

Her gift is metamorphosis.

Maryam. The poet who must never sing.

Dastgah

SOMEONE CRAWLED IN HIS EAR. POOR ROBERT, WHAT A pain it was. He could feel the man as he moved slowly into his head: a junkie who-would-just-not-shut-the-fuck-up. The stranger's tongue made sleazy sounds. There was something wet about the words that poured straight into the mind. It was not a good feeling and he grimaced to try and tighten his skull against every word sliding forward.

Robert had been reading a book, waiting for his local tea house to open in the middle of Tehran. It was a bad area. He knew that. But it was morning time, safe enough you would think.

There was weirdness right from the start. First an old man with sunken cheeks had wanted him to come around the corner, deep into the park. 'Something about how "Michael Jackson used to be a man, now woman, come around corner." And how I could fuck this half-man, half-woman. I dunno. I dunno…'

Robert shakes his head. The pimp for the half-man, half-woman un-settled him. 'Even though it was kind of funny too. I just told him to fuck off. He kept saying "Michael Jackson, Michael Jackson" and pointing towards the bushes. Like someone was waiting.'

He laughs about it now. He laughed then too. But screwing Michael

Jackson was just an entrée. The junkie was next.

Wild times in a country where women must cover themselves from head to toe. An Englishman sitting on a bench reading Persian poetry, while pimps tout trade for transsexuals and heroin addicts come to drag you inside their stories.

'The junkie was doing the strangest exercises I ever saw,' Robert explains. 'That's how I noticed him. Like tai chi and aerobics put together, but more demented. And when he knew a Westerner was looking, he got more theatrical about it. I tried not to look after that. There was something heavy about him and I didn't want to catch his attention. You know how it is with mad people. Then the guy came over and said something to me in English. He was quite aggressive. So I answered back in Farsi, hoping that would make him go away. But he just got really insulted.'

He stood there glowering over Robert. Became even more determined to make a connection. 'He just wouldn't leave me alone. Turned all friendly, but you know that type of friendly – when it just gives you the creeps and you can't escape and they won't let you go.

'He started acting all important, like I was lucky to meet him. Told me how he used to play with Carlos Santana and John McLaughlin. At first I didn't believe him. Partly because he said he was American, but his accent wasn't good enough to be American. He spoke excellent Portugese too and he told me he was born in Portugal. I'm British obviously, but I was also born in Portugal. And he didn't look Portugese to me – and the way he spoke it – well, it didn't sound right. But he didn't speak very good Iranian either. So I couldn't work out where the hell he was really from.

'Anyway, he pulled out a photo of himself in the 1970s with this amazing Afro surrounded by all these Iranian guys and their instruments. So he'd obviously been here a long time. And he had definitely been a musician. He told me he was more Iranian than Iranians. Kept going on and on and on about that. "I am more Iranian than the Iranians!" Something about him made me feel I had to hold on tightly to my own sanity. You know how it is with some people: it's like their skin is buzzing or something. They're not intact inside themselves, they have this energy that's crawling all over them. And they let it go all over you. That's what they enjoy about themselves.' He shivers in the heat, remembering. 'I dunno, I dunno. He was just strange.'

The crazed musician had probably come to Tehran for cheap, high-grade opium back when the Shah was in power. He'd stayed on after the Revolution. Got lost in the secret life of Iran. '"I know this place," he kept saying to me. "I know it."'

Tehran is now filthy with heroin. It rolls in from Afghanistan across the deserts in 4-wheel drive convoys that do not bother to use roads. The smugglers travel at night to avoid satellite tracking. In small battalions of smack, armed with night-vision glasses, hi-tech weapons, rocket missile launchers. The heroin spills into the major cities of Iran. But it mostly goes out through Turkey and into the Western world. Turkey proudly claims to stop some 70 per cent of the flow of heroin into Europe; Iran claims similar astronomical figures. Imagine how much there must be out there at night, coming through, confiscated, profiteered again back onto the blackmarket. The Iranian police are fighting the real 'drug war,' but they are poorly armed because of US trade embargoes and are often outmanoeuvred or slaughtered by the smugglers, who are rich, dangerous and well-organized.

In Tehran you see educational posters that try to address a reluctantly acknowledged problem. For a long time, the ayatollahs did not want to admit such a thing was happening. Apart from desperate policing and capital punishment, they've tried to answer the problem with naive images of a butterfly and affirmative slogans, or the cartoon horror of a spider on the cheek of a young child. Just say no. Stop the menace. Live purely in the name of Allah. The invocations are futile.

Under Islamic law, many pleasures are hidden from view. Especially the pleasures of the young: a kiss, a drink, some pop music, a couple holding hands. You can be arrested or beaten for such things. What to do with all that energy, all that suppressed desire, but to have parties behind closed doors, to get sexy in secret, to go wild and keep it a conspiracy among like-minded friends. This secrecy breeds a fearful, corrupted life: out of sight, out of mind. No one must know but us.

This is night life.

'I couldn't work out what he was going on about,' Robert says of the junkie, 'but something made sense – amongst all the bullshit, I mean – if you could tune out the shit and listen to what he was saying that *did* make sense.

'He kept saying Iran was a sensual place. Very feminine. But he didn't mean sensual or feminine in a good way.' The word 'sensual' comes out of Robert's mouth like the word 'poison.' It has a sibilant and evil tone. Robert apologizes in his ever-so-English way to Lisa. 'I don't mean to be sexist. But I understood what he meant. I – I really did.'

This was the real Iran, perhaps. A nest of dark babble that disappeared into itself like the infinite, interlocking patterns in Persian carpets or the elaborate mosaics on the walls of mosques. Or Robert's own special interest, the *dastgah-ha* of musicians like Lotfi and singers such as Shajarian.

Robert had originally learnt clarinet as a boy, 'but I was crap.' So he turned to ethnomusicology and the study of Middle Eastern music. He preferred Iraqi music to any other flavour. 'It's wild,' he growls. He thought the Azerbaijanians knew 'how to have a good time, how to let go.' But Iranian music was 'full of miserable bastards,' just too 'dense.' And yet Robert felt something attractive in its mournful shadows that he couldn't resist. And so the *dastgah-ha* held a fascination of their own, even if he was bothered by their sorrowful complexity and darkness. 'I just like the way it begins and you never really know where it's going, or where it's going to end up. With most Western music there's a beginning, middle, end – or a few themes that are developed maybe – but this music is not like that at all.'

He explained how great singers like Shajarian semi-improvised their lyrics over the top of the music, freely quoting from the enormous texts of classical Persian poets like Hafez, Sa'di, Rumi, Khayyam and Ferdosi, praising Allah and sensual love, feeling the mood and finding the words in an awesome web of recitative memory. Shajarian was regarded as the greatest singer ever in this tradition, a phenomenon of the twentieth century and a culmination of the art form. He was from the holy city of Mashad. Like his father, Shajarian had started off as a religious singer of the Qur'an – until he was fifteen, when he deviated into the *dastgah-ha* and what was considered decadent Persian classicism. He was like a gospel singer who had been turned on to soul music and jazz. Originally divine, now lost from God.

Upon his return to power, Khomeini had immediately outlawed this musical form because it was so sensual. So primal to the Persian mind. Shajarian had personally prevailed on him to lift the ban, and after a few years, Khomeini relented. Shajarian's voice had seduced the stone-faced Ayatollah. The *dastgah-ha* played on.

Robert wanted to meet Shajarian, or at least to see him perform. He knew the singer moved often between Tehran and Mashad and sometimes toured to Los Angeles, returning home to Iran like a dark prince, unveiling new works with grandiose titles. His latest and finest recording was called *The Secrets of Existence*. We'd bought the cassette at a record store, heard a voice of liquid and smoke and bereaved, erotic yearning.

We loved the pained ecstasy in the music. Robert was equally enthusiastic. 'I heard a great description of the music's structure: that it's like an underground bazaar. You enter it and you come out on another side, but you can travel through it many different ways, take many different paths – and that's how the musicians play it. Each time they improvise. But there are strict rules, paths they must follow. In each *dastgah* there are anywhere between a dozen and 50 main *gushehs* which is the Farsi word for "street" – or "segment" – or "corner," really. They can travel down these different streets in the bazaar, then turn left or right and *go*. Just play and move. It's not written down anywhere either. It's taught by ear. The only way you can learn it is by listening to a master for years and playing and playing and playing until you know each *dastgah* off by heart. The musicians have this huge knowledge, almost like maps they improvise, but in this incredibly disciplined and defined way.'

Robert was now trying to read these maps. These *dastgah-ha*. And remember them as best he could. Which of course he could not. To try to hear the minds that move through these spaces is like following tracks through the sand. Each time Robert looks at mosaics on the walls of mosques or the patterns in Persian carpets to help get a grip on this conceptual penetration of reality, 'It does my head in.'

Sometimes Robert just wants to stop thinking about all this. To go to his room and hide from Iran and what makes it. Three months of this stuff has freaked him out. 'Even just the fact that they write backwards on a page compared to us, from right to left. There's a whole different way the brain moves, the language moves.'

Robert's father had warned him before about thinking too much. That it was bad for you. The junkie was a walking example of what happens. You get lost. You go mad. And yet there was *something* in the knots of his thought, Robert kept arguing (to no one but himself).

The junkie had claimed that life is like a *shabob*. Like a shooting star. 'It's an old Persian saying. But when they say "shooting star" they don't just mean the star itself. They mean the trail of the star. And that's how they write the word here,' Robert says, making a long elaborate stroke in the air that slowly falls away and is gone. He adjusts his glasses. 'I dunno. I dunno.'

'I guess the junkie really got to me,' Robert admits. 'He summed something up. I still can't explain why. Just the way he talked about the sensuousness of the country. How Persia was a very soft place, but very hard and very complex too. It's like the way people will say things to you here that you'd laugh at back home. But here they sound meaningful. I dunno, I dunno.'

It's then I remember our own first day in Iran. A man on a bus, sitting behind us, whispering into our ears as he leant forward uninvited between our seats. He had a sweet, strange voice, a wheezing melodious tone that reminded me of a cat. He said to both of us, 'Life is not a day passed by. It is a day remembered. I hope your time in Iran is remembered well.'

His breath touched our necks with a disturbing intimacy. I could not delineate between his formality and good wishes and a more sinister shadow. A confusion that echoed again as Robert told us his own story of complexity and invasion.

Robert had hoped the junkie might be able to tell him something about the music he was studying. But there was only rambling without end in the conversation. A desire to draw Robert deeper into an intimacy that locked in around him and went nowhere. The muso junkie was insane. A living maze.

'I tried to ask him about the "Esfahan Dastgah" because I thought he might know how to play it. It's so well known. But he just laughed and said, "It's a good city to be watched in." Then he started humming some part of it, I think. He said I should visit the Golestan é Shohada, that then I would know real music. He was so intense about that. "Maybe you can go there with me. I take you." Then he laughed again and put his hand on my leg. I got up and started walking away. He shouted at me, just filthy stuff in Farsi. I was frightened he might come after me, but I didn't look back. I just kept walking.'

We had visited the Golestan é Shohada, the war martyrs' cemetery in Esfahan. A hundred thousand graves of young men killed in the war with Iraq. A hundred thousand large photos of their faces used in the way we use tombstones, all looking out into the bright, glaring day, an endless field of thick lips and thick eyebrows, such spent voluptuous youth.

In the graveyard we could hear a distant helicopter chopping the air. I could smell bitumen and looked over to a roof where men were sealing it with steamy black tar. Banalities that echoed the sounds and smells of a battlefield. There were also large pictures of the Iran-Iraq War at each intersection of the Golestan é Shohada. Billboard-size images, violent and familial: of young men hunched in bright blue parkas with bullet holes in their foreheads, of an army preparing wildly for battle, of soldiers in a tent smiling and sharing slices of watermelon.

At the entrance to the cemetery, a woman in a black chador sat reading the Qur'an, reciting it under her breath. A few soldiers strolled around. A mullah talked to an old man. A darker-looking old man, probably a nomadic tribesman, was bowed down at a grave site and talking to his lost son, pulling at a small tree in a white pot by the side of his son's photo. The sight of the old man's hand on the sapling's trunk, pulling and pulling as he grieved, was too much to bear.

All these young men who looked so feminine. Like bursting fruit. Fallen. Dead.

And now Robert, with his studious glasses and similar lips and nervous mantras of 'I dunno, I dunno' was falling apart slowly in front of us. Into a world that he couldn't put together, built on music and a junkie's words and the blinding calligraphy of Allah's name inscribed across the walls of mosques. His thoughts weaved through one story into another and then another until he told us about the time he'd had a nervous breakdown in America as a 19-year-old English boy just off the plane, walking right into the LA riots, the city on fire. 'I thought it would just be a walk in the park.' He disappeared in the city for days. When they found him, he did not know what had happened. His mind was clean.

Close to Us

HE HAS A BLACK SUIT, A BLACK BEARD AND A CRISP WHITE shirt with a wing-tipped collar, 1970s–style. His build is stocky yet somehow lean, not fat. You might say he is sleek with authority, but deliberately low key about it. Maybe 40 years of age; a handsome man. Someone who chooses his manner and makes it known.

Our world has suddenly stopped with his arrival. We are standing outside the entrance to a hubble-bubble shop in the local bazaar, watching him speak to our guide.

Where are they from? What do they do? Are they with a tour group?

Our guide answers these questions and more asked by the bearded stranger. They are speaking in Farsi, so we can't understand everything, but their gestures, and the mention of our hotel name, tell us a little and that is more than enough.

He has obviously been following us for a while, even knows the answers to some of the questions he asks. It is as well that the answers he gets from our friend are consistent with such knowledge.

This does not feel good.

We start walking to a carpet shop in the square, where our tour guide bases himself. It is not where we were originally headed.

More questions are asked of the carpet shop owner, a brazen, sly fellow who tries to take charge of the matter. We made friends with him as we sat admiring his collection of nomadic works from the Bakhtiari, the Kurds, the Lurs... Iran is a place of many peoples and carpets, of many tribal identities and languages weaving into one nation. Some patterns are simple, others dense and interlocking, a few become a little frayed.

The manager answers the questions, smiles, assumes the easy confidence of business. This is something like an equality, though not quite that. No, it is more like a mask. Easily pulled off.

There is a feeling that one small turn could put the situation in a spin.

Finally the interrogator leaves. We are still not supposed to know he is a policeman, but it has been so easy to tell: the body language, the persistent questions, that bubble of fear floating around in the blood.

The tour guide and the carpet shop manager continue speaking in Farsi to each other. They know that we know it was a policeman. But they aren't supposed to tell us. Yet it's something they can't avoid, so they begin speaking in English to us. It feels like a piece of theatre they have agreed on in order to pacify us.

'It is good,' says the manager, 'that they worry like this. For our safety. And for yours.'

They joke a little about it. We are all sophisticated people here after all. The tour guide, who is younger, more rash in his attitude, scoffs. 'What do they think? You are stupid people? You can't see? All these questions, questions, questions. How he makes me come back here. He tells me, "Don't say to them I am a policeman." What I say? Tell you he is selling me carpets? They are stupid to make me lie!'

The manager restrains the guide's words with a stern look. Then it's back to business as usual: *chai* and carpets rolled out endlessly. But maybe we won't go on a tour today or even tomorrow, as originally planned. Our guide does not have a licence, you see, and, he admits, 'Maybe they are watching me. I will phone someone and see.'

We don't want to get anyone into trouble. We are only looking for lamps and beads and yet more carpets. And a good time too. Of course we want to have fun.

But now an authority has pressed itself upon us ever so lightly. Why, we wonder?

Already some friends in a circus troupe have been moved on. In their bright bus with their clumsy show and feral looks they weren't considered the right type of tourist for this city. Bussing their way from London to Australia, and performing along the way, we'd seen their leader juggling fire in the main square. Setting up a race with local children on pushbikes, and competing with them while he rode a monocycle. It was a popular act. People laughed.

That night we saw their bus had been moved away from a quiet lane and into the main street. It was dark and empty looking, like no one was aboard. By morning it was gone altogether.

Have we overstayed our welcome as well? Drawn too much attention to ourselves? Associated with the wrong people – from this city, from Europe, from the rest of the world? Is it our clothes? Our attitude?

There is nothing specific we can identify. It may well just be a routine check. An unlucky collision in the bazaar.

But this is something you *feel* in Iran. Borders holding things in, borders you can't quite see. A constraining tension, a quiet sense of pressure out there somewhere.

The manager says something again about the policeman. 'He is religious. They worry. That is why they ask questions.'

He wants us to forget this incident. This faith that encircles people. With its men in black. This faith that works like a shadow.

Maybe that's why people seem to be acting for us. Acting proud of their country. Acting a little wild and crazy when they play some banned Western pop music in their *taksi* or do a banned dance around a room or play banned female singing in a shop late at night.

Or the opposite: seizing a magazine off us, not realizing we'd bought it legally around the corner from a bookshop where it had already been censored. How strange that moment was. A waiter in a restaurant at a plush hotel, grabbing the news magazine from me, reciting 'pictures for you' again and again with fervid disapproval before I could show him my receipt and the torn plastic cover that demonstrated it was Iranian-approved material. Look here, I showed him angrily, the women's bare arms and legs are blotted out with black texta. Look there, words are obscured! Safe, safe...

The waiter calmed down, handed me back my magazine. It had felt like a citizen's arrest was underway up until that moment. A lesson for a visitor: here you never know who is watching.

Now a policeman has followed us through the bazaar.

It's a trivial thing really, as common as a traffic infringement back home. It is Iran: secret and tight and close to us.

Coffee in Tehran

IS COFFEE THE TASTE OF DECADENCE AND DISSENT?

In Tehran only the wealthy or those with Western affectations would dare drink or desire coffee.

Iran is traditionally the land of *chai*. Wherever you go, *chai* is the communal drink, the perpetual backdrop to business and socializing.

Amid the teahouses, the bubbling water pipes and carpet salesmen of the endless bazaars, *chai* sustains Persian ideals of hospitality, acts as an aromatic reminder of the days of desert trade, the caravansari and *The Rubaiyat of Omar Khayyam*. The most sober and socially delicate of past-times in a country where alcohol is banned.

Coffee is a reminder of a more recent history – and a premonition of the future. It calls to memory pre-Revolutionary times. These were the days of the corrupt Shah and his cruel programs of Westernization and modernization at any cost. But older Iranians and those with aristocratic tastes still enjoy the scent of coffee in Tehran, its bittersweet trace on the tongue. Young people, often students, revel in its Western flavour, its liberal fumes.

Past and future: coffee takes people out of time, out of now. It is regretful, nostalgic, bitter and sweet and seductive. Like the word 'Persia' itself.

Coffee is a rare café on a side street and the society that it cultivates. It is women in tight blue jeans, bodies hidden by their shapeless *manteaus* (raincoats) and how they are sealed up with coloured buttons, a decorative feminine protest against Islamic stringency. It is an old insurance salesman who no longer works for reasons he cannot say, who talks to me with sad eyes about the past 'when it was better' like a character out of a novel by Gabriel García Marquez. It is a sexy, modern woman in a black chador seated behind the cash register, dark graphic eyebrows, bright strawberry lipstick, pale blue thin-framed reading glasses, a newspaper in her hands to kill the downtime. It is a young man in a light green-brown leather jacket with a gold chain around his neck. It is brightly coloured head scarves, sharp business suits, smoke, gossip, crossword puzzles, urbanity.

It is revolution by osmosis. The taste of dissent and longing. It is coffee in Iran. And I drink it slowly. Slowly on a late morning in Tehran.

Motherless Child

IT IS 17 NOVEMBER, MAB'ATH FEAST, THE ANNIVERSARY of the day when the Holy Prophet Mohammed was appointed by Allah as the last divine messenger.

We are cruising down the Bozograh-e-Modarres, Tehran's main northern highway.

Our *taksi* driver, an enthusiastic man with a perennial Middle Eastern moustache, is singing. Singing for us.

It is a wailing sound, chopped up and quivering, like a yodel cut off and recommenced again and again with renewed confidence. This is the tahrir: a form of classical Persian singing taken to melancholic heights by the great Iranian vocalist Shajarian.

But as our taxi driver's voice struggles free of his cigarette breathlessness, so do his words and their strange familiarity: 'I feel like a motherless child…'

He carries the song and that particular line in English on and on, improvising and distending it for us, words circling in words, higher and lower in the vocal cascade.

We sit in the back of his 'pay-can' applauding. Tehran stretches out like a jewel in the early night below us, spasm after spasm of light echoing the spidery, ecstatic artwork of Persian miniatures as the city winks and glitters awake into the freshness of the evening.

'Do you love your wife or not?' the driver asks me suddenly, breaking his tune.

I'm taken aback by the directness of the question. I say, 'Yes, I love her.' But his boldness throws me. And his words travel deep.

'How many children?'

We lie and tell him we have two, a boy and a girl. That they are staying with our parents while we travel. We have long ago learnt it is easier to give people an image of our imaginary family than to bear the pitying looks and words that loom over a barren marriage. He is happy because he too has a boy and a girl.

'It is a quiet day,' we comment, trying to change the subject. 'Not much traffic about for the feast?'

The driver, whose English is not bad – though he says, 'please forgive me' whenever he tries to speak with us – wants to know this word's meaning. 'The street is *quiet*, yes?' He gestures to the relative emptiness of the highway.

We agree that he has used the word appropriately. But I try to refine the word beyond traffic, and talk about how when music is turned down 'it is quiet,' and when it is turned up 'it is loud.'

It's odd to see your own language's ambiguities. The word quiet: it's about volume, it's about sound, it's about a mood or someone's character. A lack of cars, a song, a feeling of emptiness or peace.

'You can use this word many ways.'

The taxi driver nods. Turns some music up, then down, on his stereo. 'Quiet,' he utters, pleased with himself.

He reaches into his glove box and shows us some recordings he has. He tries to sell us homemade tapes of a singer called Ali Reza Eftakorie, as well as some sitar music and 'a girl singer.' The last offer is put to us like heroin. He wants double the price of cassettes in the shops. It's a testament to his charm that we think about his offer before declining and leaving him with a tip instead.

'Iran is a hard place with no money,' he says coughing flatly. It's not a sob story, just a fact. He's grateful for the tip anyway.

I think about his poisonously bad cough. His son studying something at university that he can't explain or translate, 'medicine but not medicine.' His son, whom he taught to sing just like him, 'but good.' His daughter who plays sitar, 'beautiful.'

He has travelled this long road many times before. Knows the history of its name, can even point to a great mural half-hidden by housing blocks that tells the story. 'Modarres Ayatollah Modarres. He is on the money. Note ten.'

The Ayatollahs' faces have flowed into the currency, the river of authority. Just as he flows down the highway and sings a poor man's tahrir. He follows an anonymous path from the outer suburbs to the heart of Tehran and back again. He sells tapes from his glove box. He teaches his children music. He sings like a motherless child.

The Call

THERE'S A KNOCK AT THE DOOR. A NERVOUS BOY WITH dark thick eyebrows pointing back downstairs. Telephone.

I've been laying awake on one of our sunken single beds, talking with Lisa across the squeaking metal springs. I pull on a pair of jeans and a coat and run downstairs.

At the desk both public phones sit on the shelf, clearly not in service. 'There is a phone call?' I ask.

The desk clerk does not speak English. I point to the phones and he shakes his head.

A new and unwanted friend in a sharkskin suit with a hungry look on his face offers to translate. He talks to the desk clerk, then turns to me: 'The phones are not working.'

'But I just got a call. The boy came to my room to say someone rang for me.'

The hungry young man looks at me. Talks to the desk clerk. Turns back to me: 'Yes, the phones are working now. You can make a call.'

'I don't want to make a call. Someone phoned for me.'

'Maybe you can call my girlfriend,' the young man says, smiling racily. 'She speaks very good English.'

'No,' I say, beginning to laugh.

'She speaks very good English. You can call her.'

'No! Someone rang for me.' I say it again emphatically, pointing to the phone and putting it to my ear, miming the whole concept. 'Have they gone now? Were they cut off?'

He speaks to the desk clerk. Then turns to me again. 'Yes, they have gone now. Do you want to call them?'

The Azerbaijanis

THE AZERBAIJANIS ARE ON THE MOVE. GOLD TEETH GLOW-
ing in the blue and yellow lights of the courtyard.

Flash, dubious personas for the men, like a dodgy gathering of *The Usual Suspects*: a pinstripe suit on a five o'clock shadow; a vinyl black jacket on a bushy moustache; a fur, oblong hat perched jauntily on wily grey eyes.

As for the women, my god! They're big, busty and brazen, broad-arsed as barns and loud-voiced enough to fill one or even two of them, with dark-ringed eyes and a no-shit readiness to do business day or night so shoo! The women wear grey cotton raincoats and black scarves in sloppy deference to Islamic dress codes, but there's a Western trashiness to them that won't be suppressed: a polka dot handbag, a splash of peroxide blonde hair and red, red lips, a whole way of walking that suggests these women shop to kill and it's best you stay out of their goddamned, hotsie totsie way.

The women also know a special whisper that makes all the hotel cats come to them. But they don't give the cats anything when they arrive. Still they whisper and seduce them, time and again. What bitches!

Loud as foghorns, jolly as a trading fleet, the Azerbaijanis converse across the hotel courtyard by yelling. Yelling from flat to flat, yelling from upstairs to downstairs, yelling to each other at their tables over *chai*. Their communication verily eats the word 'hearty.' Manifests the adjective 'beefy.' Not talking, yelling. Always bellowing, the hotel reincarnated as their import-export factory, booming to mercantile actions and the law of being heard.

Around the courtyard are their spoils. Thousands of plastic coat hangers wrapped in bundles man-high and higher – mostly red in colour, followed by a little orange, and some luxury stock in a rare baby blue. Boxes of something marked 'whitener' that is probably bleach. Giant-size, lumpy sacks of cloth and cotton for clothes-makers. And a few large electric heaters for the exclusive warmth of limited purchasers back home.

Every night a bus arrives. Every night a bus departs. With different communities of Azerbaijanis, mobs of shopkeepers who all seem to know each other and bargain with each other and help each other out. After a few weeks you notice a rotating pattern of personalities, of familiar faces yelling their way back into your world.

They load their booty onto the hired buses for their return trip. Night after night, out front the Hotel Gilano on Ferdosi Street in Tehran. The pavement is chock-full with their boxes and sacks and human industry, everything squeezed onto the vehicle, till the people ferret and push their own way in like human plugs. A job well done.

Among them I have been given one friend. The man in the sharkskin suit.

He always has a cigarette loosely at hand. Eager, hurt, dark eyes, straining, hinting at an intelligence that evaporates into the open bafflement he expresses about his life.

'You are from Australia? I have a brother in Toronto.'

Toronto is in Canada.

'Yes, yes, yes,' he says, like there's no difference. 'He is a dentist.' And then he whispers. 'But I have much trouble getting a visa. My brother try for me.'

There's an implication I can help. But I just nod sympathetically. I feel embarrassed and ashamed. Again and again on our travels through India, Turkey and Iran, we encounter people who ask why it is so easy for us to visit them, and so hard for them to visit us.

Visa. That magic, dirty word: 'visa.'

One obvious reason why they can't get an Australian visa is their desperation to get out of here – and run like hell into the Promised Land. Wherever the hell it is. But even the rich or the studious, the genuine holiday makers, find it very difficult to leave these countries. You feel privileged, elitist, to be standing in their home when they cannot visit yours.

'Yes, I have trouble with my visa.'

I act mystified. Put the blame on strange, contrary, distant Canada. 'Hmmm...'

'When do you go to Istanbul?' he asks. 'I go to Istanbul soon.'

The inference is that perhaps we will meet there. But I just go 'Hmmm...' again. I'm a real sphinx tonight.

And then Sharkskin shakes my hand passionately. 'Australia is a good country!' And that's where our conversation ends, more or less, because it seems to be all the English he knows. This is tragic for me. Because we have the same conversation, pretty much word for word, every night. Till I dread the sight of him.

The dentist brother. The visa. The conflation of Toronto, Canada and Sydney, Australia – anywhere out of here will do, he seems to be trying to say. Istanbul. When are you going to Istanbul? His curiousity is frightening and urgent.

His greetings to me are always happy, keen, wishing me all the best. I start to feel like a brother, like his brother – but also as if I am a man *already* in another country, even while I'm still in his country – and that he can only watch me helplessly, a fool of fate from behind some invisible window pane between us.

One night he finally varies the content a little. I get the feeling he has been studying his book of English phrases. Out of the blue, he turns and says to me, 'Azerbaijanian people are very stupid,' and waves his hand dismissively at the rest of his group. Then more sadly he adds, 'They are very poor.'

At the next table a big woman prepares snacks for her typically moustached husband: bread, pickles, tuna in a can. Perfect food for a cat, perhaps, but not today – nor any other day. They offer for us to join them in the meal. And we accept.

I now realize why every single garbage bin outside every single room is knocked over and spilled around the halls of the hotel. As if drunks have been upending rubbish constantly around the premises every night.

Each evening the Azerbaijanis put their finished snack tins out. And each night the cats go absolutely mental, teased into fury already by the whispers of women.

You would think this might invoke some change in the system. But the Azerbaijanis still have their pickles and tunas every night. And the hotel still has their plastic bins set outside their rooms. And the rubbish-strewn morning still comes, stinking of fish.

The funny thing about Sharkskin is how cheerily he greets those people he has whispered to me, or tried to suggest to me, he is somehow apart from. He greets them with love. Heartily. In a big loud voice that tells me he is definitely one of them. He laughs with them as they approach the table we have now joined. And calls out across the courtyard. And loads up the buses busily. And dreams and schemes secretly like each of them. Melancholy and aware of the world's bad luck, its short straws, but still getting on with what has to be done here: the talking, the eating, the working, the bus. Part of a dark-eyed Azerbaijanian mystery, a rhythm, a commerce.

But that's all philosophy and speculation and maybe a little romantic bullshit from me too. Sitting here among them with a tuna and pickle roll. All of a sudden I sneeze like a cat – 'tchew!' – and a woman says, I think, whatever the Azerbaijanian word is for 'bless you.' Then another woman at the next table starts quietly laughing – and laughing – and laughing – which makes her husband laugh, till he throws up his hands because he can't stop. I sneeze again and pretty soon the entire courtyard of Azerbaijanis is laughing and I get the feeling sneezing is like farting. By the time I sneeze a third time, people are almost falling from their chairs with laughter, and we have joined them, roaring with tears.

The Gifts

THIS IS A LIST OF WHAT WE TOOK BACK FROM IRAN. THINGS that we could hold and show you:

A large camel bell made of iron with a mythical bird-lizard creature engraved on the outside, and a diamond shape marked on a smaller inner bell.

A silver ring with an 'atomic' ruby.

A small wooden box painted with a green-and-gold mandala, with an opening for a pack of cigarettes or a deck of cards.

A handmade silver mirror with blue enamel and details of women dancing, playing music, serving food and drink, and catching a bird in flight. On the back, a surprisingly debauched scene of harem revelry.

Old paperback copies of *Seven Pillars of Wisdom* by T.E. Lawrence and *Tropic of Cancer* by Henry Miller, both bought from a street vendor on Ferdosi Street in Tehran.

Two iron antelopes braided with silver detailing and shaped in long, feminine, almost erotic curves.

Islam for All, Simple and Easy by Reza Isfahani, bought at the airport on leaving.

A battered silver section of a smoking pipe, adorned with old coins on chains, to be turned upside down and used as a possible candle-holder or light shade.

A set of stickers for children to learn the letters of the Persian alphabet.

A lacquered wooden painting done in black strokes, with dreamlike images of a hand and a woman's face, like a warning or a prophecy.

One box of *gaz* (nougat) and one circular container of sesame-covered toffees the size of fingernails.

A wooden chess set with rough carved pieces and an underside *nard* (backgammon) board also with pieces and a dice which we were not allowed to post because all signs of gambling are 'prohibited.'

Miniature hand-done paintings torn from old books and framed.

Papier mâché pencil cases with artwork depicting scenes from mythical Persian stories.

Sunglasses cases using pieces of hand-sewn old material: velvets in blues and browns and greens, gold braiding, rough cottons.

Two large Baluchi carpets: one like a sandy profile of the rainbow, the other a mix of wines and aubergines.

A leather bag coloured bright purple, crocodile brown and sharp white, all zig-zagging into oblongs like a swinging 1960s accessory. On the back, formal court scenes of ancient Persepolis.

A painting of a goat woman in a dress holding a king inside a disk or a bubble.

A pen-knife from Shiraz with nude ladies pictured in the handle. Made by an old man who had just died, we were assured.

A mirror on what looks like a small golden egg with a long stem that has a perforated, peaked cap for the purpose of sprinkling rosewater.

An embroidered curtain covered in red and purple flowers on a faded black background from Turkmenistan.

A curved, triangular blue jug with fish painted on the sides, all cracked and dirty like it has been buried for a 100 years.

Mirrors surrounded by blue diamonds and green-and-gold birds.

Hand-printed table cloths with gold and red flowers.

Tapes of Shajarian singing a Persian dastgah, *The Secrets of Existence*.

A green hand-blown glass bowl cased and decorated with brass ribs.

Locks in the shapes of birds and camels and deers.

A woman's face covered by a chador, eyes staring out, graphic slashes for eyebrows, all imprinted on a transfer to be placed on the window of a Tehran truck like a *sharia* beauty queen.

A ring of blue and red and silver, like a segment from the back of a playing card.

A ring with an ancient Persian king stabbing a lion with a sword, his other hand seizing it by the mane.

A miniature of a reflective woman with a knife (or a leaf) and a wine cask.

A miniature of a reflective man with a delicate axe and a musical instrument (or a bowl).

Help!

A MAN, appealing for assistance on
a Parisian street corner, but no one speaks English.

Paris Help!

Paris is a Mist of Zeroes

PARIS. ZERO DEGREES CELSIUS. MINUS ONE AT MIDDAY. A mist so thick I almost jump out of my skin when the plane clears the clouds to reveal a landing strip coming in fast a few metres below us.

We seem to hit the ground faster than we should, and harder. Everything looks icy and wet.

In about ten minutes Lisa and I will part company. Gobs of emotion come up in my throat out of nowhere, a wild redness threatens me with tears as my whole face rushes with pain – then it's all gone again. As if everything is normal, nothing much is happening.

But Lisa is going to New York. And I'm going to stay in this cold world.

At the airport terminal she tells me she loves me as I am. That really does it.

'I love you as you are,' she says. Then she shoos me away from the glass doors she's heading through. Both of us crying our eyes out.

I hesitate to touch her hair as she moves away from me.

Two girls are watching us cry and they're laughing at our emotion. I don't know how to hide from their gaze. My hand half-reaches for Lisa's hair. And then she's gone.

Robbed and Crying: A Poor Man's Ballet

IT'S A COLD NIGHT IN PARIS. MINUS THREE DEGREES AND sinking. Fat gloves weather. With a hooded jacket zipped up tight to my chin to keep the wind out, I look like Kenny from *South Park*. Like I've been stuffed into my winter clothes and may never get out again.

I know it's not an entirely flattering outfit. At least not the way it 'sits' around the face. But walking down into Pigalle, the red light district of Paris, I'm depressed by two tall beautiful black girls who openly laugh at me.

The jacket is military issue from Iran. I was hoping they might find me 'adventurous,' that I have a 'just back from the front' intensity. No such luck.

After they pass, I loosen the hood a little. My neck freezes.

I don't own a watch and have awoken in a room without a clock. The radio is useless to me, and since I can only ask the time in schoolboy French – 'keller-hAY-teal?' – and won't understand whatever answer people give me, I'm too embarrassed to ask people at all.

The exactingly prissy night manager at the hotel already hates me for resting my foot on one of his chairs. Despite my profuse apologies it is clear I have done something unforgivable. So I choose to avoid him in the cupboard that passes for the lobby – let alone ask him for the time.

Which is how I end up three hours early for a concert by a Morrocan DJ and rai singer in freezing cold Pigalle. *Merde*!

I go to a small café, at first for a cup of coffee, then a glass of red wine, then, yes, another. A giant black drag queen in a red mini-skirt with black lace stockings is entertaining the proprietors with wild tales I can't understand a word of. At one point she amuses them all in grand style by bending over and making a farting noise. They all roar with laughter. I smile from the periphery, like an unwanted priest.

Opposite me a Japanese guy appears to be typing his novel into a micro-laptop. I'm scratching a few thoughts and a bad poem into my notebook with a pen. A very old, very well-dressed couple come in for a beer, waiting for the stage musical *Baz* to open its doors across the road. A few hookers walk by towards the long string of sex shows a block down from us. Then a gang of about six young boys runs through the traffic in front of the café, pursued by two bouncers shouting into their walkie-talkies.

Another Saturday night in the city.

I know this area of Paris is dodgy. So I have purposely gone out with a limited number of francs – and my bank card, of course, should an emergency occur. I have left everything else, including my wallet, back at the hotel.

Two hours pass in the café as I idly watch the scenery, not a word of French in me to help participate. I reach into my pockets knowing I am running out of cash already. The francs have fled from my hands.

Out I go out into the streets looking for an ATM. Multilingual pimps yell to me in various languages, trying to guess where I am from and get my ear. There's a competition between them to see who can best pick the nationalities of likely clients, hitting them with the right call first time up.

Out the front of a McDonalds there's a brawl going on. Nothing new there. Around the corner I see an ATM at last. Two guys hover suspiciously nearby. I glance at them – then away real quick – but there's that super-fast catching of eyes I always regret when I check out guys like this. Looking has its own wild politics, a kind of street diplomacy, and it is always, always better to take someone in rather than be taken in.

It's a busy intersection and my momentum has already carried me to the face of the ATM. I figure it's best to look confident now, so I proceed without missing a beat.

Bad decision.

I am breaking the first law of travel: always listen to the buzz of your intuitive radar.

An icy wind cuts through me and I have to put my gloves back on again once I slide my card into the machine. I start punching the numbers. Then give the OK instructions after a question about which language I want the transaction to proceed in. I'm hesitant at the machine – thanks to the gloves and my appalling lack of French.

Suddenly a young man is beside me, his hand reaching into the panel of the ATM. 'Excuse me, *monsieur*,' he says. I jump right out of my skin. And immediately start pushing him back from the machine and away from me with my right hand, half-guarding the money being spat out with my left, never quite taking my face from the ATM itself. Everything happens at a slow and steady pace. No jot of menace at all. He is explaining the machine to me in French versus English, offering to help, so polite, but I say I am fine, fine.

I calm down when I realize he is not one of the characters I first saw on the corner. But I turn back to the machine quickly and with a lingering territorial edginess. I'm outta here.

That's when I take the money. Reach for my bank card. And see it's not there.

I start pressing buttons frantically. Where is it? Then I turn around. No one there. He's taken the card. Fuck, he's taken the card.

My mind is spinning. I look down the street but I can't see him anywhere. I'm in a major commercial district: restaurants, theatres, book stores, that weird proximity of jewellery shops and strip clubs and pawn brokers that always characterizes a red light area, traffic everywhere, neon irradiating the landscape. He's long gone into this nest of light.

I know for sure he is on his way to another ATM this very minute.

He wouldn't have taken the card without having seen my pin number. I gotta cancel that card – NOW.

There are two phone booths nearby, both occupied, with people lined up and waiting. I can't speak French and I am starting to crack up. I ask two girls who approach the ATM if they speak English, but they veer away from me till I try again and they realize something is the matter. 'I've been robbed,' I say. I can hear the cracking weakness of my voice and feel embarassed by its helplessness. '*Parlez-vous Anglais?*'

They understand me well enough. Clear a path for me at the phone booths. But as I try to call for help I just get a long waiting message, and finally a phone operator who can't speak English. Click. One of the girls dials again for me, gets a number, but it is only the day phone for the bank back in Australia and a remote message: 'Business hours between 8 a.m. and 8 p.m., please call…' Fuck you!

I don't know the emergency number. My diary with it is back at the hotel. I'm starting to FREAK!

The police! I have to go to the police.

The girls load me into a taxi and wave me goodbye without much confidence, having instructed the driver where to take me. Almost as soon as we get rolling it's obvious he doesn't have any idea what he is doing, despite his confident replies to the girls. He begins to consult street directories, roving up and down the back-streets looking left and right aimlessly.

I eventually lose my temper and stop the taxi, arguing fruitlessly and having to pay what precious few francs I have left to an idiot who has helped get me lost in the back-blocks of Pigalle. I start running up a street to what looks like a phone booth on the hill and suddenly find myself running straight past a police station. Thank god.

I bolt in. Start babbling my story. They don't speak English. A guard stationed outside is dragged in to translate. He tries to be helpful but the officers on duty are very, very bored by my difficulties. It's like being trapped inside a disastrously bad French version of *The Bill*. One of the two officers does not even pretend to listen. Instead he leans back in his chair, foot on his desk, and turns away, firing staples at a wall with his staple-gun. The senior officer is fat as a sleepy cat with a droopy moustache and a thug-like air. He will not let me use the phone to try to call Australia and cancel the card. He has no advice. Does not want to file a report. Suggests I go to the phone booth up the hill. Points in the general direction and goes back to reading his newspaper.

As I leave I am almost crying. I hold back out of rage and the need to do something. The young guard looks at me pitifully as he resumes his post in the cold. He can see the trouble I am in.

I get to the phone booth. It's been vandalized.

I start running again. Spot a taxi, hail it, and head back to the hotel. I have to get that emergency number for the bank from my diary. At least an hour has now passed. I feel myself losing the battle here. But I have to call them and pray that guy hasn't cleaned out my account yet. My credit card is already over the limit. And I only have $800 left in my savings. If he takes that I'm fucked.

I pay the taxi feeling sicker as I hand over even more francs. Doing nothing since the robbery occurred but pay taxis to drive me vainly around Paris. I'm surprised to find the door of the hotel opening as I slide in my key. I almost fall into the entrance as it swings forward in front of me.

Oh no, it's the night manager – and once again he is unhappy with me.

'Mark, when you leave, ze door is not shut properly.'

'I've been robbed,' I say breathlessly, barely able to talk at all.

His English is not so hot, and he is not focussed on whatever I might be saying anyway. 'You shut ze door like this. Mark?! You see. Open ze door,' he says swinging it back and forth. 'Close ze door. Open ze door. Close ze door. Understand?' His head vibrates as he says the last word, a touch of moronic punctuation.

'Yes,' I say, beaten down to anything, anything he wants. Just leave me alone.

I bolt up the stairs, get my diary and the emergency number. Run out of the hotel again to nearby public phones. But my fucking phone card now hasn't got enough points on it to make the international call. And as I dial number after number for almost an hour, freezing my arse off, it becomes clear the free emergency phone services are either off or not functioning or that the numbers I have are no good. Operator enquiries are just as futile all over again. Finally I get an answering machine in Sydney: 'Business hours are between 8 a.m. and 8 p.m.'

Useless, useless, useless …

I run back to the hotel. The proprietor is now furious. In my panic I have again failed to shut the door properly. He recommences his routine contemptuously as I try to tell him I've been robbed. Till I am screaming at him, 'I've been robbed! I'VE BEEN ROBBED!'

He lowers his head unsympathetically. Tells me there is a police station back down the road.

Off I run again. Into another world of bored police officialdom. Two girls are supporting a young and bloodied male friend who has been bashed out front of a nightclub. I find myself vaguely flirting with one of them, gazelle-beautiful in pale blue hipsters and jacket, all the while she continues to support her injured friend and I try to report my robbery. I sense the drift of her attention towards me as she begins to let go of her friend and her girlfriend absorbs the extra weight, and for a moment the bank card becomes meaningless, simply floats away, but they are shuffled off into another room and my reality snaps back into 'play.'

The desk officer doesn't speak much English and haltingly tells me there is nothing the police can do for my problem.

'You speak French?' he asks.

'No,' I say.

'You cannot speak French. What we do?' He shrugs his shoulders.

'I want to at least file a report.'

He groans. Indicates he is too busy. That no one can help me there. Suggests I go home and forget about it. But I insist. If I don't file a report there is no hope of ever reclaiming the money. I have to file a report.

A detective is passing by. He says something disapproving to the desk officer. That my report of a crime must be accepted. 'Who will do this report?' the desk officer sneers. 'I am busy.' There is no one here now and the phones are dead silent. It is late and he is busy with nothing.

The detective tells me to wait and that he will help me soon. About half an hour later, as I sit exhausted by the flouro drear, the detective finally returns. Between our clumsy conversation in bad English, we file the report. I am so grateful for this man's patience on such an awful night in Paris. I go back to the hotel, tell the proprietor I must leave tomorrow (I have no money to pay for another night) and stagger up to bed.

I wake up and pack my things. It's 9 a.m. Sunday morning. I have to call a girl I have met once before and beg her to let me bring my baggage around and sleep on her floor that night till I can get my life reorganized. Amazingly, she agrees to help. All the while I am doing my best not to sound too desperate.

I have more than I can carry but the night manager does not assist me leaving the hotel. I leave the door ajar for him and drive off. Jam my finger badly in the boot of the taxi when I arrive at my temporary home. The girl has left keys for me at a flower shop next door to her apartment block. Somehow I manage to lug all my gear up three flights of stairs (she did say there was no elevator).

I call Lisa in New York and begin to tell her what happened. But after such a long 24 hours my words crumble and I begin sobbing, my story breaking up into heaves and tears. Before I know it I am crying and crying.

Having parted from Lisa at the airport a bare two days ago with dreams of being Henry Miller in Paris, I have been robbed and am just another hopeless tourist down on his luck. I feel awful. Broken-spirited. Lisa tells me to fly to New York and stay with her. I have the air ticket, just come to America and forget it all. Eventually my tears ease and I tell her I will make the flight arrangements and see her in 24 hours. That I love her and I can't wait to be with her again.

What I don't know yet is that my finances will be so tight I will get to the train station the next day with just 50 francs. Tickets are 48 francs to the airport. And so I leave Paris with two francs in my pocket, with quite a grilling at the airport by security who suspect me of being an international terrorist because of my visit to Iran. It's not all over yet by any means for me. But today I am just so happy to speak to Lisa and hear her reassuring voice.

'How did he get your PIN number, though?' she asks.

I replay the moment in my mind. The cold, the fat gloves, the way the keys are lit up and set low and big like the operating panel of the Starship Enterprise. You could probably see me pressing numbers all the way from the corner. Those two guys.

Then my helpful friend. The way his left hand moved in to point at the keys. He was so polite. My instinctive response: to cover the money with my left hand as it was being spat out. Not looking at his right, which must have hit the top part of the machine, where the card was being returned. His hand was there at the exact moment it was coming out, his voice startling me and obscuring the sound of its return. He had obviously done this a thousand times before. 'It took about three seconds. It was like a ballet when I think about it. Not one move was wasted by him. Not one.'

I deny it, officer. I fell ashleep.

A DRUNK
on the New York Subway.

New York Ash Sleep

I Get Lucky

I GET LUCKY IN AMERICA. FIRST OF ALL LISA GREETS ME and takes me to an apartment where I have an unexpected week with her before she really does leave me for good. We won't see each other again till I get back to Australia.

I am going to have my solitary writer's season after all – but in New York, not Paris.

The problem is, I still have no money. Lisa lends me some cash to tide me over for a few weeks, but if I plan to stay here for the winter I need a job of some kind, and I certainly need to sell a few stories to a newspaper or magazine. I start looking around at all the publications, new and established, planning my assault.

The end of the week comes quickly. Lisa flies back home to her family for Christmas. It is a repeat of our previous airport and terminal goodbyes. We laugh about it, almost free from tears. How many times can we do this?

I have to be out of the apartment she has rented within 24 hours. I don't know where I will go. A hotel if I have to. I phone friends and contacts to no avail, getting the harsh truth about living space in Manhattan. But an hour before I am due to leave some friends of friends call me back. Yeah, sure, I can stay a night with them.

I arrive looking like a bag man but the couple who greet me don't seem too put off. The night turns into a week once they decide I am okay. The guy smuggles me into his work one morning so I can borrow a laptop computer to work on at home. I type up a story venting my hatred for 'Cool Britannia' and the way the English have encoded a latent imperialism into cultural and media manipulation. I am determined to bring down the Empire!

I hand the story in to a magazine called *Madison* on Thursday. Friday morning at the internet café I have two messages saying they must speak with me urgently. I get home and they have also phoned. By mid-afternoon I am in a boardroom meeting with them on Madison Avenue itself. As we talk I mention my trip to Iran, which unintentionally creates the impression I'm a wild frontiersman – an impression I don't deter. I then retell my Paris robbery tale, my favourite story of the moment.

'So Mark, you don't have any money?'

There's a sense of deep American horror to this question. I don't want to look like a loser to them, but I'm flying wild, and my response is genuinely hopeful. 'No, but that's okay. I'm sure something will work out.'

The publisher and the editor confer. Then they write me a cash cheque for US$2,000 on the spot, 'an advance' on the story they have accepted. It is more than I have ever been paid in my life for an article. They apologize for not giving me a larger sum but they are a new magazine, a brave independent. They give me a promotional t-shirt as well. Walk me down to the street and wish me well, tell me to stay in touch with my ideas. I march along the bold streets of Manhattan laughing, almost hysterical, singing 'God bless America. Far out!'

Land of the Giants

A COLOSSAL, DENIM-DARK JACKSON POLLOCK LUNGES OUT over a sprawl of basketball courts on the Avenue of the Americas. His brow is tight with concentration, a large wet paintbrush in his hand, whorling fresh snow across the asphalt, turning hydrocarbon black into stone blue and cold white.

From a billboard he bursts forth, dominating the world: a god of action.

The basketball courts flow forward beneath him. An hallucinatory extension of the canvas he is pictured pouring over. I feel as if I am with him on the first day of creation. As if the image of Jackson Pollock at work nearly 50 years ago and the outside world are tangling into each other, becoming one. Everything cool in the early morning light, the air spored with moisture, dampening my clothes.

The painter is so intense, so there, nothing can stop him – not the poise of a documentary photograph blown sky-high, not New York City in crazy turn of sun and snow at once. He is mixing this world up in that domed head of his, holding us in a moment of wild balance. What a buzz to see him go at us after all this time.

Jackson Pollock may be dead. But today he leans into the city from billboards everywhere advertising a retrospective of his work at the Museum of Modern Art in Manhattan. His paintbrush reaching down from rooftops and skyscrapers like some elemental wand. Be excited! Feel it happening!

Welcome to New York City: land of the giants.

The city pumps itself up out of the pavement. The Empire State, the Chrysler Building, the inevitable tides of humanity on the move. Manhattan has a beat that seems to enter into people if it doesn't crush them altogether. A great big heart beat. It swells the best of them here into something bigger than I can explain. They have concrete in their blood, glass in their eyes, steel in their bones, and something else flooding through them: it's the city, the city…

Yesterday I saw the legendary singer Patti Smith at a corner grocery store. I had a bag of tomatoes in my hand when I turned to face her not more than a few feet away. To be truthful I felt her first, the doorbell jingling as she entered. Then her presence: an electrical message shooting through my back. It's what made me turn around more so than the sound of that bell.

She had on a scruffy suit coat that was too big for her, baggy pants, old running shoes. As if she were carrying a man's body over her own. Her raging grey hair was in pigtails. That Indian squaw look she has, domestic and calm, ready for war if you wanna try it on with her.

She put her reading glasses on to see something on the side of a food packet, to make sure it was right. I turned back around as fast as I could, away from her, dying to say hello, yet not wanting to intrude on her private space. Standing there in a narrow grocery store aisle with a brown paper bag wrinkling in my fingers, the ripe tomatoes hanging stupidly by my side.

I was surprised by such an attack of nerves. That I could be so overawed. I wanted to go up and tell her we'd met before, but I doubted she'd remember. And even if she did, why couldn't I just let her pass freely into the day?

It had been a press conference in Sydney. Patti Smith had come in dishevelled, a human storm getting out of bed to deliver whatever. Everyone was frightened of her, all the journalists – including me. She was funny, she was unpredictable, she was passionate. Everything you could hope for. And when the truth arrived as she spoke – well you tried to stay out of the way of her mouth. Her words could be surprisingly kind, or flamelike. A searching quality she could just as easily turn on herself.

The press conference was an edgy affair. It had only been a year since her husband and her brother had both died. She was out on the road promoting her requiem *Gone*, if a word like 'promote' suits someone such as Patti Smith and the exorcisms she was dealing in: part-warm New York rock 'n' roll, part-Native American mysticism, crossing over to the other side. Towards the end of the discussion she had asked us all about Australia's phenomenally high youth suicide rate, about Aboriginal culture and the landscape. She wanted to know what was 'really going on here. Can't anybody tell me something?'

Words were few in coming.

As she left the podium I caught up with her. I can't remember if I called her 'Patti' or 'Ms Smith.' Sometimes you can never find a name for someone.

I started to talk to her about Uluru. That great sun-red symbol at the heart of the Australian outback. I told her something I'd learnt from a poem. A story about a terrible drought that brought all the Aboriginal desert tribes together, encircling 'the Rock' in a ceremony appealing for water. Three days of singing passed, the various languages of the tribes unified by a commonly understood song and story, of which they each owned a 'piece.' Despite this long and ancient song, the sky remained hard and clear. On the final day, the singing reached its sonorous, earthy climax: didgeridoos, clap sticks, voices all calling and uniting with the harmonic drone of the land. At that moment, with the sky still blue and burning, the great rock Uluru bled water.

Patti Smith was not entirely grateful for this tale. In fact she was angry with me. 'That's a great story. That is a great story!' she said again, deeply frustrated. 'Why didn't you tell everyone? Why did you hold that back? Why didn't you speak up when I was asking about these things?'

I said I was shy. She said, 'No, you're not!'

I was shaking now and so was she. I almost thought she might cry. It was not the response I had expected. But then other voices came in and I was pushed back into the crowd of admirers.

Patti Smith was half-right. I could have shared the story. But I didn't feel badly castigated – at least not in the long run. Because what she was really telling me was this: I had a chance to say things; I had an obligation as a storyteller and a fellow human being to share my voice.

But there were other things I wanted to say in order to justify myself – things I couldn't get out quickly. I wish I could understand why I become so inarticulate at times like these, even when I know deep down what I think, why I act the way I do. Sometimes the force and language of other people's thoughts simply blows me away from my own words altogether. I can't seem to get them off my lips. In a more complicated way, I doubt the conviction of my own uncertainty, but sometimes learn to appreciate it later. Hesitation can be about sensitivity too, not just cowardice.

As much as Smith was correct to think the way she did, I wanted to tell her today in New York in this tiny shop that I hadn't wanted to draw attention to myself at the Australian press conference by trading in what I suspected was a sacred story. Aboriginal people tend to believe in their more precious stories being earned before they are passed on. That you have to be ready for them – and that they are not to be given cheaply. Honouring that feeling had informed my hesitation to speak up as well as 'shyness.' And yet I still wanted to give Patti Smith that story anyway, to connect with her personally. Maybe there was some false vanity in that, a lack of sharing with everyone, as she indicated. I still wonder about all those reasons running through my head. There's no clean split in the trail.

What I also couldn't go on to tell her – then or now we had collided again – was that her voice had reached out to me in another time, another place. As a 15 year-old boy in Australia tuned into an alternative rock station after midnight. Out through the radio came 'Piss Factory,' galloping, hot, angry. The piano and her Beat blast of poetry reciting her rage against a boring factory job. It was Smith's first single. Full of the energy of her brewing escape from New Jersey to a dreamed-up new identity in New York.

And there I was – thousands of miles away in another industrial suburb in another country – a sudden witness to refusing conformity and finding a route to prose freedom: some kinda sister-man, maybe, in love with her words – and then with making my own. She made me wanna go.

Patti Smith helped set my imagination moving to the nearby big city of Sydney – and in a connected way to Uluru and now New York. To becoming a writer more than anything else. And here I was in the 'Big Apple' feeling her standing near me once more. Frightened she'd recognize me; wishing she would. Her corner shop ordinariness another tribute, in my mind, to her democratic voice and the way she connected to the street.

Back when I was fifteen, I must have heard New York racing through her. How I love that beat now that I am here. Just to see her passing by for real. To see her walk in and out and know that maybe I will see her again.

So I get to walk tall in this new world – to dream I can become a part of it. Standing on the Avenue of the Americas, looking up at Jackson Pollock looming over these empty basketball courts, the pavement warming to the new morning and a long, long street roaring upwards into uptown steel and glass. That sense of a monumental lift-off, the drama of architecture taking my head! Is it any wonder people liken skyscrapers to rocket ships? Oh man, *blow me away.*

A week earlier, this thrill had turned to tears. Lost downtown by the World Trade Center, darkness closing in, a bitter wind coming in off the waters of the Hudson. I felt tiny as an ant. It was the first time I thought the city was too much for me. That I just wanted to go home, please. How could I ever hope to be something in a place so big? I was actually having trouble breathing. My fears enveloping me like an asthma attack, pressing down on my chest. I leaned against a wall at the base of the towers, using both hands to steady myself, looking for some calm moment within me.

I had become hopelessly lost on the subway system. Looking back it's funny now. Thinking 'Downtown' was a place, I had kept travelling further and further away from where I was actually going – the Village area. I had ended up at the World Trade Center in lower Manhattan in a peak hour atmosphere that seemed like a mad exodus, a desperate act on everyone's part to desert the district before night and its terrors visited. Despite

all the talk about New York's safety and the police policy of 'zero tolerance,' I still had an image of the city as an unpleasant secret held down
at night by sheer force. I returned to the subway and worked out what
was now obvious – that 'downtown' and 'uptown' were directions as well
as generalized locales, and made my way back to the apartment I was
temporarily renting. Beaten down from lofty dreams to the street, a man
turned into a boy.

These wild dilations and contractions are part of the life in this city, I
believe. Its monumental being. And how one tries to live with it. Swinging to its big, big moods.

A few weeks later I'd go uptown to see Arthur Miller speak at the 92nd
Street Y. At least I knew where I was headed this time. 'Miller fever' was
building for the fiftieth anniversary of *Death of a Salesman* and a new season
of the play on Broadway. Along with an amazed sense that this guy was
still alive and walking the earth at a ripe old 83 years of age.

The Paris Review was holding the talk as part of their 'Writers at Work'
series. I could see silver-haired editor George Plimpton outside the audi-
torium, holding court with a few exclusive guests. Long and tall and slyly
dignified, Plimpton made aging itself an ironic gesture, something good
to wear with a suit. I wanted to stand among them, to be noticed quietly
and respected for things I could only fantasize about doing and being.

There I stood, instead, for nearly two hours in a line, hoping to get
into the already 'sold out' evening. As luck would have it, I was the last
person given the chance to buy a returned ticket. The last person to pass
through a silk rope. The main doors are opened after the regular subscrib-
ers are seated first, and the crowd floods in. I find myself a few rows from
the very front, dead centre between two grand dames who have helpfully
signalled a vacant place between them. 'Over here, dear...'

Arthur Miller enters and I am surprised – and pleased, selfishly pleased,
I admit – to see how tall he is. It's silly, I know, but I am able to see a tiny
part of myself in his height, able to imagine myself being a fine old man
like him. If only height guaranteed ability! He is well over six feet tall,
broad shouldered, arms by his side, his weight towering forward from
the hips. Like a big, strong farmer. So alert behind his glasses it stuns you.

Begging off the applause he gets to work, weighing questions, speaking clearly, a practical man.

Miller is introduced to us as someone who has 'not only dominated American theatre, but world theatre,' an epithet supported with the note that he is 'the most performed playwright in British national theatre with the exception of Shakespeare.' What a life to have led across the century: the Depression, the Spanish Civil War, World War Two, McCarthyism, the Cold War, the 1960s, Vietnam, Kennedy, Nixon, the Berlin Wall, Gorbachev, Reagan, Clinton. Miller had not only seen it all, he'd spent most of his time operating somewhere near the eye of these events and figures, trying to get at the American condition and the moral struggles that enveloped its men and women.

I thought back to studying works like *The Crucible* and *Death of a Salesman* at school, and his screenplay for *The Misfits*, written for his wife Marilyn Monroe just before she died. Today he describes the desert cowboy futility of *The Misfits* beginning with 'an image I had of that area, of people who were floating in space.'

It had seemed to me there was always some sense of disconnectedness at work in his writing, a spiritual untethering that troubled him despite the political convictions that power him forward. Contesting that view, Miller claimed, rather, a fascination with the question of 'What is real? How do we constitute reality?' Then he went on to rephrase this obsession as another kind of question: 'How do we get to be sincere with another? Which is maybe a more concrete term for "reality".'

His deepest and darkest and best feeling is that we are all 'creatures of our past.' Something he references to a recent play of his called *Mr Peter's Connection* and a main character 'who can look at a building and remember what was there before. And before that. He's walking around New York with layers of the city in his gut and trying to find some connection.'

Miller was obviously also talking about himself here. What he felt as a man native to the island of Manhattan, and to America. Trying to adjust to the history and movement of the city, these great erasing or enriching forces. But it could be just as true for me, a new arrival looking for a place to fit in. How does one find a reality, a connection, when one is new? I took some courage from Miller's jovial response to defining what a writer is: 'I have the image of a man wandering around in a lightning storm with an iron rod in his hand.'

It is a Christmas morning when I see Jackson Pollock over those basketball courts. A light snowfall had come down the previous evening. Right on midnight. I'd noticed it falling and gotten dressed again just to walk out in the streets around Little Italy. My first White Christmas – and only the second time I had ever seen falling snow; the first time a bare six months earlier trekking in the Himalayas. It was fun to feel so excited by such a simple thing.

The next day the sun was out. The ice was melting. Buds of fresh snow were falling with an unbelievable lightness from some invisible cloud above. Sixth Avenue, the Avenue of the Americas, was 10 a.m. fresh. I could see the Empire State off in the middle distance. It was time for breakfast: a bagel, a pot of coffee at my favourite French café on lower Hudson Street. Too early yet to ring my friends here, even if it was Christmas morning. Just some slow time for myself in the sweet freshness of the city, to stare at familiar buildings which I felt something for as I passed them, and were, I began to believe, now part of a new pathway I was making and finding agreeable to myself.

Looking up at the giant billboard I could feel Jackson Pollock's brush running right through me with the breeze. Patti Smith and Arthur Miller's words were approaching me too, rolling like distant thunder from my past, down through these mighty streets. Their art seemed to fill their bodies and make them bigger and nobler as human beings, and do some little good for me as well. This was New York and I loved it so.

Pissing in the Wind

YOU KNOW, WHENEVER I PUT NEIL YOUNG ON THE STEREO, I find myself fifteen years old, learning to drive on the long free roads of Australia's Northern Territory, a bauxite redness in the land and the pale, ghost greys and lean tawns of the gum trees jittering past like wilting bones. The air seems to burn in the bush, to crackle in the sun, hot breath in an old man's ribcage. Nothing is moving, but the whole place seethes. This big, vast silence, crackling, while 'Vampire Blues' pumps on the cassette player and my mother has to keep seizing the wheel and pulling it towards her as I keep getting hypnotised by oncoming cars, drifting toward them as I watch them approach. Took me a while to get the hang of watching where I was going. Watch the fucking road, for god's sake, watch the road. Jesus.

I'm 38 years old now, listening to Neil Young in New York City, snow-flakes out my window, getting carried home to Australia and the dry heat of growing up in an isolated mining town. To those times. It's his voice. The weight of his guitar. Both embedded in me.

My mother had picked up on Neil Young from a couple of Canadian hippies who lived across the road in Nhulunbuy. They were mostly famous for smoking pot, walking around their house nude, and their two young sons, who had nearly waist-length blond hair and seemed to run feral, although Carol, their mum – who the kids called by her first name – used to teach them herself and they usually got good grades that no one felt they deserved. The boys were twins. One would grow up to be an artist in Sydney, the other stayed in town as a miner.

It could be a brutal town for choices. I used to watch the next-door neighbour's husband falling asleep standing up at the 6 a.m. bus stop opposite our home. His wife was fucking another guy, and he was trying to literally work it out, doing 'doublers,' long 24-hour shifts in solid blocks of two by twelve hours. As if he could pummel himself back into shape. Eventually he couldn't take it anymore, and he left town in a 4-wheel drive. There were no roads in or out of Nhulunbuy, so this was a danger-ous business at the best of times. About a week later they found his truck bogged in a dry riverbed, with him crouching dead beside it. My father was called in to identify his friend and neighbour, but he came home weeping, not able to recognize his dark-haired workmate at all: his whole body had been cooked black, his hair had turned white as a ghost. The sun had made him into something else.

Down the road from us were the Stevenses. Nothing but trouble. The older brother Tim was a skinny guy with black hair, a bad tattoo of a heart on his arm and a leather jacket in tropical weather. Just fucking dumb, acting cool without even knowing what cool was. By the time he was seventeen he would already be in some kinda jail for a few break-and-enters in a town so small everybody knew who was having affairs with whom, and when you went out to buy groceries, and probably what you bought as well.

My best friend when I was fourteen was his younger brother Steven. Steven Stevens. You'd think they could have come up with something… more. He always seemed to be in the shadow of his brother, who hadn't been arrested then, and I didn't understand then what I do today: that there was an anger starting to sprout up inside of him. I can't even remember Steven's face now. Just the sinews on his arms turning tighter. And how there was something prematurely manly about him, as if the boy in him didn't last long. But when I felt I knew him there was a looseness to what we did. We could just wander all day. Things weren't hard. Whether we took an axe to the tops of termite mounds just to see how long they would take to grow back, or simply walked down to the local garbage dump to scrounge in the smoke, we were animated slowly, hovering in our scenery, not quite shaped in what we did, what we were.

I was also slowly drawn to his sister Jenny, who was just a year older than me and Steven. The way she could glance at you. The cup of her neck.

One time I went to Steven's place to see if he was there. I knocked, called out and walked in. It seemed like no one was home, even though the door was open. The dry season heat streamed in like a balloon sagging over the entrance and into the air-conditioned room. I was glad to get inside, to pull myself beyond its weight and into the centre of the room. It was midday. Most sensible people were staying still, staying under cover. I stood there nervously in the lounge room, and called out again.

I heard a voice call me back deeper into the house. It was Jenny. So I walked down the white hall, past paintings of horses drinking and purple-blue impressions of Spanish señoritas. When I came to Jenny's room, she was still getting dressed. It's the first time I can recall having an erotic moment, her back, its nakedness, the false way she pretended to cover up, but unhurried, brazen, inviting me into her room without saying a word – if I wanted to make my own decision, I could.

I backed away, frightened, wishing I could somehow step forward. Not even understanding what I was feeling. She just called out then that Steven wasn't home. 'Okay, see ya later. Tell him I came over,' I said in a flat, hollow way, making how I spoke rougher, as if to protect myself from her. To sound further away, less interested, drier than I really was.

Later that same season Steven and I would go spearfishing in a local mangrove. We had our own spears of bamboo with three metal prongs made out of clothes-hanger wire, and we chased fish through the open, undulating shadows and shallows that faced onto the sea. The water was so peaceful you could still see footprints in the sandy beds where Aboriginal people had been there hunting earlier and smarter that morning. I didn't know what sunstroke was, and after a few hours I began to feel faint. I went to sit under a saltbush. But it made no difference to the nausea spinning over me. Steven didn't give a fuck and went back to hunt in the mangroves. Eventually I realized something was seriously wrong and I started to walk home, staggered really, losing my head to the sky.

It was a half-hour walk through the bush to town. The noisiest silence you could ever struggle through. A goanna came running, like a fuse along the dry ground, *so fast*, rattling twigs and leaves. I had startled it, and it me. Its whipping run caused me to go off-balance and almost vomit with a rush of fear. It slithered up a tree and some bark peeled slowly to the ground from where it had furiously scratched its way up the trunk. Birds screamed, something whistled a way off in the distance, I heard my own footsteps as if they were coming from someone near me.

Finally I passed through the local 'golf course,' really just cleared ground then on the outskirts of town. The greens weren't anything more than flattened sand and clay beds. Pathetic shit. It mocked itself and the fantasies of leisure that the town was trying to have.

I had that head-tipping momentum, where you start to fall forward rather than walk. It may have been 30 or 40 minutes since I had left the mangroves, but it felt like hours.

Later my mother would tell I had walked straight through the fertilizer sprays. I was so out of it I didn't even know. Walking through all these trucks set up to spout out some noxious shit to make this new world grow. Just desperate to make it home.

It was a brand new mining town and the whole place was still being set up. Still being civilized, from cyclone-proof homes to the golf course. The sprays were part of the making of the town, the invention of lawns. Quite a process. It had taken weeks. First people were encouraged to dig up and soften their yards with hoes. Then trucks had come round with decent quality dirt to make a topsoil. They'd dumped it in giant mounds out the front of each person's home. Then it was a case of spade or wheelbarrow, just spreading the dirt, beautiful and sweet, shit brown, rich, all over your yard. People had then been encouraged to go out into the bush and look for grass roots and runners to help with the next phase. So we went out and pulled them up like green rope, then replanted them, yellowing already. Giant trucks then came around and sprayed the lawns on, with what were like fire hoses spouting out this blue-green algae, a high-powered mix of seeds, mulch and fertilizer. Then it was a case of water the hell of it in this dry season. And water it some more. A whole suburban landscape drenched in psychedelic blue.

I came stumbling through a fortnight later, having spread some of the original dirt myself, the blue magic already comfortably, normally green, blades sprouting in fresh earth. A new round of trucks was respraying with a softer, clearer essence. And I just staggered through the fertile mist.

My mother started yelling at me about what the hell I was doing you bloody idiot, swearing at me in a kind, worried way. I just tried to act like I was all right. Not wanting her to know what I had been up to. They hadn't wanted me going to the mangroves, didn't even know I'd gone – now I remember the day, it was probably lucky we didn't get taken by the crocodiles that hunted there. Innocence is bliss sometimes.

Whatever my story, it became pretty apparent to my mum that I was in a fucked-up state. She was relieved to realize it was sunstroke rather than the sprayed poison I'd been blasted with. Figuring I was dehydrated, she made me drink water, lots of water, then she offered me a cold, sweet, strawberry lemonade that I promptly vomited back out.

Don't remember much else. Apparently I lost almost 24 hours in a delirium. Thinking of fish in pools darting away from me, cars coming towards me, bush ghosts, lizards, blue grass, blue skies, sweat, and me running, staggering, not even knowing my own name, not even lying down on a bed, just spinning through space.

When I came out of that world I felt so weak it was unbelievable. Sticky and drained. My mother had water for me, bread, some chicken soup with not too much chicken. I could barely make it through this geriatric's meal. Where had I been? It was frightening to land back in my own body and realize I could go so far away from it.

I didn't see Steven after that. And I was kinda pissed off with him for leaving me to make my own way home when I was so sick. For deserting me so he could keep spearfishing.

Then all of a sudden the holidays were over and I went away again down south to school. Didn't see him for a whole year. When I came back it had all changed. By now Steven's brother was in jail, no longer the rebel, just a dickhead loser. Steven's sister Jenny looked sexier than ever, but she was known as 'the town bike,' easy to ride. No decent guy should go near her. And Steven was headed down the same road as his brother, dropped outta school, no job, getting pissed, doing casual vandalism on phone booths and street lights, and small-time theft that everybody knew he'd done, or said he'd done, though somehow he hadn't been caught yet.

I'd already been told to stay away from him and his family as soon as I arrived. His sister smiled at me down at the shopping centre and I had to just smile back and ignore her then with a nod of the head and I'm on my way. She knew straight away what I was doing and I burned with shame. She was wearing tight jeans and a soft, old checked green shirt. She didn't look like a slut to me.

Steven called round a few times but I didn't call back. He finally caught me at home reading one day – there wasn't much else for me to do that holiday – and we sat on the morning verandah in the rising heat and talked. But it was all stiff. I couldn't invite him inside, though my mother did relent and bring us out some soft drinks. Then Steven tried to intimidate me into being his friend, to threaten me somehow. He had become much harder and I was repulsed by this toughness and frightened too. I did not know how to remake our old familiarity. Or even if it had existed.

He'd get busted trying to break into my parents' car a week later. My father just kicked his arse. Told him to fuck off and never show his face anywhere near him again. And that was the absolute end of Steven Stevens for me and my family. I don't know where he or Jenny ended up, what happened to them – eventually they just all moved out of town. I heard stories about jail and babies, but nothing certain. I was away studying and when I came back they were just gone. That was what a mining town was like. New people were living in their house. It was like they didn't exist anymore, except in old talk – and because of it being a mining town, with lots of people coming and going, not many people could talk the old talk anyway.

Funny to think how it all began with whispers that I could sorta hear. Then it became a fact without hardly anything being said. They were just an untouchable family. Then they didn't exist any more.

I felt like a guilty witness to something. And I found it hard to go from being best friends with someone one year to not speaking to them at all the next. It just wasn't my way. But it was imposed upon me – by my family, by circumstances, by Steven too and the way he behaved. Like he challenged our friendship out of existence.

I was pretty bored whenever I came home after that. So bored I used to kill time riding around town on the free bus, just sitting up the back, looking at the streets, watching the few passengers get on and off. This wasn't an uncommon way for Nhulunbuy youths to entertain themselves. Round and round a two-suburb circuit.

Alternatively, I'd cruise the sports shop, mostly running my hands over fish-hooks, diving masks, snorkels and shark chains, feeling the thickness of lines and weights, all the murder of the water. Or I'd go down to the chemist, which had a records section where I pondered *Kiss Alive* for a whole three months like it was an indecipherable mystery before I finally bought it. Read *Catch-22* in like three days. Then ploughed through a bunch of *Archie* comics, plus my dad's collection of crap westerns, a lesbian vampire novel and heaps of science fiction. A highlight was seeing Bruce Lee in *Enter the Dragon* at the local pictures when he had to fight in a hall of mirrors. I gave the trees, the telegraph poles and my sisters hell on the way home after that.

In the end though, I was experiencing most things on my own, trying to deal with how my world had shifted. Trying to fill up the space. Or live with it in my head.

My mother had changed a lot in this time too. I arrived back from studying to find her doing the vacuuming to 'Get It On.' She switched me on to T-Rex's *Electric Warrior* completely and at least a little Neil Diamond, though I could never hack my father bellowing 'Song Sung Blue.' I started to explore music then, to find out about stuff that wasn't in the Top 40. To listen to things I didn't even understand. That was when my mother started to teach me to drive on red dirt roads just off the highway to get me away from those oncoming cars. We'd listen to Neil Young's *On The Beach*, our mutual favourite, and sing 'they're all just pissing in the wind' and laugh and drive down to the sea, where a blue-pocked moon could sometimes be seen on pale afternoons, half-formed, hanging like an ear in the sky.

New York Conversation

'HOW COME EVERY BOYFRIEND I HAVE IS BROKE?'

'God's Judgement Day is coming. It's gonna be a bloodbath.'

'But I used spellcheck.'

'Are you a dumb sheep or are you a hard-headed goat?'

'A square is less funky. A triangle is prettier.'

'Men aren't like us. They just don't think about it. They just don't think.'

'Secret Service men don't get up early anymore. They get up at like two in the afternoon.'

'You know who a lotta people look like?'

'Oh no, it's a tall guys' convention.'

'I would assume part of the pressure you are feeling is that you are two big guys and one dog in one very small apartment.'

'Taxi. Taaaxi. Ah fuck it! Goddamned fucking taxi!'

'So I go down south. I've already been looking nine or ten times, and they're all dead except one guy – and it wasn't him. They're all old, whoever I look for. So I arrive and knock on the door and this guy answers. I ask for Larry and he won't tell me where he is. "Larry's in a lotta trouble right now. There's been bullets flying around here and everything. Call back on Thursday – by phone." So I call back on Thursday by phone. Larry's there. He says come on over. So I come on over. And as I'm walking up the path, I see inside the window. And he's sitting there. And it's me. Me sitting there. And I know rightaway it's my father. It's him.'

Scene: winter subway entrance, Union Street, New York. Four young black dudes, dressed up to the nines in their best sports gear, Nikes, windbreakers, tracksuit pants. All standing around rapping to each other without making a sound. Butterfly fingers and arms flapping and snapping and shaking. Deaf and dumb. Rapping the silent rap.

'Because everybody floats away.'

'We do not coincide with each other. If we coincided with each other I would have said, "Hey let's get up and dance!"'

'That's air regular. Sorry, sir.'

'Rock garden. Mushroom. Cactus. Pits. Bromeliad – there's nine. I know there's nine. What are we leaving out?'

'I'm gonna propagate money.'

'I wrote to Herb Flubber.'

'Well she came up with seventeen questions for us.'

'You are such a jerk. You are such a fucking jerk. We had a cab and we were going to have such a good time. You are a jerk. You are such a fucking jerk.'

'So you thought they was coming at you?'
'Yo, they was comin' at anybody.'

'Don't go in. It's shit.'

'We could go to the White Horse Inn where Dylan Thomas dropped dead from drinking. Or do you want to visit my cousin?'

'I know my son is deeply mad at me now.'

'…like white trash…'

'My sex life lately. Those two guys, man…'

'You know I've ordered pizza?'
'Oh my god!'
'Oh my god, yes!'

'I'm a real penny pincher. I don't buy this deal that because it's 1995, 1996, 1997, whatever, everything gets more expensive.'

'You know I was just watching TV. That picture with Farrah Fawcett. And it was just awful.'

'I caaaan't do up my shoelaces.'
'Well, you know, you got to learn. Don't be lazy. You learn to tie up your laces. What if nobody around? You got to do things for yourself. You want something done, you do it yourself. That's what you got to learn.'

Scene: a guy on the #1 train to the South Ferry, Manhattan. Searching himself all over for something he can't find. Jingle jangle hands like Parkinson's disease has him in its grip. Trying to get his hands into his own pockets, terror growing.

'New York's one of the safest cities in America.'

'My wife's gonna kill me.'

'Quarters, dimes, spare change?'
'No change, sorry.'
'How about a buck for luck?'

'Help me, help me, please help me, you've got to help me.'

'Well, movement is hard. Just sitting is easy.'

'I had this dream last night that all the tablecloths for my wedding were glittery green. It was terrible.'

'I used to have to beat 'em off with a stick. Now I'm 24 years old and I can't even get a man to use me for my apartment. And I live down the road from a men's home! And they say men come a dime a dozen. Well I got a whole dollar and I can't get any action.'

'Oi loik a ham sanwich.'
'Yep. Me too.'
'Oi loik ham in the sanwich. It's good.'
'Me too. I like ham sandwiches too.'
'Ham's good...'

Scene: the broken squealing of the #1 downtown train arriving like Indian war cries through Times Square Station.

'And then she meets this movie star. And the movie star is arguing with his lover. And then she runs away in a car and whatnot...'

'He knows he's in danger of his life here.'
'Judy, I'm a peace loving man.'

Scene: three street tramps drinking leftovers from Coke cans out the back of a supermarket, flapping their arms, slurping and swigging from hundreds of near empty cans, tossing them away and laughing on an overcast afternoon that threatens rain.

'One tea, very hot. With lemon. Teabag on the side, please. Croissant with butter. Two prune Danishes cut in half. Bagel, no seeds, extra on the cream cheese. One coffee, black. One light sweet 'n' low.'

'I love fuckin' talkin' to you, man.'
'Yeah.'
'Every day I fuckin' ring ya, you know what I'm sayin'?'

'Yeah.'

'I'm gonna clean my slate and start again.'

'Yeah.'

'I am. It's like gambling. I dunno.'

'Yeah. In the 5th.'

'No more steppin' in line. Now it's my time to shine.'

'You are so nice, Jim. Stay nice. Be sweet. Be your self. May God bless you.'

'Fuck him. Fuck him. Fuck him. Fuck him.'

'You invite me over to dinner and now you tell me you don't have any food?!'

'It's a transaction.'

Scene: two railway security guards with crackling walkie-talkies and guns strapped to their waist, laughing like thugs.

'Teo dropped his gun. 110–7th. No further. No further...'

Static smothers the message radiating from his hip.

'Teo dropped his gun.'

'How'd he do that?'

The static completely dies away on the walkie-talkie. They listen for more. Silence.

'Keep thy Jones to thyself.'

Laughter.

'...the people that are accusing you. That's right. Your grand style. You're shit. Listen! Listen!'

Scene: Beggar on the #6 train downtown. 'My name is Moses and I am homeless.'

'They don't care.'

'No. They don't care.'

'They don't care.'

'Stupid sack of shit. Ha ha ha. I'm a veteran, why should I have to pay. I'm a Vietnam veteran!'

'You got to learn to mind your own damn business.'
'They makin' it my business.'

'May God bless you all.'

'I'll calm down. I'll calm down.'

'Free information. Free information. It don't cost you nuthin."

Scene: A man out front of an apartment block, walking back and forth, looking everywhere but up.
'Hello Rudy! Hello Rudy!'
'I can hear your voice. Where are you?'
'Up in the sky, Rudy. It's your conscience.'
'Where the fuck are you?
'Up in the sky, Rudy. Up in the sky.'

'Hey, I'm a nigga!'

'Excuse me, do you know where *Garden Monsters* is playing?'

'I know my son is deeply mad at me now.'

'Ring the king.'

Scene: a drunk is awoken on a subway train with the sharp rap of a nightstick against a pole. He starts speaking straight away. 'I deny it officer. I fell ashleep. I fell ashleep.'

S&M: An American Express Story

IT'S LATE AT THE PARTY AND MARK V. NOTICES I AM NOT shaping up too well at all. He asks me if I want to go for a walk, 'take some air. There's a bar just a few doors down from here that you might like to see. C'mon. Let's go check it out.'

I'm happy to agree. He helps me to my feet. The halls, the elevator, the lobby, it's all snakes and ladders to me as we move down and out. But the oxygen on the street slaps me awake instantly, tiny snowflakes drifting to my cheeks, burning them.

We enter the doorway of Le Nouvelle Justine, walking over an elaborate wooden platform that turns out to be a gallows when I look back at it. An s & m bar. But kinda downbeat, struggling to be wild. It doesn't look like they do in the movies, all designer edges and slick sex under strobes and shadows. Instead the feel is ordinary drinking saloon tarted up to look dark and erotic – manacles on the wall, Helmut Newton prints over by the spirits bottles, queer touches that don't quite measure up to decadence. It's all a bit weary. We order a couple of over-priced beers, sit back on our stools and look about us. There's not many people left here tonight. Those that linger are a normal, even bland bunch – but for the handful of dominatrixes who get around with whips, mesh, brassieres, masks, black boots and general vampire bitch gear.

One of the girls sidles up to us, tapping a riding crop harshly in her hands. 'So boys, have you been bad?'

'Not me. He has, though.' I point to Mark V.

Mark V. pleads his innocence, laughing nervously. Like we're all in on the joke. I turn away. There's some 1960s French pop playing, just loud enough to mean everyone has to whisper into each other's ears. I guess that counts as intimacy, or conspiracy. I start looking at a guy who is laying himself down on the floorboards of the gallows. As I watch him, I don't realize Mark V. is now pointing back at me, telling the dominatrix repeatedly, 'He's been bad, very bad…'

'So what do I call you?' she asks me with a challenge.

'This is Mark,' Mark V. leaps in, proffering an unneeded introduction.

'And this is Mark,' I say, trying to include him.

We both laugh like schoolboys. Maybe we're more uncomfortable than we think.

'Yeah – like I'm your mother and I haven't got much imagination,' she drawls. 'Are you sure it's not Michael and Michael? Guys seem to like Michael as a fake name around here. I figure it's a Jackson thing.'

She looks around now at the gallows. Spits out a bored whistle as the guy on the floor is bound to some pillars. She raises a nastily pencilled eyebrow for effect, slaps the riding crop in her hand a few more times impatiently. 'Sorry, guys, but I have to keep working the room,' she says. 'Bye,' she adds sweetly. 'I might see you boys later.' Then she struts off on her particular, precarious black heels. Black knives on wooden floorboards. Stab, stab, stab.

Now our attention is fully focussed on the guy lying on the floor where the gallows are. Another girl in a dominatrix outfit is placing a credit card across his mouth. She struts around him in her stilettos. Then she starts to walk slowly across his chest, his body wobbling under the pressure. She puts one hard heel on his forehead. Surveys us all imperiously.

His arms are spread outwards, Jesus style, softly tied to the wooden pillars by light white cord. The girl takes a grip on both pillars and steps up onto the edge of the credit card, balancing herself as her weight drives the card down, stretching his mouth hard. I'm surprised it doesn't shatter or cut into him. Drool starts running down the sides of his now distorted face. I can see he has a hard-on through his white chinos, even though I try not to look. He is so turned on he is beginning to tremble all over. It's repulsive, but compelling viewing. Then he starts trembling even more, his chest swelling and subsiding quickly, sucking hard and desperate for air. Coming his brains out on the floor.

'American Express,' the girl announces flatly to everyone as she steps off his face. Her foot lands unevenly, one leg buckling awkwardly before she rights herself and parades off, reclaiming her dignity.

He just lies there. Not moving. With the card between his lips.

Gay Talese is Hungry

GAY TALESE IS WALKING DOWN THE HALL, RATTLING American coins in his closed fist. I hear their friction, the slide that is almost a jingle as they move. Sense the nervous energy radiating off him and into me.

He wears a tight-fitting blue pin-striped suit as if he is ten, twenty years younger than he actually is, cut too sharp, accentuating a clothes horse intensity, a gangster femininity to his long body. Where did he pull an outfit like that from? Tailor-made from the past?

He walks lightly. Looks away, haughty and frightened, rearing his head.

It has been a fine night. With generous introductions by Talese for two fellow writers launching their new novels in New York: the Cuban-American Oscar Hijuelos, awkwardly charming and wearily sweet; the visiting Scotsman Ian McEwan, poised, humorous, detached, all British charm with a stab.

Back in the 1960s Gay Talese was the man for whom Tom Wolfe first coined the phrase 'New Journalism.' He was one of the pacemakers for a revolutionary movement in writing. It's been a while since he set the world into a cold excitement like Ian McEwan has now, or captured the more pregnant, uncertain sensitivities of Oscar Hijuelos.

Is he jealous of these men, I wonder? Is it their limelight that has set him jangling and flashing with energy?

I hear him in the lobby talking enthusiastically, almost violently, about Hijuelos. 'Think about it,' he says to an older couple who look a little overwhelmed. 'There is no other Hispanic writer in America. Think! Can you name one?'

It is the crime of absence that angers Talese, an Italian immigrant's son who made his mark early as both a writer and an underclass champion. He still believes in the missing American voice. What some people call a dedication to 'losers.'

Of course there are Hispanic writers out there, somewhere. But Talese understands the way a big name can occupy the centre ground. The need for someone who can stand tall, act as a giant for all those disenfranchised and inarticulate and hidden.

McEwan has entered the main arena from a very different angle. With an eye for the bland fact, the facetious, the surgical flick of emotion: a somewhat frostier view of human nature. His is a most impressive reading tonight from his recent Booker Prize-winning novel, *Amsterdam*. We all laugh on cue, dancing to his words. Jerking wherever he wants us to go.

McEwan's American publisher is Nan Talese, Gay's wife and one of Simon & Schuster's most highly-regarded editors, so regarded she now has her own imprint. Gay Talese tells an amusing story of the literary infidelities that have gone on across the sheets of their marriage bed. The manuscripts of writers like McEwan nudging at their toes. The brilliance shining or being shaped up when you yourself lack a bestseller or something of fresh significance. 'In 40 years of marriage, I don't remember a night without other authors' works in the bed!'

McEwan is most flattered, able to smile. Talese is a very generous man, he says. Talese gave up his own study to serve as their bedroom for ten days when McEwan, his wife and two children first arrived in New York on the heels of his debut novel, *The Cement Garden*. That was twenty years ago. Now McEwan is the prizewinner and a British literary superstar. The trans-Atlantic friendship has endured. The weight has changed.

Oscar Hijuelos has only known Talese for five years. He seems embarrassed by the brevity of their history in comparison to the McEwan years, a little overshadowed personally and professionally today. Nonetheless Talese ranks him a great American writer, the first Hispanic novelist to win a Pulitzer Prize back in 1989. Did you know that? 'I think he is our answer to Gabriel Garcia Marquez,' Talese declares passionately. Talese jests about an employment history that included Hijuelos doing a stint 'writing advertisements on the subway… for hemærrhoids among other things.' It is the profile of a humble man.

After Talese's introductions and the authors' responses, the night rolls on. Oscar Hijuelos reads from *Empress of the Splendid Season*. He is a diffident speaker – stumbling once or twice over a word or an emotion or a scene. His story seems small and sensitive, nervous about its own existence. When McEwan starts with his opening gambit from *Amsterdam*, he is much deadlier, captivating all before him with a knife-edge humour.

Like most people, I will be so dazzled by McEwan I will join the much longer of the two lines for these authors as we all wait to buy autographed books after the show. Almost as soon as McEwan signs my copy, I regret this decision, the blank icy look in his eyes when I say how funny I thought he was. He is unpleasantly polite, or so I imagine. And I see Hijuelos sitting next to him, signing copies of his own book, not nearly so many, looking beaten and trivialized by a new monster in town.

All these thoughts and moments are held suspended along the hallway that night for a few seconds. As Gay Talese strides along in his pin-striped suit, a dandy on some invisible tightrope. Those coins rattling alarmingly in his fist. The currency of a peculiar type of American starvation oozing from him like static: the need to regain public attention, to be a great writer again.

The Chelsea Dilemma
An Investigation into a Forgotten Citizen

There has to be something called reality in order for us to come to its rescue.
— JEAN-LUC GODARD

1.

MARIO FATTORI IS DOWNTOWN. PAPER CUP OF COFFEE. Dead Visa Card. What to do?

It is late and he needs a room. But the Chelsea Hotel is as closed to him as the mouths of the desk clerks in the lobby. Outside the neon has crapped out in the cold January winds: the sign above the entrance reads 'HO…CHEL…' A few residents snigger by and into the elevator, shouting the new abbreviation to the boys behind the counter. Their voices cut back and forth through Mario, jovial and jabbing.

Some coffee sloshes over his fingers as he tries to explain his situation again. A waste of time, a waste of coffee, he thinks. They forget him; they *want* to forget him. Why?

A young man with a cocksure Sinatra walk approaches the night desk. Fine leather jacket to the waist, Mafioso style. He spies the older man in a fire red jumper and a brown suit arguing with the staff. Decides to ignore him at first. Other things are on his mind, like women and drugs and keys. But this old man, there is something about him.

'Excuse me, please?'

Mario Fattori grabs his attention.

'*Buon giorno,*' the young man smiles, picking the older gentleman immediately as a fellow Italian. He shoots the greeting a little smartarse and quick, *Milano* style.

Mario Fattori is amused by this young rooster. And his polite accuracy, the northern twist of his tongue. But things are going wrong tonight. How to contain it? Nobody in this world wants a desperate man. He knows it is best to hold on, to control himself.

'My name is Mario Fattori,' he begins proudly. 'Film producer and director!' He bows slightly.

'Tony. Tony Navarotino.' The young man shakes his hand. '*Fotògrafo.*'

The formal introductions still the waves rising in Mario. He takes a deep breath. No words follow. Tony waits – asks finally if he can 'be of assistance?' Then it all tumbles out. 'The stupid bitch I speak to on the phone won't help. Now these pigs here refuse me a room when I have stayed here many times before. Many times!'

'*Aspetta,*' Tony says, slightly overwhelmed. 'I don't understand, *signore.*'

'My card, these bastards say my credit card is no good. I am trying to ring Italy but the banks are all closed. I don't know what to do. I can't get a room. I can't make a call. This is criminal. Criminal!'

'There must be an emergency operator at your bank. Someone?'

Mario Fattori does not answer.

The desk boys at the Chelsea Hotel smile wornout smiles. It's about 1 a.m. One of them smokes like a chimney. The smoke disappears, but the used-up smell lingers around him. The other looks like a fat Puerto Rican rapper jammed into a secondhand suit that is falsely conservative. They act more tired than they really are.

'Monkeys. Bastards,' Mario curses them in Italian. 'And the manager! He is a thief! This is why they refuse to help. I threaten to sue the manager for what he tries to charge me last time for my room. This is the real problem. Why they make my life so difficult.'

Mario's rage pops out in a hot flush over his face and neck. Like a hand made of water spreading beneath the skin. The night staff pretend not to overhear, not to understand his abusive fits of Italian, not to understand his anger either. They do a lot of not understanding – it is their form of expertise.

Tony turns to the desk grandly. 'What about it, fellas? Aren't you going to help an old man in trouble? You've got to do something here.' He slaps the counter ironically.

The skinny one answers, 'Ah, he's talking bullshit, Tony. He's got no money.'

Mario bristles. 'You lie. You know me. You know me! Always I come here.'

'Yeah, yeah,' the desk clerk mutters, turning his head away, 'we know.'

Tony sees the situation has long ago reached a dead-end. He quickly whispers something to the fat boy in the suit, another arrangement, 'okay?' At the same time he begins to lead Mario away from the counter as a good son would an ailing father.

They stop near the elevator. Tony reaches out a calming hand to Mario Fattori's shoulder. The old man holds his steaming coffee cup close to his face. It makes him look lonely. It's then Tony notices a cluster of flesh-coloured plastic bands on his right wrist. Hospital ID bracelets. Curious.

'Try the public phone over here again, *signore*. Try Italy again. There must be someone. And when you have finished, please, come to room 507A. We are having a party there. Please join us for a drink.'

'Thank you, thank you,' says the old man, placing his paper cup beside one of the phones. He searches his pockets. Pulls out an expensive gold fountain pen, tries to scratch the room number unsuccessfully on a piece of paper. The ink in the pen is bone-dry. Mario shakes it, tries again with an exaggerated effort. 'It is not my day.'

UPSTAIRS THE WORLD IS ROARING. LAURYN HILL IS ON THE stereo, then some frenetic Miles, then Astrud Gilberto stepping light, followed by the rush of Beck's 'Beer Can.' The CD player is a battlefield for the taste masters, the jag of moods. Vodka is being poured into tumblers, coffee mugs and what looks like an old jam jar. Someone accidentally explodes an ice tray over the table. Everyone just picks up the cubes and throws them in their drinks laughing. A bag of mushrooms sits open over a pile of magazines – a few people reach in and taste the dried, chewy fragments.

I sit on a chubby black leather lounge. It reminds me of a swollen piece of licorice, an ideal set piece for a porno film. Deep inside it, I find Tony whispering at my ear. He is leaning over the backrest, squelching down close. 'Follow me.'

I get up with an effort, pushing myself free of the lounge's sticky grip. By the time I am standing up, Tony is already out through the door and into the hallway. I chase after him. 'Where are you going? What are we doing?'

Tony laughs. He's high, smiling. Waving a finger onwards. 'Just come with me,' he says like a boy who is about to do something he shouldn't. He reaches into his pocket as we hit the main stairwell and start heading upwards. Pulls out $60 and says, 'When we get to the door, I'll knock. Okay? A girl will answer. You show her the money and say, "I want one gram."'

'What?!'

He hands me the money. We're at the door already. My mind is still catching up. I'm feeling stoned – and a little paranoid. A girl answers. Tony steps back to let me in first. Having thrown me in the deep end, he's enjoying my struggle. I show her the money. Then I say, mumble really, 'We'd like a…gram?'

The girl smiles, leans past me, kisses Tony hello. She's beautiful in a way I can't define. An above-average blonde, short curly hair, dressed cool in jeans and a dark blue glittering top. Witty somehow in her movements, her facial expressions. Alert. 'Fred's out back,' she says, leading us through a cave of wires, electrical cords, computer screens, keyboards, musical instruments, amps, speakers, TVs, tools, torches, toys, with lights positioned amongst the man-high electronic rubble like glowing eyes.

The tangled hallway opens into an equally crowded room with a low ceiling and a disco ball sparkling over patches of yellow-lit life. A bunk bed is established on a pallet above the melee, and I see that beneath the bed there is a small recording studio.

A thin corridor between all this expensive junk leads to the end of the room where I am surprised to recognize the notorious film director José Garcia, the auteur of corrupt cops, rape and Catholic dementia. He's standing in a kind of enthusiastic stoop, grey hair wild down his back, body like a loose piece of flesh on a bent bone. Another attractive blonde is beside him, dressed tip to toe in a tight black leather outfit. Garcia keeps putting his arm around her from time to time, squeezing her in closer to him.

She keeps knocking his hand away, or wriggling free somehow, never moving so far away from Garcia that he won't be tempted to try again.

His enthusiasm for her is unstinting, with patches of distraction where his gaze spins floorward, or up into an idea he starts discussing with another man, who I now see positioned at a narrow table behind yet even more electrical crap in a tight corner of the room that passes for the kitchen.

'Oh I hate that fucking existential "I have my own religion" stuff,' Garcia laughs at him. 'Jesus, Fred, everybody's got their own religion!' He starts to cough roughly over the last word, lights up a cigarette. Some low jazz and night talk feeds from a radio by the sink. It sounds like someone speaking in Russian, cheap and far away.

I realize the blonde who opened the door is no longer beside us. She has somehow travelled parallel to us, straight under the bed and into the studio space. I can see her blue top making little pins of light in the shadows. She passes the guy in the kitchen 'my' sixty dollars through the framework of the bed. He is wearing a porkpie hat and has black eyes like an evil possum. This place is his drug warren, his nest of demented circuitry. It reminds me of the inside of a badly damaged battery.

I notice Fred turn to a cupboard near the sink then turn back with a dusty white sphere about the size of a tennis ball. He starts cutting into it. For some stupid reason, I don't know why, I push apart some wires and gear dangling from the ceiling to get a better look at what he is doing and say, 'Is that cheese?'

I really believe it's cheese, too. I'm not thinking very straight at all. The guy doesn't like me looking at his dusty tennis ball and moves it away slightly, muttering, 'Yeah, cheese.'

'Mark's just got back from Iran.'

So Tony introduces me. It seems pretty dramatic. I like the idea I might sound crazy, a frontline Ayatollah kinda guy. It seems to excuse completely my faux pas with the 'cheese.'

'Ireland. Oh I'd love to go to Ireland,' says José Garcia. He goes to sing a song that's indecipherable to me, then starts making a move on the blonde in leather again, who slithers out of his grip once more. He seems too out of it to realize that this is a pattern, beginning each 'feel' of the blonde as if it is a first moment, a virginal effort. Appropriately enough in this space, his short-term memory is more of a short circuit tonight.

No one seems to correct him about the Iran/Ireland thing, so I let it pass too. Tony asks Garcia if he's seen the photos that he took. 'Jesus, yes!'

Fred nods to a shelf under the bed. Tony signals the girl shining in blue from the shadows. She grabs a red box and pushes it through a beaded curtain that clatters lightly. The box is large, maybe three foot by two foot. Tony flips it open and starts to lift out two big black-and-white prints. In both shots Garcia has the same dangling posture he has tonight, a slightly out of control sense of leaning forward. He appears ready for some pained act of conjuring, hands casting a spell. In one shot he is open-faced, haunted, a tormented magus. In the other he wears a cheap party mask with spiders printed all over it. He half slaps the picture with the spiders and shouts at us, 'Leave that poor bastard alone!'

Everyone laughs.

Tony puts the photos away, seemingly satisfied. Garcia tries to discretely manhandle the leather blonde again. I get a small folded paper package – it goes from Fred to Shining Blonde then to me.

'There's a party downstairs if you want to join us,' Tony says.

Fred nods. He has a permanently neutral expression, vaguely friendly – but with no spark at all. For the first time I notice a video camera on a tripod just above the sink and I worry if it is filming us. Garcia seems interested in the party, and half stands up independently of the small table he's been leaning on, before reeling backwards lightly and saying, 'Sure, why not?'

Shining Blonde says to both of us, 'Maybe we will see you downstairs later.'

Fred echoes her. 'Maybe.' And we leave.

THE HALLWAYS OF THE CHELSEA ARE WIDE AND GLOWING. It is that washed-out time of morning when even light itself looks tired. The paint on the walls – mustard yellow and a weak rose or candy colour – eats the low wattage, dopes it out. Everything is slow-mo.

Mario Fattori shuffles along, shoulders hunched, neck and head turtling out to see what is going on in the world. Up and down the long corridors, listening to his shoes slide across the floor, their sandy echo. Me, and me again, he laughs.

He has a cup of coffee – the same one? – half-drunk in his hand. The cuff of his suit jacket is wet. You see the damp marks as he reaches out to closed doors. Touches room numbers with the delicacy of a blind man. Sips the cold coffee from time to time as a scientist might while pondering a difficult equation. Once or twice, he even knocks, small butterfly raps at silent hived-off spaces. He turns his head to the door. Nothing. Nothing. In the background he can hear the familiar groaning of the elevator shaft, always so slow. What a ridiculous hotel! *Stupido!*

For a moment there are footsteps on the stairwell. They go away. He feels suddenly, deeply sad. Why must God send him such footsteps?

He thinks suddenly of the priest who blessed him many years ago. Such beautiful, sad hands: Padre Pio. He looks at his own hands as if the priest might still be touching them. Sighs heavily. Then reaches into his suit pocket. Squeezes old rosary beads for luck. A superstitious act, he knows – sentimental – yes – but maybe Padre is watching from somewhere above.

Art on the walls crowds in around him. Some Mario recognizes, others no. In the lobby, up the stairwell, on every landing: fragments of people who have been here before, all fucking and drugging and dreaming.

Brett Whiteley's chrome-eyed mutant visions of heroin America; Vali Myers with a giant rabbit, buck-toothed just like her (yes, I remember her!); a royal portrait done with a drag queen as the subject; an explosion of semen like a large abstract nova (this one must have liked sex very much, Mario giggles bawdily); a horse's head scratched into shape, its black wildness scrapped like a negative from out of an under-colour (strong!); bad stuff, wonderful things, crazed shots of New York energy, and here, he looks closely, a tiny painting of a girl's face at a window in the rain.

Art, art everywhere, expression burning a hole in his head.

'Sometimes there are too many things in the world,' he says. 'People are too full of themselves.' He laughs loudly at the idea. Then he looks around, frightened that someone may have seen him talking to himself. Like a crazy man! He stops for a while. Sips his cold coffee suspiciously.

Wanders on. Talking some more to no one but the walls, raising a hand to invisible friends. Forgetting himself again.

IN THE ROOM MARIO FATTORI IS SEEKING, ALL THAT CAN BE heard is 'War' on the stereo. Everybody is dancing, chanting out a blankminded chorus.

José Garcia goes simian when Hendrix hits the speakers, leaps to the middle of the dance floor playing air guitar to 'Crosstown Traffic.' Let's rock! He staggers around the room, thrashing at the atmosphere. People clear the decks to make way for his moves. He's got a stadium thing going on tonight. 'Are you out there, New York?' he screams hoarsely.

There are about twenty people in the room. Settling into lounges, shaking the refrigerator open, twisting bottle caps, pulling a mirror off the wall, using a ten dollar note as a straw, exhaling smoke, popping wine corks, butting cigarettes out into beer cans and saucers, voices submerging and rising over the music, the chink of ice, clear cold liquid pouring, little detailed punctures of human air and activity amid the stew of sounds: a song, a party.

A digital camera gets thrust towards me like a bad nose. It's Otis. Right now it feels like every second person in New York is a filmmaker. I don't know when surveillance got hip, but digital cameras are shooting the shit out of the social arteries everywhere. Otis always has his camera out. A sinewy, shaved-headed six foot five inches tall, he's not exactly invisible with it either, although I spy him letting the camera 'sleep' a while on the mantelpiece. It's weird to see it and know it's there and still forget it anyway. No one seems to care. Maybe it's just part of the TV-eye fever the whole city is hypnotized by.

Things get a little flickery and I become aware of a soft heat tracing its way up my neck, so I sit down, take a breath and shake myself clear of it. I reach automatically for my vodka which hasn't moved from the table in god knows how long all the while I've been rambling about the rooms here. I can't remember when I forgot it. But the ice has almost melted. I drink the last drops, pull the slice of lemon out and suck it dry. It tastes remarkable.

Otis's girlfriend Nina starts pulling at my arm wanting me to dance, but I tell her I can't. 'Please Nina, you don't understand – I'm breathing.' I wave my hands across my face like an aristocratic lady who has just fainted. She laughs at me and says, 'C'mon, Mark' but I'm not having any of it. I cover my eyes completely. 'I'm just breathing. Ya gotta let me be!'

My heart is thumping. Rage Against The Machine get slapped on the stereo and the rushy vibe from before starts coming back on me, a quickening underdrive to the whole party that I know is pure over-stimulation, my biorhythms kicking hard to the bpms.

I try to steady my breathing. Suddenly, Tony comes in the door with a slam. I hadn't noticed he was gone. He falls down beside me. Up to mischief, I think. Always up to mischief.

'Hey,' he asks, 'no one else has come to the door tonight have they? I invited this old Italian guy up to the party ages ago. I was hoping to talk him into letting me photograph him. I was sure he'd come.'

'No. Not that I know of. But…' I wave my hands in the air to indicate the music. 'It's kinda hard to hear if he did.'

Tony starts to shout his enquiry to a few people across the room, but no one is listening. There are fresh lines on the mirror. A credit card is tapping away. The volume is going up and up, blowing everything away, us included. I feel my heart bursting to the rhythms of 'Sleep Now in the Fire.'

THE PARTY FADES. AND THE FEW OF US SURVIVORS DECIDE to go out, somewhere, anywhere. Tony, Otis and Nina. And me. We leave the party-smashed room and go back into the halls of the Chelsea. As usual, the lift is fucked so we take the stairs.

Otis and Nina stop me at the next landing to show me one of her paintings. I'm impressed it's been hung on the walls at the Chelsea, but they tell me that they just put it up themselves. What the hell? There's so much stuff around they doubt anyone will notice there's been a new addition to 'the gallery.' The painting looks like Nina's face from behind a rainy window – or as if she has scratched long downward strokes on the canvas over herself. I look at the two of them and wonder why? She stands there in a black mini-skirt and knee high boots smiling, and I look back at the painting, at what seems like another person inside of it.

We all start moving forwards again – with Tony walking backwards, talking to us. 'C'mon, let's try the s&m bar for a while, there won't – oh shit, it's him!' he says suddenly, almost laughing. We all turn, follow his eyes.

A figure in the distance moves and catches us in his gaze at the exact same time. He calls out loudly to us as the door we've just passed through swings shut, snuffing out his voice. We can still see him though, a tiny character inside the small frame of the door window. He comes racing along the hall, puts his face clownishly to the glass, then pushes it open, bursting through to greet us.

He embraces Tony first, speaking to him in a jumble of English and Italian. Then to all of us, darting back and forth like a tiny animal. 'At last I find you. At last.'

He blinks a lot and rubs his eyes, as if he's not used to surface life. He must be well into his sixties, nicotine-yellow teeth, a crusty old paper cup clutched in his hand with some coffee swill at the bottom. He keeps grabbing us like he can't believe we are real. I get the feeling he is so happy he could cry. Otis puts his camera on.

Tony introduces us all. 'This is Mario Fattori, everyone.'

'Sí. Sí,' he nods appreciatively. 'Film producer and director.' He taps his chest excitedly. His clothes look ratty. His face likewise, all thin and busy and hungry. His features remind me of Salvador Dali or Spike Milligan or a mixture of the two. Examining his suit, it's hard to believe he has 'produced' anything in a while. He looks on the skids. Like they're the only clothes he owns.

Tony suggests we all return to his room, inviting Mario to join us. 'Of course,' Mario says, throwing his hands open humorously. He swivels his body from side to side, 'Now I belong to you. We must celebrate this happy situation.'

We all laugh. He lifts his head up a little, raising his eyes towards us slyly.

Tony explains he would like to take a portrait of him. Mario is greatly pleased. 'How you see me?' he asks professionally. Tony takes his arm, explaining his Chelsea photographic project. Mario gives him an approving, executive nod. '*Documenta*! Good. I like the reality, not the pretend. Everything pretty, covered up, no!' he says firmly. 'We must move towards reality, always,' he says passionately. 'This is another kind of beauty, *un giaco di contrasti*? Yes?'

As soon as we get to the room, Tony starts setting up his huge stills camera in the blood red alcove. Otis still has his digital panning over all of us. I get drinks while Nina rolls a big fat joint for the team. Mario starts sweet-talking her straightaway.

He holds his hands up to her face, making a square. 'Oh, *bellisima*!' he sighs extravagantly. '*Essenziale, pura*. Too many men must love you. Be careful,' he says affably, shaking his head. 'Too many.' He holds his heart like it won't last the night. She laughs, charmed.

As I begin handing everyone their drinks, Mario quickly reaches for his, taking it without even looking at me, still focussed on Nina. I'm surprised at how adept he is, like someone used to being waited on. To having what he wants right where he reaches for it.

He looks at her with a flash of inspiration. 'I want you to be in my film. I know!' he says loudly to Nina. 'And you,' he points suddenly to Otis, filming the semi-seduction of his girlfriend. 'You can work with me as my assistant. For my company. Aquarius Enterprises. Please, I hire you.'

Otis keeps filming. Says, 'Thank you, Mario.'

'But first,' Mario says, dominating the room. 'You must promise me you will be kind to Nina. Promise me you will be kind to her.'

Otis pulls the camera from his eye. 'Of course, Mario. You don't need to make me promise that.'

'Perhaps my production company will also produce ideas you have.' He raises his finger admonishingly to Otis, 'Good ideas. They must be good ideas.'

Mario returns his gaze to the beautiful young woman with jet-black hair. He keeps stroking the back of her hand. Nina laughs softly, glitters him a smile. 'You will be star for me, please.'

He tells her, all of us, that he has made 'many, many, many films.' That he has an Academy Award, 'Best Foreign Film, 1971.' That he is very well-known in Europe. That he is here in New York working on a very special project.

'I have a new movie I research,' he explains. Mario waves us closer, secretively. 'A woman, experienced in the city,' he says. 'A village girl, sweet,' he counters, reaching his fingers to his lips with a kiss. 'The two young women meet. Here. On 23rd Street. What will happen? Who will be happy?' He spreads his arms out widely, taking us all into a suggestive embrace. 'Who knows?! I call it *The Chelsea Dilemma*.'

Tony signals he is ready to start shooting. Mario asks for a comb to tidy what little hair he has. Suddenly we are all around him, taking his coat, finding a comb, handing him his drink again, taking the comb from him, handing his coat back – all dancing to his tune. He puffs himself up like a little rooster. 'Tony, are you ready?'

'Yes, Mario, please – over there.'

'Tell me "Now", Tony, when you want to take image for me. Tell me "Now."' He lunges forward from the red wall where he is positioned. 'Tell me "Now," please!'

'*Aspetta*,' Tony says. '*Aspetta. Aspetta*.' He makes a slow-down gesture towards Mario with both hands. Adjusts a light so that he can get a sharper sense of Mario in the morning darkness of the room. 'More red, more heat,' he says to himself, moving a second light in closer. But the subject will not stay still. Mario runs up to Tony, brushes his finger around the circumference of his face and nods, directing him on what to focus on. Otis videos the photo shoot, as the photographer chases the Italian film director back into position.

'Tell me "Now!" Tony, tell me "Now!"'

'Yes, yes! *Aspetta!*'

'Looks like it's now or never,' I joke quietly with Otis.

Mario slings his brown suit jacket over his shoulder in a cavalier pose. Then he calls out 'Now!' loudly and lunges forward again like a bird of prey.

Tony does not take the shot. Mario looks frustrated, beakish and annoyed. PHOOO! A huge electronic flash system goes off like a blinding gunshot. Mario is stunned. 'Not now, Tony, "Now!"' Mario says, striking the same bird pose to nothing but the stillness of the air around him.

'I like to catch people off-guard sometimes,' explains Tony. Otis zooms in. Mario moves about, blinking in confusion, nodding. He throws his coat away, grabs his old coffee cup and strikes a pose. Tony goes to take his photo, but Mario suddenly holds his hand up in a stopping motion. The next minute he has a banana in his hand which he begins to peel and eat. It looks ridiculous.

Otis and I laugh. 'He's obviously a props man.'

Mario throws the banana skin away. Gestures for his coffee again. Drinks whatever might be there in that filthy cup. It seems like nothing but air. Tony shoots.

2.

ST. MARY'S HOSPITAL, WARD B.

A painting of a big-eyed, friendly dog greets you upon entry. Further along the main hall, some toy plastic sharks and killer whales are suspended in green shadows behind the face of a small waterless aquarium inserted completely into a wall. Turn right past this sinister still life, through a doorway, and you'll see foldout cardboard logs 'blazing away' in the fireplace – some Pop Art absurdity for the group therapy room. Above it is a Dutch map of the world, seventeenth century, imaginatively deformed with estimations and fantasies of uncharted lands.

There are just a few decorations in the psychiatric wing, a locked-door ward of the hospital. But what piece of mind do they belong to?

We've taxied our way uptown to St Mary's after repeated phone calls from Mario to discuss his film project. He calls at midnight, he calls at 8 a.m., he calls whenever a thought grabs him and a phone is free. We hear the chink of coins, the background of half-yelled conversations. He explains he has not been well, a foot infection. 'Please visit. I have not many friends in New York anymore.'

A big black orderly lets us in through a heavy door. We anticipate something out of *One Flew Over The Cuckoo's Nest*. But it is gentler here, duller too. I'm reminded of a bus-terminal cafeteria. Mario stands behind the orderly as we enter, hunched with excitement. He acts amused by his situation, self-consciously acknowledging the scene around him. 'There is no room in hospital upstairs, so they give me a bed here,' he tells us quickly, gesturing to his white room. 'I no mind. A bed here, a bed there, what is the difference? As long as I get out soon!'

We try to look convinced.

He is mildly distressed that Tony is now away working on a photoshoot. 'I have much ideas to speak about. Maybe I phone. I try him. You must tell him I try.' The worried moment passes. And the fact Otis, Nina and I have turned up starts to send him into a hyperactive spin. Into his room and out again. We follow him like donkeys on a winding trail. Mario begins taking us on a tour of the ward, introducing us to patients, nurses and doctors in a vague way that leaves you wondering who is what, treating the sane as if they have cracked and the broken as if they are whole. No one seems offended or surprised.

He leads us into the recreational room, which doubles as a communal kitchen. Picks up a small portable CD player off a shelf and rests it on an oil heater, plugging it into a nearby outlet on the wall. A large handwritten sign is taped to the player: 'DO NOT FRY OUR CIRCUITS. KEEP ME AWAY FROM HEATER.'

Mario hits the button, shifting the CD onto his favourite track. Billie Holiday starts singing a ragtime number. He begins to dance, turning his legs and feet in and out, his hands and arms the same way, a funky hieroglyph.

'Ooooh, oooh, oooh, what a little moonlight can do!'

He sings along with her, swings his index finger in a jaunty circle beside his head. Jives about apparently unhindered by his bad foot.

As the song goes on, he forgets words and ad-libs, 'Va, va, va vey-hey!' Claps his hands loudly, hits a stream of cutout pink hearts pasted onto a notice board, tapping them one by one. 'Mine, mine, mine!' he trills proudly.

The CD begins to speed up and skip at the same time. Mario keeps dancing. Vibrating across the room, speeding up himself. 'Va, va, va vey-hey!' The skipping of the CD gets even more jagged and ridiculous. Like a Chipmunks interpretation of Billie Holiday, a B-grade lunatic movie theme. He turns it up more. He is so happy.

'I *love* Billie Holiday.'

He flicks the CD player to some reggae for a few seconds, then back to the jittery Holiday track which he seems to prefer. 'Billie Holiday was my lover. For a year!' Mario declares. 'Yes, we used to sing together – only for fun. She was wonderful. That was a very special relationship for me.'

'Oooh, oooh, oooh what a little moonlight can do!'

He snaps his fingers to the spastic distortions of the music, smiling like a band conductor high on orchestrated bliss. His eyes shine. 'I love her.'

OTIS OFFERS MARIO A GIFT WHEN WE GET BACK TO HIS ROOM. A colour printout from his night at the Chelsea Hotel, taken off the digital camera.

Mario is triumphant. 'This is me,' he says admiringly. 'This is me!'

He goes out the door and begins declaring to everyone in the ward that we are journalists and documentary makers here to 'make a story' on him. We cringe, hoping no one will believe him or ask us to explain what we are doing visiting a virtual stranger in a psychiatric clinic.

Mario grasps the image tightly and marches ecstatically down the hospital hall. He meets a man in a kimono whose glasses appear thrown onto his face rather than placed there.

'Look,' says Mario. 'This is me! A portrait.'

The kimono man leans into the photo. His disarrayed glasses don't help a need to get closer and closer till his nose is touching the picture. He looks up at Mario, then back to the print, then to Mario and to the print again.

In a deep, droogy voice, he says, 'You look like God.'

Mario laughs. Points to the man. Then rubs his fingers together as if they are holding a pinch of salt. He throws the imaginary salt over his shoulder.

'Like God,' Mario repeats to him, beginning to laugh again. He looks at the photo, then straight at us, shaking his head.

I TAKE TO VISITING MARIO EVERY DAY OR SO WHILE HE IS IN hospital. Everybody else gets sucked back into their lives. I'm the only tourist in town. The only one with time to burn. And I'm genuinely curious too about who Mario really is.

One morning he wants to discuss 'a collaboration' with me. A film script. 'I think you understand my ideas,' he says passionately. I say 'sure.' But he picks up immediately that I am humouring him. I feel suddenly naked with what it says about me: visiting a disturbed man I hardly know.

Why am I here at all? If not to believe him?

Mario chooses to overlook what I am sure he has seen, all my thoughts netted in a single action. I feel him letting me go, setting me free again. As if he needs to believe in me and not let these questions invade the relationship.

By his hospital bed, I see that Mario has some musk cologne 'For Men' and a book, *The Anderson Tapes*, an old hardback by someone called Lawrence Sanders. It looks like an airport novel from an age when airports were novel. The room is stuffy, stale. A tap drips into a small wash basin where Mario keeps his milk container and some fruit, one pear and one apple. When I look at the dripping water he says, 'It stay fresher this way. My own refrigerator, I make. An innovation!'

I look across to Mario. His eyes are bloodshot and weary. It looks like he slept in his clothes last night. I think he might cry.

'Thank you for visiting me,' he says, tears welling suddenly. 'Thank you. You give me ten years. Just by coming to see me. You give me. You give me…'

MARIO'S JOB TODAY IS TO TIDY UP ALL THE PULP NOVELS AND magazines left around the ward and stack them neatly together in the reading room. We are in the ward 'library' now, a motley collection of ad-hoc bookcases full of tired-looking copies of Reader's Digest. He flicks at them distastefully. 'For my mind,' he scoffs, 'for my mind!'

'Have you got any cigarettes?' he says sneakily, looking over his shoulder.

Before I can answer, he tiptoes to the doorway, looks down the hall towards the main desk. Turns back and whispers harshly across the linoleum space between us: 'Three cigarettes a day they give me.' He holds three fingers up like a crude insult and shakes his head. 'And I smoke pot! This is ridiculous.'

'Look at what I do,' he adds furtively, weaving my attention towards him with those same fine fingers. He creeps to a cupboard. Holds it as he silently slides a drawer towards him and pulls out a few hidden butts. He lets out an evil giggle. The trivial malevolence in him unsettles me.

He is dressed in black suit pants and an old white T-shirt with the giant face of a teenage boy printed on it. He looks like an aging gentleman punk. It takes me a long while to work out that the face belongs to a very young Leonardo DiCaprio. It's probably a collector's item, not that he'd know or care. But stretched out disproportionately across Mario's chest, the boy star looks hideous, a Hollywood imbecile melting down out of an old man's throat like a misdirected genie.

There are some severe marks at Mario's inner elbows where needles and drips have been inserted. He also has three new plastic bands on his wrist. He has been around the institution since we last spoke. Trying different techniques, different medicine, before returning to Ward B. The wrist bands clatter thinly when he moves.

HIS BRIEFCASE IS SITTING SHUT BESIDE HIM ON THE BED. IT is covered in a garish vinyl pattern made up of car registration plates from all over the USA: Florida, Arizona, Seattle, Washington, Texas, Montana...

Visible inside once he flips the lid: a leaflet for back-pain; decade-old head-shots of models, dated by their hairdos; crumpled faxes with telephone numbers all over them; rolly papers, but no tobacco or dope; a black-and-white picture of a woman that he pries out and shows me. 'She was my lover. She died of cancer. Beautiful. I never forget.' He shuts the case again quickly on her.

Mario then pulls a pale white paper plate out from under his pillow. Ideas, names, phone numbers, addresses, little arrows and diagrams are written all over it in black texta: 'This is my movie. *The Chelsea Dilemma.*'

Mario opens his briefcase again narrowly and puts the paper plate inside it for security. Before he can close it, a small religious photo catches my eye as it slides into a corner. 'Who is the priest?' I ask quickly.

'Father Pio. He can be in two different places at once. He have ability of bilocation. Yes. Two man at once. He also have the sign of Jesus Christ,' says Mario emphatically. 'Blood.' And with that he points to his own palms, meaning stigmata. 'Blood comes for him every day. He die in 1969. After many miracles. Always his bleeding disappear then return, day after day. I follow him.'

HE PULLS A LITTLE TAPE RECORDER OUT OF HIS BRIEFCASE. 'It is like a talking book for me. I say what happens everywhere to me. My dictaphone for ideas.' He clicks it on. 'Hello? Hello?' He is joking. 'I'm here.'

He laughs and clicks it off with a flourish. 'Please, now, interview me.' I do not ask a question.

He starts talking about his friendship with Jimi Hendrix. How he was in London the day he died. He thinks Hendrix was an alien because of the way they communicated, hinting at telepathy. 'I make a lot of film, 8 mm, with him. We spend weekend together, always he play. He hardly say a word, but we speak.'

Inevitably I ask him about Billie Holiday. 'That I think the most important meeting of my life. She revealed to me the *dimension* of music. Three months before she died she was in Milano. When she feel worst,' Mario says, making an injecting motion into his arm. 'She didn't like no more to live. She give up.' He looks devastated. 'She say, "Mario, I can't live this way. World don't respect me. So I leave." I have letters,' he nods, becoming very melancholy. Then slaps his thighs and points at me and says, 'She have a lot of humour.'

He thinks we should remember this laughter in her.

'Gerry Mulligan is a musician I also like very much. He has a record called *Summit*. With Astor Piazzolla, who plays the accordion. The music is incredible. So fantastic! Especially done for my film. I will send you copy.'

This was when you got an Academy Award?

Mario gets confused. 'No. Yes. The Academy Award film was *Investigation of a Citizen Above Suspicion*. The director was Elio Petri. I co-produced with Danielle Senatore. *Indagine su un Cittadino al di Sopra di Ogni Sospetto*. 1970.'

He says all this very proudly. But like someone who has lost something he cannot find. A nurse enters the room. Lithium time. He pops it into his mouth, drinks a tiny cup of water. Smiles. She leaves. He stands, goes to the sink. Pokes his tongue out with two pale blue tablets on it. Spits them out. They land with a chalky clink into the basin. He turns on the tap and lets the water wash them away.

'If I take that, I don't feel Mario Fattori. At this point, I rather take cocaine.'

I ignore him because I think he is showing off. But I really start rolling with our interview now. 'Did you ever meet Fellini?' I ask.

'Fellini was a close friend. Fantastic man! A poet. Also Tonino Juerra who wrote all Fellini's films was very good friend. Part of my heart. He believe in me very much. He say, "Mario, you got to do something more. Do something more."'

Mario shrugs his shoulders. 'So, they teach me. All teach me. But I have my own personality. I am always reaching for my own way to communicate.' This is why he is now obsessed with the digital revolution and the independence it brings, he explains. He puts his hands around something invisible in front of him. Holds the vision. 'I work like a mosaic.'

Right now he needs to get out of hospital and go to Los Angeles. CBS are interested in a made-for-TV project he has. 'It is called *The Sandy Story* or maybe *The Tender Trap*. It is documentary fiction. A real person. She call me in Italy. Ask me to come to America again – tell me she has a problem. We know each other because we have love affair 26 years ago. She is alcoholic, drugs. I make a movie with her in six days about her life. CBS cannot believe it!'

He says David Letterman liked it too. 'Next week, I am on show. I have been on before. He is a friend of mine. Always he is very fast. Last time I see him, I go like this,' Mario says, making giant sniffing noises. 'I say, "Hey what is quality of your Colombia?" He go, "Ha, ha, ha." Then run away.'

Mario sniffs again. He can't stop laughing. 'Letterman.'

Mario has many film ideas 'in development.' One called *The Power Against the Power* that he cannot say anything about. It is a secret. 'Another film I have is *To Be or Not To Be, That is the Joke*. Who say to be or not to be is a tragedy – no, is a joke! The most important thing is to be – and to love each other!'

And, of course, *The Chelsea Dilemma*. Mario repeats 'the scenario' again. Saying it seems to make it real for him. 'In the world-famous Chelsea Hotel live a top model, very lucky. She is the best. In another Chelsea

Hotel across town, same name, different place, live another model. No one knows her. Her hotel is small hotel, filthy but fantastic, run by Indians. It is terrible, but wonderful, you understand?

'So, in New York two Chelsea Hotel exists. Two beautiful girls. Then an exchanging occurs,' he says, swapping his hands back and forth. 'Who will be happy? Who is the Chelsea that is the best?' Mario shrugs his shoulders joyfully. 'Who knows?'

'You must go to the Chelsea Inn. Go there. It is at 23rd West right till end at the river. On the Chelsea Pier. Ask for Mahni, she is beautiful. Oh you must ask for Mahni. Say you are a friend of Mario. She will know you.'

He has all the details written on that white disposable paper plate of his. A crowd of phone numbers, locations, dramatic phrases, his heroines Nina and Mahni…all in black texta colour.

Mario eyes me quizzically. Points to the paper plate in his hand. 'You like this very much. My paper plate. Yes?'

'Yes I do, Mario.'

He laughs. 'Columbia Pictures like this idea very much too.'

'Have you seen Andy Warhol's *Chelsea Girl*?' I ask him. Mario ignores the nature of the question. 'Andy Warhol was clever,' Mario says, raising his eyebrows. 'Clever.' There is a long pause. 'He was a friend of mine. He build up an image of him,' Mario says, passing his hand over his face like a moon, 'for make a lot of money.'

'What about where you came from, Mario?'

'I was born near Milano, in a little village. And I dream since I was young to make a movie, to write a theatre. And I wrote it! Many pieces.'

A woman dressed in white now enters. Another nurse, I think. Mario flirts with her. Puts his finger into a small blood-pressure device applied to his index finger. 'I think I have the pressure like a baby. 120 over 70 is really like a young man?' She agrees. Sticks a thermometer in his mouth, waits, plucks it out, shakes it. 'Temperature 98.6.'

'So I am well. I can fly away,' says Mario easily. 'Soon I fly away. Not tomorrow, not the next day, but the next day, I fly.'

Mario grows thoughtful. 'When I leave here, I leave a piece of my heart,' he says sadly.

I'm surprised. 'Why would you miss this place?'

'The crazy people – I have a special consideration for the crazy people. Like the Indian has a respect for crazy – they have a vision in the mind,' he says tapping the side of his skull. He gestures out beyond his hospital room to the whole ward. 'I prefer these people to certain people.'

He gets up off the bed and limps out into the hall. His foot seems to be getting worse not better. A man with a deformed, elongated face is sitting in a wheelchair dribbling. I'm repulsed. But Mario goes up to him and starts stroking his head, stroking it softly like a baby. He whispers to him in Italian, kisses his head. Keeps patting away as the man dribbles and makes noises that somehow approximate joy.

THE NEXT TIME WE MEET, THE LAST TIME WE MEET, MARIO does not speak much and is very serious. He is being returned to Milan. A doctor stops by the room to inform him that the Italian embassy is sending a car tomorrow morning to take him to the airport. Tickets have been arranged. He will fly to Munich first via Zurich, where he has stop-overs for a few days. 'Some business. I like Zurich.'

His son will pick him up at the airport in Milan. It will be spring in Italy. 'My favourite season.'

'What about *The Late Show with David Letterman*?'

'What?'

'David Letterman.'

He says nothing.

'I thought you were appearing on it.'

'No.'

There is silence again. It is a violent silence, like something has been broken. I instantly realize he does not want to talk about Letterman. That Letterman no longer exists as a subject.

Mario apologizes to me, but he has a group therapy session soon and cannot talk for long. His eyes are heavy and bloodshot like a beaten hound. I feel more uncomfortable about being here than at any time since I have been visiting him.

He gives me his address. 'Maybe we will meet again in New York.' The words feel hollow. Meaningless. But I know that he recalls my visits, our conversations. At the same time he is suspicious. After all, who am I?

We say our goodbyes. Mario shakes my hand. I can't tell if there is any closeness, anything left between us. I am let out of the ward by the same male orderly who first let us in twelve days ago. A female doctor is also leaving. She asks me how I know Mario and I explain, in the vaguest terms, our Chelsea connection. I finish by saying, 'He seems a little down today.'

'No,' she says, 'I don't think he is down. I think what you are seeing is the real him. I think he is a very serious, quiet, creative man. But when he has these episodes and takes cocaine he is very different to the person you see today. The Mario you met today is probably Mario as he really is.'

We're outside the hospital now. It's a windy, half-wet winter's day, lost between the morning snow and the light rain of the afternoon. When we spoke inside, Mario told me he disliked heavy weather days such as these. 'People do not like each other on such days. This is no time to speak. New York, on days like this, is not so good. I see it in faces. They have not time to be a human being. Not time to look at each other. Running always, above ground, below ground. Where they go in such a hurry?'

3.

FOR A GOOD YEAR I TRY TO TRACK DOWN ANYTHING I CAN find about him through the internet, through books and casual enquiries, without any success. There is no mention of him either when I eventually find the production notes to *Investigation of a Citizen Above Suspicion*, an almost forgotten Academy Award-winning Italian film from 1970. All the people he spoke of are there in the credits: his so-called 'co-producer,' the director, the actors too. But no Mario Fattori.

I am not disillusioned – there are still shreds of possibility. Nothing he has told me checks out as untrue. Indeed I'm surprised how accurate his ravings are. Maybe he was financing it from behind the scenes? It's possible.

But I can find nothing on him anywhere else that would suggest a place in Italian cinema. And I start to give up on his story. Then I discover and order the CD *Summit* ('*Reunion Cumbre*') by Astor Piazzolla and Gerry Mulligan. I don't expect much to emerge. It's a last gesture. I'm just glad it exists.

It arrives in the post and I put it on the stereo: rich, over-romantic music latticed with an Italian ache. It does not support itself as a stand-alone work of art, despite moments of beauty and drama. One actually sees things happening with it, a beautiful woman walking down a street or a handsome man driving a car. It is obviously a soundtrack. But there is no mention of any film accompanying it.

Credited as the producer of the recording, though, is one name: 'Mario Fattori.' And in seeing that name some piece of reality falls through time towards me to the melodic squeezing and smoke of a *bandonéon* and a saxophone.

Hearing it, I imagine seeing Mario again: down that long corridor at the Chelsea Hotel. Far from us, touching the numbers of doors. In a wilderness of light. He turns and spots us and opens his arms and eyes in a wide expression of disbelief. Then he moves towards us like long lost friends. We know him not. But he embraces us. 'At last I find you. At last.'

Wild Girl in New York City

So you're a wild girl
with your blonde hair
and your canvas bag,
your acne breakouts
and slouchy cool,
pizza fucked!

the city after 12
on your black-nailed fingertips
in your spooky blue eyes,
the greasy straggle
of your stolen-drinks wit
and the way you eat alone

careless as a vixen
in the early a.m. takeaway.

Are you outta school?
Are you on the street?
Are you playing games
that can take you down?

Wild girl
I see you twice
in New York!

the next night
catching the 'B' downtown
with an ugly girlfriend
laughing and whispering,
'Diamond Dogs'
graffitied on your jeans.

Are you going to be a star?
Are you gonna break a heart
and be remembered
long after you fall
as a wild girl
in New York City

bad skin,
body like a lamb,
beautiful
temporary
eyes
like a clear February sky
blue, blue, blue.

I Sat Down by Columbus and Wrote

I SAT DOWN BY COLUMBUS, EATING A HOT DOG WITH mustard ketchup on a broken bench in Central Park. Looking at the dark, shining coldness in his face, wondering if you could describe his lips as sensitive? Spilling sauerkraut on the ground in a great filthy splodge, along with half a bottle of Coca-Cola all over my jeans, like I'd just pissed myself on a sunny New York winter's day.

All sticky and oniony and sated once I was done. Burping loudly because no one else was close enough to hear me. Feeling the warm sun on my face, closing my eyes and quietly laughing at my own rudeness. Seeing warm reddish spores of light move over my eyelids. Thinking about my terrible temper and how I needed to control it better. To not let small things *get* to me in the way that I often did.

Why couldn't I let things go more, I wondered? This anger that tore through me on trivial currents. I breathed inwards deeply and wanted to phone someone close and apologize. To say I was sorry for the awful things I had done.

The feeling slipped away with the sun as I breathed outwards again and visualized my breath as a colour, a cool ultramarine blue. A beautiful demon leaving the soul. Free for a little while.

I opened my eyes and looked at the man whose Spanish name means 'dove.' Statues can be such funny things – it's as if there is someone inside them for real, an undeparted mortality. I always feel as if they have sacrificed themselves for me. That I owe them something and they are waiting for me.

I imagined Columbus as an astronaut on the ocean, ready to fall off the edge of the world. Landing here and being turned to stone. Locked in his greatness.

America hummed in the distance. An almighty turning of car engines and wheels through skyscraper streets. Somewhere in the park loud music was playing, indecipherable faraway raucous music, the melody hanging in the air like soft, frayed wires that teased electrically at the ears. I wanted to know what song it was but I couldn't quite hold it together in my head.

It slipped away on the breeze, came back in spirals and thumps and buzz-ing clouds. A dance song.

Children were back down along the path, through a tunnel and past a grassy embankment. Playing around a statue of 'Balto the wonderdog.' I couldn't see them from where I was sitting but I knew they were there.

'You don't know who Balto is?!'

I had met a family down there and learnt all about Balto from their children, who sat on his back and hugged his neck and had their photo taken. They had seen the animated video of his life 'five times' and could report to me in detail on the true story of his very fine adventure – how Balto had led a crew of sledge-dogs through the Arctic weather to fetch medicine and save a town of children dying from whooping cough.

Was there ever such a thing so brave?

Balto: symbol of everything good in the world.

It put Columbus and me to shame.

I fancied I could hear them still, but it was other children's voices float-ing over me. The whole park was full of children's voices that day, a bright Saturday. I wouldn't say their sounds made me lonely, but they gave me a strange feeling of silence or stillness inside, as if I was remembering myself. Their voices made me feel cleaved from my body yet more alive inside it as I watched this feeling grow, a boyish feeling, accentuating something that had not quite died in me and which it relieved me greatly to discover again. I seemed, therefore, to be looking at myself as if I were an old friend coming back to visit after a long time, not dead or lost at all.

I faced Columbus, rubbing my belly. Not really looking at him any more, but past him now to another statue of Shakespeare. This version of the English playwright didn't look anything like the actor Joseph Fiennes, whose film *Shakespeare In Love* was the hit of the moment in New York. There was no handsome romantic genius apparent in this dark statue – instead the tight dome-like baldness of a middle-aged man predominated. His cold head reminded me of a globe of the planet. And I smiled at this coincidence and at the way he and Columbus had this section of the park as their own.

The trees around me looked petrified by the last airs of winter, bare as light poles. A woman park-keeper hunted for rubbish with a two-pronged calliper, giving directions to yet more young Balto fans, rattling and crinkling along as she awkwardly squeezed her callipers to catch some drifting plastic bags.

The whir of bicycle wheels. The rattle of roller blades on uneven pavement stones. A mother dressing her baby girl in a red parka, whispering to her while the little one stared towards the sun, thrown in and out of balance as her mother buttoned her coat and tugged to straighten her clothes. Spitting on a handkerchief, wiping her mouth.

A Puerto Rican family stopped to look at Columbus. '*Que?*' The questioning word rose like a bubble from their conversation. Their youngest boy, who was maybe seven years old, explaining in Spanish to his nodding parents. The mother raising her eyebrows at the statue, then shooing her son along.

Traffic passed by in a soft rubber *whoosh* on the nearby road. Joggers pounded the pavement. An airplane high above in the silent blue, droneless, burning a white vapour trail in the sky. Two men in black efficient suits. Then an old grey-haired woman, her daughter and granddaughter, all with the same hairdos, all with the same red lipstick and overly pale faces shining with makeup, a walking advertisement for plastic surgery.

A backpacker dragged his feet along in a sandpapery walk towards me. Ironically enough, he asked me, a visitor, for directions to a railway station. I gave him very bad ones – convoluted and contradictory, a maze of choices that would surely see him lost in five minutes time.

Two girls with glasses and curly hair, like sexy librarians, leant forwards with their arms crossed, as if they were afraid of their breasts. Then two boys with slick-backed slouches and leather jackets strolled by, looking *Happy Days* tough. Chipmunks snuck across the neat lawns, darting easily between the metal fences while a woman walked her distracted Scottish terriers, stepping along at hyper-speed as they strained madly to go in two different directions at once.

The road and paths around me snaked away in long curves and disappeared. Small dry leaves blew over and over across the ground in a crackling fever. Columbus and Shakespeare and I watched it all pass, while Balto waited just over the hill, beloved.

I stood up to leave. It was getting colder, I realized. But a cloud passed and the sun returned in a sudden blaze, warm light in a great bucket splash pouring across the park from end to end.

So I sat down by Columbus and started to write. Slowly, and without a purpose. Keeping the lost softness of America in my eye.

On Hudson Street

A BEAUTIFUL MIST HANGS OVER DOWNTOWN, ROLLS LIKE sleep down the streets, around the buildings. Wraps and forgets them before your eyes. The whole of New York is disappearing in a wet greyness. The engine of a bus, a mother tying a scarf around her daughter's neck, the footsteps of a young woman in a fur-trimmed coat, the smell of grilled fish, a 'don't walk' sign in pulsing red... it's all going away. The sky is moving in. Trees, bare and winter fine, touch it before me. Their branches like exploded chandeliers dipping into the fog. Up there in the disappearing, a fourteenth floor apartment window light is on. My page begins to dampen. The wind blows cool and soft. New York is disappearing...

'You know,' said Port, and his voice sounded unreal, as voices are likely to do after a long pause in an utterly silent spot, 'the sky here's very strange. I often have the sensation when I look up that it's a solid thing up there, protecting us from what's behind.'

Kit shuddered slightly as she said: 'From what's behind?'

'Yes.'

'But what is behind?' Her voice was very small.

'Nothing, I suppose. Just darkness. Absolute night.'

THE SHELTERING SKY
Paul Bowles

Sometimes I wish I could fly like a bird up in the sky,
A little closer to home.

'Sometimes I Feel Like a Motherless Child'
Traditional gospel blues

Let's get back to the prayer of touching.

DE K–BAND

Australia The Prayer of Touching

When I Wake Up

I WAKE UP FRIGHTENED. WITH A BEAUTIFUL YOU AM I song flowering into in my mind, these words about how he 'wrote it all down on the head of a matchstick'.

I was glad to find you there beside me. And I rolled over in the bed just to feel you and make a lover's question mark as I shaped myself into your body. I could hear your breathing.

Outside a car started up – the first worker leaving the street. It was 5 a.m. exactly, the alarm clock glowing red.

I hadn't written with any love or strength for weeks. And I was still trying to finish this book, the document of a journey we had both been on. But there were two journeys, really. The one we experienced as we travelled around the world. Then the one I took writing.

I was writing my way back to you – and to myself too. Some cliché about finding myself in foreign places and then refinding myself with the words that bucked and flew up out of an emotion or a sideways thought some two years later. So this is reflection.

I've always been frightened I could live more honestly on the page than in my life. For the past few years I'd been on a journey with words as well as the physical journey that inspired them. Not really understanding what those words were about or where they were going, but groping through them into myself and out into the world. Crossing the river stone by stone. Thinking in the worst times that these words might take me apart from you for good. That I was just running into them, running into words and getting lost.

Now I wake up frightened on a wet spring morning still in darkness. Not out of a dream, but out of a non-dream. I may as well have been dead.

It's happened before. A nothing-there feeling inside of me. I wonder where these emptying, unsoulful aches come from?

But this time I'm lucky. A song lands in my head and makes me feel better straight away. So I go downstairs to find some pen and paper and get a feeling down.

I think back to you meeting me at the airport, how you held a postcard of that great red stone Uluru high above your head. How I could smell the electrical charge of a summer storm sweeping through the air-conditioned terminal. You turned the postcard around when you saw me, like a hostess waiting to help a tourist from another place. No name on the card, just a language that I knew. It said, 'You're mine'.

Now here I am. Writing notes to you in the dead of night.

I think we are in danger of losing our grace all the time. That just lying on the lounge downstairs now as I write, finding these thoughts inside me and hearing a bird's feet on the roof and a metal gate open and shut in the street can be the most beautiful and redeeming things in the world: the only sounds at this early hour, and oh so necessary for me.

How lonely I would be without you upstairs sleeping. Without the world moving around me. The weight of you beside me in the bed: the felt possibility of living with someone when I do wake up so scared.

I wish I could tune into the radio now and find that You Am I song, whatever its name is, wherever it is, out there drifting somewhere on a wavelength in the universe, and turn it up loud and sing along and ache with it happily for a while. Let all my feelings go.

I hope this book makes sense like that to people. As a love letter you can join in with, like a good song, the melody of a heartbeat. So that in the frightened dawn hours when people are waking or sleeping nervously, some little part of it might enter into their unconscious to let them know they are not lost from the world altogether. So that I can feel peace and warmth too and finish with all these stories and words – part of some bigger secret story inside of me that is still unravelling – and hold the world close again in a lover's question mark.

Acknowledgements

MY GRATITUDE MUST TRAVEL THE WORLD.

In Calcutta: Well, straight off there was the unforgettable Fairlawn Hotel (kooky). And these two New Zealander guys whose names we have forgotten. Australia was getting murdered in the Second Test against India, the year was 1998. You gave us your tickets to Eden Gardens and told us a funny story about a bus running over a dog. We liked you because you made us laugh so much. We were going to meet up again in Kathmandu but that didn't happen. What did happen was we arrived in Nepal to brawling taxi drivers and some Nepali boys carrying a sign that said, 'LISA AND MARK, THE AUSTRALIANS.' Assuming these were envoys of love sent by our Kiwi mates ('what nice guys'), we immediately went with them. An error in judgement. You weren't at the hotel and the room we got conned into sleeping in was five times the going rate around town. It was mid-evening, we were tired, no one could explain anything. In the morning they finally handed us your envelope – inside was a note to let us know you had set off for points unknown on the trekking compass. They had made their airport sign for us by copying the front of your envelope exactly, and spent every afternoon waiting for us to arrive on the only flight from Calcutta – until they finally got us. You indicated in the note that we might not want to stay at this hotel. You were right. We left.

In Nepal: 'Namaste' to the Shanti Guesthouse, Lake Side, Baidam, Pokhara, a must-stay establishment gently attended to by the proprietor Basu Pahari and his beautiful family, its courtyard enlivened by travellers such as Swiss-French Daniel (another? why not?), Italian Adamo (still wearing those shorts?) and South African George (maybe you and Adamo should have done it backwards?). In Kathmandu the Red Planet was our rapidly-assembled concrete home conveniently close to Just Juice & Shakes, the very best coffee and breakfast spot in all of Nepal. Our karmic love to Robert Talbot, a vision splendid on the Annapurna trail, the only Englishman to climb the Himalaya in an all-white suit (very pukka) with ski stocks, a diamond geezer on the trail to nirvana. We are honoured to know you. Take note, trekkers: Nepalese guesthouse menus offer 'maxed potatoes,' 'screambled eggs' and 'wall drop salad' and urge you to 'please enjoy the heart taking scenarios'.

In Varanasi: The Sunview Hotel near Kedarghat is highly recommended to the budget-conscious – it sports a direct view of 'the Ganga,' psychotic thieving monkeys and other eccentric charms, including its manager, Ashok the astute, his lovesick friend Rajoo (I can still taste that fucking awful pahn you gave me to chew) and their club of kindly gentleman bachelors who sell an excellent array of postcards. What I want to know, though, is this: whatever happened to the young Canadian poet who got heat exhaustion after sleeping with his socks on in 48 degrees Celsius heat?

We later travelled north by hire-car from Delhi to Dharamsala/McLeod Ganj and back, with much thanks to our chicken-loving driver Wakil Barshad of Sandu Tourist Transport Service (white Ambassador vehicles for hire 'round the clock'). Wakil, our lives were in your sure hands and we remember you in our hearts forever.

A traveller's warning: there is something evil going on around the Kullu and Parvati Valleys, so watch your back.

In the UK: London was a dog that gnashed its teeth politely and tried to bite. It's so dreary to be a visitor from the colonies. Special thanks to Samantha Nicol, who saved us from the Glastonbury mud (and ain't there a lot of that!). Josh and Jan Swirsky, you opened your beautiful house to us when we were down for the count. Yasmin Huseini, I'm a low-down lousy emailer but I still depend on your kind ways to persist! Roger Grierson, the Groucho Club was great and your sister Adrienne really can heal with her hands. Polly Borland you were beautiful and funny to talk to – I hope we work together again one day. Jarvis Cocker, hey man, I knew what you were talking about, 'turned up to ten.' Finley Quaye, you got me fucked up before I went to catch the London subway for the first time in my life (um, thanks). Alex Garland, I am glad we met to talk about writing – yes, *The Tesseract* is miles better. Pamela Smith, you're the princess of Clerkenwell and it all worked out okay.

Up in Edinburgh, we got misty and lost in 'the Haar'. Catherine Gunning, you were the girl in a party hat who kept us alive and kicking. De

K-Band and Leonardo's Bride, you really saved my soul with music. Huun Hur Tu, you took it to another place: free space for some wild horses to run. Christa Hughes, I never hit the floor, but thanks for looking out for me – by the way, I hear those Tuvan throat-singers really know how to pash! The New Eritrea restuarant in San Francisco sent me fresh-baked bread from far away – thanks Mussie Manna for helping. Fiona and Gavin Boyter and Nicola Meldrum at the top of the stairs, you were my Edinburgh lights in the dark. Stuart Brown, my great friend, I walked your old footsteps and felt less alone.

A sociological observation: did you know the Scottish have fist fights during screenings of *The Horse Whisperer*? They're a passionate people.

In Paris: The irresistible yet invisible Nicole Lobegeiger saved me (yet again!) – I love you. Billy McKinnon, you were a prince and the red wine was fine (see ya in Baghdad one day). Ciryne Berra from the net cafe, thanks for showing me where the Champs Elysees was on a rainy day when I was lost. A small warning to all: beware thieves in Pigalle (not to mention farting transvestites and bored police with staple guns). Mary D'Andrea, I had only met you once before when I called you up at 9 a.m. on a Sunday morning, robbed, desperate, broke and out of luck with nowhere to go – you said, come on over.

In Turkey: The Nayla Pension in Sultanahmet, Istanbul is the coolest, whitest place to stay. In Olympus we lived in tree houses and were entertained by a busful of loons called The Nashville Sprockets, a circus that went down the same road as us – more or less. I never made it to Gallipoli and I don't know why. But I heard stories of bullets bent together in mid-air and still findable in the melancholy sands. Kelebek Pension (the name means butterfly) is without compare in Goreme, a real home in an unreal place – thanks to everyone there, especially Jenna Breines, the best banana-cake cook in all of Anatolia (long live satellite TV and Letterman, baby!). Pat Yale, thanks for being a friend and showing us Cappadocia from the inside. Bill and Mary Searle, you married us off with a certificate of love (we will never forget our Humptydoo blessing) and some liquid white-out so we could cross the border into the world of Islam and be allowed to share a conjugal bed. We're now wondering if it was legal?

In Iran: Our love to Jasper Credland, a poet-adventurer and lifelong friend, the only man to have filmed his own car crash (including an entire backflip within the vehicle). Where will the road lead you next? Closer to us we pray. Speaking of which, my best to all the Buick 59 road gang – maybe I was too hard on all of us for the sake of a good tale. If you ever head down Esfahan way, let's meet for coffee and carrot jam at Amir Kabir, the only place to stay. Christiane Bird, I hope you found the book that you were seeking. Hossain and Ali, you opened your homes to us and showed us a kind world we did not know before. Most of all thanks to the friendly and generous people of Iran – I wish I could name you all. As a great carpet seller once tried to tell me, 'Let us look at it from an open window.' Through this I hope to fly in again at your welcome one day.

A Persian entertainment note: the only Western film we saw in Iran, screening in a hotel lobby to immense interest, was *All the President's Men*.

To New York, the city of kindness: My gratitude to everyone at *Madison* magazine who gave me a break, notably Pam Schein, Fred Moore, Scott Cohen and Jennifer Stroup. This book would not have happened without you. Pru Smith and Tim Brown, your floor was the best, thanks for making me a cappuccino tramp (love that inflatable). Emma Fletcher, that day I chased you through the streets, your stunned husband, those steps to your apartment, the back of Jim Jarmusch's head! Ian Keldoulis and Sahara Briscoe, New Year now spells 'new fear' (American style) for me, but hey I could have gone slower between the bongs and The Cramps. Kim Frankiewicz, you're a sweetheart of generosity and I loved *Ray of Light*, but your TV is still too close to the bed! Tony Notarberardino, Mark Vassallo, Olivier French, Nicole Langelier and all the Chelsea angels, you guys are so bad it's good. Mario Fattori, you're an inspiration to me – or as Leonardo da Vinci once put it, 'No matter whose face he paints, the painter always paints himself.' Jim and Chloe Osborne, thanks for Christmas dinner and the Alice Coltrane CD and the white snow so quiet out your windows. Nikka Costa and Justin Stanley, you took care of me like family and we discovered The Saints on vinyl too (let's rock again soon). Katie Siegelman, thanks for the computer and the pasta. Gregory Harvey at the Australian Consulate, you are the cultured traveller's best friend. To the Harlem

Young Women's Tennis Association, my appreciation for showing me the good part of town – I owe you a story. Hello to Café Gitane and that French place on Hudson Street (most especially the rainy morning you were playing Keith Jarrett's *Köln Concert*), you were my little caffeine homes. Arthur Miller, Patti Smith, Jackson Pollock, Rufus Wainwright, You Am I, silverchair at the Bowery Ballroom (it was like hearing my hometown Newcastle blow: all that steel and surf in your sound), The Black Crowes (hey guys, I was with all your fans smoking weed and drinking and singing and getting arrested for no-nothing offences and having fun – can't wait to see the show one day if that's what it is like just lining up for tickets), and all those black girls phoning up to sing love songs to Isaac Hayes on the morning radio, oh yes! I guess I should thank Balto too.

In Millthorpe: Frannie Hopkirk – what can I say? Your flowers and your home, Putu and Buster barking and slurping up my leftover coffee, my work-shack up the back garden – I'm indebted to you for letting me live in Millthorpe to write my heart out in solitary divinement. P. S. Sorry about leaving the hand-brake on in the car that time, and the headlights that other time, and the, well, you know. I just hope Rod de Vries is putting it back together round at his Bulletproof workshop (when the going gets tough, the tough get creating).

Allen & Unwin: I owe everyone in the company my thanks, of course, but most especially the publisher, Sophie Cunningham, for commissioning this book and believing in me. You're one hot babe! Simone Ford, I know you must have nearly torn your hair out trying to get the manuscript in on time (I'm nearly finished now). Jane Gleeson-White, thank you for the fine edit. Designer Brett Cheshire, you're a saint of patience and a friend as well (let's play *Prussian Blue* again soon).

Jenny Darling & Associates: Jenny Darling, Jacinta di Mase and Sophie Lance, you are the best agents in the world. The fact that Jenny D. is a Neil Young fan just confirms you all kick arse. Let's whack 'Cinammon Girl' on the stereo and party like it's 1975 real soon. It's that *Almost Famous* feeling.

To my friends too numerous to mention, I thank you from across the years. But there are a few I must include here for helping get this one through to the keeper: Robert and Sara-Jane Miller, Michael and Megan

Sherman, Andrea Healy and Michael Wee, Gerald Jenkins and Eva Ara, Wayne 'Iggy' Eager and Marina Strocchi, Carolyn Constantine, Annabel Barton, Shelley Reeve, Helen Eager, Lucia Eliot, Marcelle Lunam, Shalie Sweetnam, La Passion du Fruit café in Sydney (please, not too strong!) and all the 713 Bourke Street gangs who ripped it up with me. Some little part of you is here in the heart. And to Ellen Comiskey (RIP), hey, you're still a sweet fire in my mind. As some strange passing Persians might say, 'shabob'.

To all the Nicol family who love and support both Lisa and me, my profound gratitude.

To Cecil and Pauline Mordue, my father and mother, and all my family, more love than I can express. You bring me back to earth, yet you've always let me fly.

Most of all I want to say thanks to Lisa Nicol for showing me the way. I wouldn't have made it without you. I didn't know it when I started, but I guess this book is for both of us – and for our first child, still on the road and getting closer to us every day.

Credits

'Superstition kills woman': Story on page 29 is verbatim news article from *The Kathmandu Post*, 1 April 1998. Reprinted with kind permission.

'Roadkill': Economist Devendra Raj Panday quote on page 32 from *The New York Times*, 6 June 1999. Discussion of Maoist motivations on page 32 from *The Kathmandu Post*, 19 November 1999. Thanks also to Kiran Basnet at *The Kathmandu Post*, Greta Rana at ICIMOD (www.icimod.org.sg), Deepak Thapa at *Himal Magazine*, Professor Linda Iltis at the University of Washington and Anup Pande for their contributions in helping me to develop the story.

'Double Cross': Allusion on page 136 paralleling the smell of roses and mint with Iraqi gas attacks is drawn from a book review of Jonathan Randal's *Kurdistan: After Such Knowledge What Forgiveness* (Bloomsbury, 1999) by John Sweeney appearing in *The Guardian*, 17 January 1999. Discussion of Ataturk Dam on page 135 sourced from Robert D. Kaplan's *The Ends of* the *Earth* (see bibliography). Thanks to Turkish journalist Jon Gorvett for generous critical advice and research assistance.

'Land of the Giants': Discussion of Uluru and gathering of Aboriginal tribes in search of water on page 259 is drawn from a collection of poems by Billy Marshall-Stoneking called *Singing the Snake* (HarperCollins, 1990).

'The Chelsea Dilemma': Jean-Luc Godard quote preceding this story drawn from a Kent Jones profile of American director Abel Ferrara called 'The Man: Who Cares?' in *Lingo* 4 (Massachusetts, 1998).

Writers depend on independent publications and journals to carry their voice through loud and clear and true. 'Pissing in the Wind' previously appeared in *Purple* 3 (Paris, Summer 1999) and *Overland* 158 (Melbourne, Autumn 2000), and 'The Dead' (under the title 'A Still Wind') in *Madison* (New York, April 1999). 'Roadkill' (under the title 'A Bend in the Road') previously appeared in *Madison* (New York, March/April 2000). 'Dead Flowers' has been previously published as 'Dead Roses' in *Madison* (New York, June 1999) and as 'Painted in Blood' in *The Australian Magazine* (Sydney/Melbourne, 12-13 June 1999). 'Double Cross' appeared in *Speak* (San Francisco, March 2001), 'Waiting for a Chance' in HEAT 13 (Sydney, 2000) and *Salon* (San Francisco, 23 July 1999), and 'Land of the Giants' in *The American Muse* (Huntsville, Alabama, Spring 2001). Ivor Indyk at HEAT, thanks for your advice with 'The Chelsea Dilemma'. I tried to take at least some of it! Dan Rolleri at *Speak*, you are brilliant, the only editor I know to so totally 'feel' a magazine into existence with each issue (I hope you live to fight another day).

Bibliography

Robert D. Kaplan, *The Ends of the Earth: A Journey to the Frontiers of Anarchy*, Vintage Books, 1997.

Sandra MacKey, *The Iranians: Persia, Islam and the Soul of a Nation*, Epilogue, 1998.

Jeremy Seal, *A Fez of the Heart*, Picador, 1995.

The *Guardian* and the *New York Times* websites were also indispensable, not to mention the inevitable copies of *Lonely Planet*.

POETRY/PROSE

Excerpt from *The Rubaiyat of Omar Khayyam* is a translation by Edward J. Fitzgerald, London, 1859. It is believed to have been written in Persia circa 1120 before being rendered into English verse in this famous translation.

The quote transcribed from Oscar Wilde's grave in 'The Dead' and the lines used within the Leonardo's Bride song 'Oh Yeah' in 'No Stars in the Sky' are both drawn from *The Ballad of Reading Gaol*.

Line by Rumi introducing chapter on Turkey taken randomly from a fellow traveller's handwritten notebook. James A. (Sandy) Hill, you sang it as a cracking song to the Cappadocia sky. I only heard it later. Thanks to John Moyne and Coleman Barks for their assistance in tracking it down. It is drawn from a poem called 'Undressing' in the collection *The Glance* (Viking, 1999) and is a translation by Coleman Barks and Nevit Ergin.

Excerpt on page 92 from *A Good Hanging* by Ian Rankin, Orion, 1998.

Excerpt on page 317 from *The Sheltering Sky* by Paul Bowles, Penguin, 2000.

SONG LYRICS

Special thanks to Rebecca Foulcher at the Australasian Mechanical Copyright Owners Society (AMCOS) for her assistance in contacting publishers. With the exception of 'Sometimes I Feel Like A Motherless Child,' I have listed songs from which I sourced lyrics in the same order as they appear throughout the book:

De K-Band: I wrote to your post office box at Bowling Green, I searched the net, I emailed Edinburgh Fringe Festival, but I still couldn't find you. I hope the prayer of touching does.

'Oh Yeah': Written by Dean Manning and featuring a 'lyric sample' courtesy of Oscar Wilde. Performed by Leonardo's Bride. Mushroom Music Publishing.

'Ambulance Blues': Written and performed by Neil Young. ©1974 (Renewed) Silver Fiddle. All rights reserved. Used by permission of Warner Bros Publications U.S., Inc., Miami FL 33014.

'What a Little Moonlight Can Do': Written by Harry Woods. Performed by Billie Holiday. Reproduced by permission of Warner/Chappell Music Australia Pty Ltd. Unauthorised reproduction is illegal.

'Damage': Written by Tim Rogers. Performed by You Am I. Festival Mushroom Music.

'Sometimes I Feel Like A Motherless Child': An old gospel blues spiritual from the turn of the century, songwriter unknown and usually credited as 'traditional'. The lyrics in full, as sung to me by a Tehranian *taksi* driver, are as follows:

Sometimes I feel like a motherless child,
A long way from home.

Sometimes I wish I could fly like a bird up in the sky,
A little closer to home.

Motherless children have a hard time,
A long way from home.

Sometimes I feel like freedom is near,
But we're so far from home.

Sometimes I feel like the Kingdom is at hand,
But we're so far from home.

Notes for the American Edition

THE JOURNEY DESCRIBED IN THIS BOOK WAS WRITTEN AND
completed before the events of September 11, 2001. It was published a
matter of weeks afterwards in Australia and New Zealand by Allen &
Unwin.

I'm now indebted to Hawthorne Books for releasing *Dastgah* in the
U.S. in its original form (including the Acknowledgements). I'm particularly grateful to Rhonda Hughes and Kate Sage at Hawthorne Books for
appreciating the unity of the pieces and the chords these stories and impressions continue to strike as time moves on.

The almost premonitory quality of the writing would take me by surprise as our world moved so quickly into that condition referred to as
'the war on terrorism,' a state of mind as much as an event. Having spent
a year traveling the globe it was inevitable that deeper possibilities would
seep through than I was perhaps conscious of at the time. It's in the nature
of writing to be 'given' a story as often as one might create or piece it
together. Certainly I'm proud of what's here and the reverberations beneath, even if it amounts to little more than a mood of misgiving and
hope.

Since *Dastgah* was first published various stories have continued to
appear internationally. 'Coffee in Tehran' in *The Diplomat* (Sydney, August–
September 2002). 'Pissing in the Wind' in both *Planet* (San Francisco, Nov.
4, 2003) and *Canvas* (Auckland, 17-18 January 2004). 'After the Rain', 'Electric Avenue, Brixton,' 'Himbasha,' 'Istanbul, City of Cats,' 'Town Hall
One (A True Story),' 'Dead Flowers,' and 'S&M: An American Express
Story' in that literary wildflower, *Gobshite Quarterly*, Issues 3 and 4/5 (Portland, 2003/2004).

I'd like to thank Derek Peck at *Planet*, Carroll du Chateau at the *New
Zealand Herald's Canvas* and Michael Visontay at the *Sydney Morning Herald*
for their continued support, as well as Art Winslow at *The Nation* and
Scott Cohen at *Interview* and now *Giant* for their encouragement from so
far away. R.V. Branham at *Gobshite* deserves special mention, the king of
the ampersand & a truly Beat soul in an out-of-whack world. Without

R.V. this book wouldn't have made it to America. Thanks also to Garrett Mok (12 Gauge), Michael Goldberg (Neumu), Derek Alger (*PiF Magazine*) and Jennifer Stroup (yet again) for keeping a few ripples moving on my behalf.

The rest of my American friends are well noted in the preceding Acknowledgements. Something of a story in their own right, the Acknowledgements should also serve a practical purpose for the adventurous traveller in need of somewhere to stay and someone to trust.   —M.M.

Titles available from Hawthorne Books

AT YOUR LOCAL BOOKSELLER OR FROM OUR WEBSITE: *hawthornebooks.com*

Saving Stanley: The Brickman Stories
BY SCOTT NADELSON

Scott Nadelson's interrelated short stories are graceful, vivid narratives that bring into sudden focus the spirit and the stubborn resilience of the Brickmans, a Jewish family of four living in suburban New Jersey. The central character, Daniel Brickman, forges obstinately through his own plots and desires as he struggles to balance his sense of identity with his longing to gain acceptance from his family and peers. This fierce collection provides an unblinking examination of family life and the human instinct for attachment.

SCOTT NADELSON PLAYFULLY INTRODUCES *us to a fascinating family of characters with sharp and entertaining psychological observations in gracefully beautiful language, reminiscent of young Updike. I wish I could write such sentences. There is a lot of eros and humor here – a perfectly enjoyable book.*
—JOSIP NOVAKOVICH
author of *Salvation and Other Disasters*

So Late, So Soon
BY D'ARCY FALLON

This memoir offers an irreverent, fly-on-the-wall view of the Lighthouse Ranch, the Christian commune D'Arcy Fallon called home for three years in the mid-1970s. At eighteen years old, when life's questions overwhelmed her and reconciling her family past with her future seemed impossible, she accidentally came upon the Ranch during a hitchhike gone awry. Perched on a windswept bluff in Loleta, a dozen miles from anywhere in Northern California, this community of lost and found twentysomethings lured her in with promises of abounding love, spiritual serenity, and a hardy, pioneer existence. What she didn't count on was the fog.

I FOUND FALLON'S STORY *fascinating, as will anyone who has ever wondered about the role women play in fundamental religious sects. What would draw an otherwise independent woman to a life of menial labor and subservience? Fallon's answer is this story, both an inside look at 70s commune life and a funny, irreverent, poignant coming of age.*
—JUDY BLUNT
author of *Breaking Clean*

HAWTHORNE BOOKS & LITERARY ARTS ∷ *Portland, Oregon*

God Clobbers Us All

BY POE BALLANTINE

Set against the dilapidated halls of a San Diego rest home in the 1970s, *God Clobbers Us All* is the shimmering, hysterical, and melancholy story of eighteen-year-old surfer-boy orderly Edgar Donahoe's struggles with friendship, death, and an ill-advised affair with the wife of a maladjusted war veteran. All of Edgar's problems become mundane, however, when he and his lesbian Blackfoot nurse's aide best friend, Pat Fillmore, become responsible for the disappearance of their fellow worker after an LSD party gone awry. *God Clobbers Us All* is guaranteed to satisfy longtime Ballantine fans as well as convert those lucky enough to be discovering his work for the first time.

A SURFER DUDE TRANSFORMS *into someone captivatingly fragile, and Ballantine's novel becomes something tender, vulnerable, even sweet without that icky, cloying literary aftertaste. This vulnerability separates Ballantine's work from his chosen peers. Calmer than Bukowski, less portentous than Kerouac, more hopeful than West, Poe Ballantine may not be sitting at the table of his mentors, but perhaps he deserves his own after all.*

—SAN DIEGO UNION-TRIBUNE

Dastgah: Diary of a Headtrip

BY MARK MORDUE

Australian journalist Mark Mordue invites you on a journey that ranges from a Rolling Stones concert in Istanbul to talking with mullahs and junkies in Tehran, from a cricket match in Calcutta to an S&M bar in New York, and to many points in between, exploring countries most Americans never see as well as issues of world citizenship in the 21st century. Written in the tradition of literary journalism, *Dastgah* will take you to all kinds of places, across the world ... and inside yourself.

I just took a trip around the world in one go, first zigzagging my way through this incredible book, and finally, almost feverishly, making sure I hadn't missed out on a chapter along the way. I'm not sure what I'd call it now: A road movie of the mind, a diary, a love story, a new version of the subterranean homesick and wanderlust blues – anyway, it's a great ride. Paul Bowles and Kerouac are in the back, and Mark Mordue has taken over the wheel of that pickup truck from Bruce Chatwin, who's dozing in the passenger seat.

—WIM WENDERS
Director of *Paris, Texas; Wings of Desire;*
and *The Buena Vista Social Club*

 HAWTHORNE BOOKS & LITERARY ARTS :: Portland, Oregon

Things I Like About America

BY POE BALLANTINE

These risky, personal essays are populated with odd jobs, eccentric characters, boarding houses, buses, and beer. Ballantine takes us along on his Greyhound journey through small-town America, exploring what it means to be human. Written with piercing intimacy and self-effacing humor, Ballantine's writings provide entertainment, social commentary, and completely compelling slices of life.

IN HIS SEARCH *for the real America, Poe Ballantine reminds me of the legendary musk deer, who wanders from valley to valley and hilltop to hilltop searching for the source of the intoxicating musk fragrance that actually comes from him. Along the way, he writes some of the best prose I've ever read.*   —SY SAFRANSKY
                    Editor, *The Sun*

September 11:
West Coast Writers Approach Ground Zero

EDITED BY JEFF MEYERS

The myriad repercussions and varied and often contradictory responses to the acts of terrorism perpetuated on September 11, 2001 have inspired thirty-four West Coast writers to come together in their attempts to make meaning from chaos. By virtue of history and geography, the West Coast has developed a community different from that of the East, but ultimately shared experiences bridge the distinctions in provocative and heartening ways. Jeff Meyers anthologizes the voices of American writers as history unfolds and the country braces, mourns, and rebuilds.

CONTRIBUTORS INCLUDE: *Diana Abu-Jaber, T. C. Boyle, Michael Byers, Tom Clark, Joshua Clover, Peter Coyote, John Daniel, Harlan Ellison, Lawrence Ferlinghetti, Amy Gerstler, Lawrence Grobel, Ehud Havazelet, Ken Kesey, Maxine Hong Kingston, Stacey Levine, Tom Spanbauer, Primus St. John, Sallie Tisdale, Alice Walker, and many others.*

www.hawthornebooks.com

The Greening of Ben Brown

BY MICHAEL STRELOW

Michael Strelow weaves the story of a town and its mysteries in his debut novel. Ben Brown becomes a citizen of East Leven, Oregon, after he recovers from an elec-trocution that has not left him dead but has turned him green. He befriends 18 year-old Andrew James and together they unearth an chemical spill cover-up that forces the town to confront its demons and its citizens to choose sides. Strelow's lyrical prose and his talent for storytelling come together in this poetic and important first work that looks at how a town and the natural environment are inextricably linked. *The Greening* will find itself in good company on the shelves between *Winesburg, Ohio* and *To Kill a Mockingbird*; readers of both will have a new story to cherish.

Core: A Romance

BY KASSTEN ALONSO

This intense and compact novel crackles with obsession, betrayal, and madness. As the narrator becomes fixated on his best friend's girlfriend, his precarious hold on sanity rapidly deteriorates into delusion and violence. This story can be read as the classic myth of Hades and Persephone (Core) rewritten for a twenty-first century audience as well as a dark tale of unrequited love and loneliness.

Alonso skillfully uses language to imitate memory and psychosis, putting the reader squarely inside the narrator's head; deliberate misuse of standard punctuation blurs the distinction between the narrator's internal and external worlds. Alienation and Faulknerian grotesquerie permeate this landscape, where desire is borne in the bloom of a daffodil and sanity lies toppled like an applecart in the mud.

JUMP THROUGH THIS GOTHIC STAINED GLASS WINDOW *and you are in for some serious investigation of darkness and all of its deadly sins. But take heart, brave traveler, the adventure will prove thrilling. For you are in the beautiful hands of Kassten Alonso.*

—TOM SPANBAUER
Author of *The Man Who Fell in Love with the Moon*
and *In the City of Shy Hunters*

HAWTHORNE BOOKS & LITERARY ARTS :: *Portland, Oregon*